Published by John Wiley & Sons, Inc., Hoboken, New Jersey.
Published simultaneously in Canada.

Wiley Bicentennial Logo: Richard J. Pacifico

Limit of Liability/Disclaimer of Warranty: While the publisher and author have used their best efforts in preparing this book, they make no representations or warranties with respect to the accuracy or completeness of the contents of this book and specifically disclaim any implied warranties of merchantability or fitness for a particular purpose. No warranty may be created or extended by sales representatives or written sales materials. The advice and strategies contained herein may not be suitable for your situation. You should consult with a professional where appropriate. Neither the publisher nor author shall be liable for any loss of profit or any other commercial damages, including but not limited to special, incidental, consequential, or other damages.

For general information on our other products and services or for technical support, please contact our Customer Care Department within the United States at (800) 762-2974, outside the United States at (317) 572-3993 or fax (317) 572-4002.

Wiley also publishes its books in a variety of electronic formats. Some content that appears in print may not be available in electronic books. For more information about Wiley products, visit our web site at www.wiley.com.

Library of Congress Cataloging-in-Publication Data:
Yenne, Bill, 1949–
    Guinness : the 250-year quest for the perfect pint / Bill Yenne
        p. cm.
    Includes bibliographical references.
    ISBN 978-0-470-12052-1 (cloth)
    1. Guinness (Firm)—History. 2. Brewing industry—Ireland—History.
3. Guinness family. I. Title.
    HD9397.I74G859 2007
    338.7'6634209417—dc22
                                                        2007024226

Printed in the United States of America.

10 9 8 7 6 5 4 3 2 1

GUINNESS®

THE 250-YEAR QUEST FOR THE PERFECT PINT

BILL YENNE

John Wiley & Sons, Inc.

At the pub on the crossroads there's whiskey and beer
There's brandy and cognac that's fragrant but dear
But for killing the thirst and for easing the gout
There's nothing at all beats a pint of good stout!
Some folk o'er the water think bitter is fine
And others they swear by the juice of the vine
But there's nothing that's squeezed from the grape or the hop
Like the black liquidation with the froth on the top!

—from the Irish folk song, "Drink It Up Men"

Fanny ate a whole fowl for breakfast, to say nothing of a tower of hot cakes.
Belle and I floored another hen betwixt the pair of us, and I shall be no sooner
done with the present amanuensing racket than I shall put myself outside a pint
of Guinness.

—Robert Louis Stevenson (letter from Samoa, February 19, 1893)

Dear Jack, this white mug that with Guinness I fill,
And drink to the health of sweet Nan of the Hill,
Was once Tommy Tosspot's, as jovial a sot,
As e'er drew a spigot, or drain'd a full pot—
In drinking all round 'twas his joy to surpass,
And with all merry tipplers he swigg'd off his glass.

—William Makepeace Thackeray (from *Burlesques*, 1880)

That's why people look for that Holy Grail of the perfect pint. They come to
Ireland looking for the best pint. People are always looking for that. Even I'm
looking for that perfect pint. That's why Guinness is such a legend.

—Guinness Master Brewer Fergal Murray

Contents

Notes on Measurements and Terminology

For historic purposes, volume measurements are stated in the unit of measurement used at the time. S. R. Dennison and Oliver MacDonagh of Cork University Press note that Guinness measured beer in hogsheads consisting of 52 imperial gallons and barrels consisting of 32 gallons before 1881 and 36 gallons thereafter. An imperial gallon is equal to 1.2 U.S. gallons. By comparison, U.S. barrels (when used as a form of measurement) contain 31 U.S. gallons. A U.S. gallon is equal to hectoliters.

Currency figures are generally given in British Pounds Sterling, the form of currency in which the data was originally calculated. In 1900, a pound was worth $4.85 in then-current U.S. dollars, and in 1939 (on the eve of World War II), it was $4.00. In 1950, a pound was worth about $2.80 and, in 1980, it was worth about $2.22. In 2000, a pound was equal to $1.45 and at press time it was around $2.00. According to the Consumer Price Index tables developed by Robert Sahr at Oregon State University, adjusted for in inflation, a U.S. dollar at press time would have been worth $0.04 in 1900, $0.07 in 1939, $0.12 in 1950, $0.41 in 1980, and $0.85 in 2000.

As for terminology, this book, though mainly researched in Ireland, was written in the United States. Therefore, the spelling conventions are consistently American with the exception of the Anglo-Irish word *draught*, which Americans spell *draft*. The term draught is part of a Guinness product variant name, therefore, we have used the Anglo-Irish spelling throughout for the sake of consistency, capitalized or not. The product name now written as Guinness Draught was once written as Draught Guinness, but we have used the current term Guinness Draught throughout for the sake of consistency.

Acknowledgments

Thanks to the people without whom this book would not have been possible, especially Master Brewer Fergal Murray. Thanks are also due Guinness Archivist Eibhlin Roche, for giving me access to many original documents—and more—and for her patience in working with me and answering my myriad questions. Special thanks also to Rhonda Evans for facilitating my research work in Ireland, to Matt Holt for believing that this book was important, and to John Coakley, who doesn't know that without him, this book would not have happened as it did. Thanks also to the beautiful ladies who have traveled with me through Ireland, Carol, Azia, and Lisa; and all the people with whom I have shared a pint at Vince Hogan's pub, including Mike, J. R., Dan, Nick, Todd (with whom I have also enjoyed some wonderful road trips involving quests for perfect pints), and Tom, who long ago helped infuse in me a passion for Guinness.

Prologue: The World's Greatest Beer

Surely this is hyperbole!

How can there be such a thing as the world's *greatest* beer?

I believe there can be, and I believe that this is it.

Even those who would quibble with such an assertion will agree that Guinness has a place of prominence among the pantheon of the world's greatest beers. As we hear in the folk song, "there's nothing that's squeezed from the grape or the hop like the black liquidation with the froth on the top."

Indeed. There is nothing quite like it.

In more than two decades of writing about beer and brewing history, I've been asked countless times to name the "best" beer, or my "favorite" beer. I've even been guilty of asking those impossible questions a time or two myself. The easy answer, and an answer often given, is "the beer I have in my hand at the moment." For me, such an answer is usually not a flippant one because, wherever I go, I seek out the local brew, and the local brew usually has two of the characteristics most desirable in a beer: It is the work of a local craftsman who takes pride in his—or often her—craftsmanship, *and* it is fresh.

A global search for the "best" beer is a moving target. It is always qualified by freshness and many other factors, especially craftsmanship. The "best" beer is many beers. It might be a glass of Anchor Steam in Fritz Maytag's wonderful brewery on Potrero Hill. It might be an astounding farmhouse brew or an exquisite Trappist monastery ale, sipped at their sources in Belgium. Or, of course, it may well be a pint of Guinness poured in Dublin itself, or at a pub called the Dubliner that may be five or ten thousand miles from the Emerald Isle.

A global search for greatness begins on the never-ending road to the "best" beers, for no beer can be great without also having earned a place among the best. But greatness is derived from many sources. For Guinness, this includes its passionate following who sip the two billion pints that are poured and enjoyed around the world each year. No other beer with a flavor profile so complex and so rewarding is enjoyed by so many people in so many places—in at least 150 countries—around the world.

While deriving greatness from its truly global charisma, Guinness also derives greatness from its unique sense of place. No other brand of such wide appeal is more endowed with roots that extend so deeply into its native soil. The Irish write folk songs about Guinness. James Joyce mentions it dozens of times.

Meanwhile, no other beer with such a complex and rewarding flavor profile has been enjoyed for so *long*. The greatness of Guinness comes also from a history that stretches back across *a quarter of a millennium*. When my mother's grandparents, Matthew Cunningham and Margaret Fennesy, were born in Ireland's County Clare in 1830 and 1840, respectively, Guinness was already permanently establishing itself as the largest brewery—and the leading stout in the Emerald Isle.

When my father's grandparents, Dennis and Margaret O'Leary were born in County Cork during the Famine years of 1842 and 1845, respectively, Guinness was one of Ireland's leading exports and the payroll at the brewery at St. James's Gate was a powerful keystone in the rapidly changing Irish economy.

Though rooted in Ireland, the greatness of Guinness is without borders. It has a unique place in global beverage folklore. Guinness is a beer with a long and colorful history and mythology—while at the same time having a passionate following among beer connoisseurs around the world today.

The global search for greatness begins on the never-ending road to the "best" beers. For me, the road that has taken me on my personal global search for the best and greatest has taken me to many rewarding places.

One day, this search led me through that big black gate on James's Street in Dublin.

—BILL YENNE

Introduction: What Is Guinness Stout?

A pint of Guinness is a magic thing—black magic. It is the rich color of dark chocolate, with an equally rich and creamy head unlike any other beer. A pint of Guinness is a magic thing that rewards the palate as no other beer on earth.

Technically, Guinness is a "stout porter," a dark, top fermented beer that is strikingly distinctive both in taste and appearance. Culturally, Guinness Stout is an enduring icon that has been deeply intertwined with Irish life and folklore—both at home and abroad—for a quarter of a millennium. Guinness is a beer apart from mortal beers, but it is even more than that.

What is Guinness Stout, and where does one go to answer that evocative question? To the source, of course.

For generations, the Guinness brewery at St. James's Gate was Dublin's largest employer. Everyone knew someone who worked there, and nearly everyone was related to someone who worked there. The address has no number, for none is needed. Everyone in Dublin knows St. James's Gate, and every Dublin cab driver I've met has a story to tell about St. James's Gate and the beer they make there.

I was still listening to my cab driver's story about his brother and his brother's friend, and his brother's friend's friend, and their perfect pint as we drove through what has been the main gate of the brewery since before George III ruled Ireland and George Washington presided over that upstart democracy across the water.

The actual St. James's Gate, for which the brewery is named, was the old medieval city gate through which people once passed on their way to the south and west of Ireland, or as they began religious pilgrimages to holy sites in continental Europe. It stood for at least five centuries immediately perpendicular to the location of the present brewery gate. Everywhere I look, I find myself staring at history and history staring back.

I'm here to meet Guinness Master Brewer Fergal Murray, not in a steel and glass corporate headquarters, but in the house where Arthur Guinness took up residence in 1759 and where his children and grandchildren were raised. Arthur Guinness brewed his first batch of beer within a stone's throw of where I'm standing.

Arthur was brewing at this place for 30 years before the French Revolution, and nearly two decades before the American Declaration of Independence. His was the epoch of Mozart and of Handel, of Jonathan Swift and of Samuel Johnson, of Voltaire and of Benjamin Franklin. This was an age, it has been said, that bequeathed to posterity many things of lasting importance.

One such thing is the black liquidation with the froth on the top called Guinness.

Having inherited greatness from that truly great era, this singular beer has been brewed fresh every day for generations by men such as Fergal Murray. He started at Guinness in 1983 with an applied sciences degree from Trinity College in Dublin, as well as an MBA, and a master brewer degree from the Institute of Brewing in London.

When I mention his scientific credentials, he shakes his head and tells me: "My heart lies in being able to talk to people about the qualities of the brand. I'm certainly more passionate about *that* than sitting back and thinking about the science of it."

When the man who makes the stuff uses the word "passionate" in describing his product, I know that I'm off to a good start. When he goes on to toss around phrases like "the perfect pint," it makes me think that I'm home in my local pub talking with friends who are ardent Guinness fans. In fact, I'm discovering that the man who makes the stuff is himself an ardent Guinness fan.

The perfect pint.

Is that not, after all, what Guinness is all about?

The pint is point of contact between all Guinness fans and Guinness, and the mythic *perfect* pint is the often spoken Holy Grail of those who drink this beer.

How better to introduce the subject of the black liquidation with the froth on the top than with the ritual of the pouring of the pint, the slow and thoughtful two-shot pour?

"No other beer has to go through a ritual," Murray smiles. "We make the ritual important. It's theater. The ceremony behind pouring a pint is essential to the consumer's requirement for a perfect pint of Guinness. It's all part of the indefinable essence. The ritual and the crafting of the pint is about serving the beverage to your customer in the right way. With any other beer, you can just put it under the tap and hand it out. But with Guinness you've got to think about it."

It is reckoned that more than four million pints are poured every day around the world, but each pouring is like a sacred ceremony. As any publican will tell you, pouring a pint is not something to be rushed. Three or four pints of other beer can be poured in the time that it takes to slowly and carefully pour a pint of Guinness.

"We do the two-part pour to build the strength of the head," Murray says, slipping back into his scientific training as he introduces the ritual. "First, you place a clean, dry, branded pint glass under the faucet at a 45-degree angle, never allowing the faucet to touch the glass or the beer. You aim the font at the harp [the Guinness logo] on the pint glass, and pull the handle slowly toward you. Allow the beer to flow smoothly down the side of the glass until it's about three-quarters full, tilting it slightly to straighten it. You stop the pour when the beer is about an inch and a half from the top, then you set the glass on the bar to allow the beer to settle."

All good things require a wait, our mothers have told us, paraphrasing our age-old cultural adage. The more theatrical among us would call this a dramatic pause. The settling is the intermezzo in the process where the thirsty drinker is given the opportunity to enjoy the pint visually before he or she is allowed to touch or taste it.

As if by magic, a reverse waterfall of tiny bubbles the color of roasted barley malt surge up though the blackness from the base of the pint.

As if by magic. A pint of Guinness is a magic thing, and part of the magic is the visual show that we are required to pause and enjoy before we are permitted to treat our sense of taste to other forms of magic.

"You give the consumer a vision of the surge," Murray says proudly. "People like to see this activity, which is unique in the beer world."

What is this phenomenon that he calls "the surge" and others call "the waterfall effect?"

As with any good ritual, there is a story. As with all the Guinness stories, we'll be getting to that in due time, but suffice to say the key word is *nitrogenation*. In my first conversation with Fergal Murray, he told me that I could do a whole chapter on nitrogenation, and I have. Most Guinness fans know that there is nitrogen in their pint, but few know the story behind it. A long time ago, in the late 1950s, a man named Michael Ash—a scientist, like Fergal Murray, with a passion—figured out that adding these little two-atom molecules would be part of the key to perfection in the head of a pint of Guinness.

"Because the surface tension of the beer is so strong, the nitrogen doesn't escape," the passionate scientist Murray tells me. "The bubbles float to the top, surrounded by the surface tension of the beer. That's why they don't dissipate as fast as carbon dioxide bubbles that occur naturally in all beer. The carbon dioxide bubbles dissipate because there is less surface tension to hold them in place. The nitrogen bubbles don't dissipate. The nitrogen can't escape because the protein-carbohydrate mix that holds the beer together is so strong. The quality of the raw materials in Guinness is directly associated with the sustainability of the perfect head. The strength of the head is one of the fundamentals of a good pint of Guinness. That's why we do a two-shot pour, to create a foundation for a wonderful head."

Pointing to the tiny surging bubbles, he explains that "during the settling you allow the consumer to see the wonderful surge, the activity of the nitrogen bubbles trying to get back into solution after they've been energized. They can't get back into solution because of the surface tension of the beer, so they surge to the top, down the outside, and back up the middle."

It is an art, but an art that can be mastered. When the surge is complete, and the beer considered "settled," the publican tops off the pint with a domed head that has the texture of rich whipped cream, unlike nearly any other beer.

"For presentation purposes, it's always best for a pint to be completely settled," the master brewer says, doubling as master of this ceremony. "If you taste it before that, there shouldn't be any difference in the taste. It just looks better."

He explains that the surge and settle time is affected by the gas mixture and by the temperature of the beer. Ideally, the beer should be between 4 and 6 degrees centigrade (38 to 44 degrees Fahrenheit). The specifications for the temperature and the mix of gas are created to provide a perfect head, which measures 18 millimeters from the base of the head to the lip of the glass, and 22 millimeters from the base to the top of the head.

Adjusting the gas mixture is a lot like tuning a musical instrument. The only criterion is the end product. In the U.S. market, Guinness is poured with a mixture of nitrogen and carbon dioxide that is specified at 70 percent nitrogen, plus or minus 5 percent. In Ireland, it is about 80 percent, although, as Fergal Murray points out, this is individually tweaked at the pubs. He adds that in Ireland there are individual temperatures and individual gas specs for each line running from keg to tap.

"During the settling, the beer is building a nice, consistent strength of head," he says proudly eying his work of art. The pint is "art" both in the work of the brewer and the work the publican, whom he compares to another profession. "It's like an architect, when the final vision of his building is to put a dome on the top. He has to have a very strong foundation to support the dome. You're allowing the strength of the foundation to occur by settling. You can't do a dome if you fill the glass with a one-shot pour. You might get a nice-looking head, or you might not, but you won't get a dome."

Then the passionate man turns to that word "perfect" again: "To pour a perfect pint, you build that strength, you allow it to settle, and then you top off the beer, allowing this wonderful, creamy head to form. You don't want it rushing into the glass, it's always a slower speed top-off. The final step is to serve the perfect-looking pint."

What is Guinness Stout?

Is this is it?

Yes and no.

There is more to Guinness than the ritual pour that is the point of contact between us and our beer. There is even more to this beer than the nitrogenated form we know in pubs. To half the Guinness-drinking world, nitrogenization does not exist. Nor did nitrogenization exist for two centuries before the epiphany of Michael Ash.

Out of the 250 years of Guinness history, there have emerged the three principal product variants that we know today. The oldest of these is Guinness Foreign Extra Stout, which traces its origin to West Indies Porter, first brewed here behind these walls in 1801. Next is Guinness Extra Stout, whose direct precursor was Guinness Extra Superior Porter—for which the founder's son penned a recipe in 1821. Finally, there is Guinness Draught, which dates back half a century to 1959, the year that Michael Ash and the Guinness scientists figured out their foolproof way to create the perfect head on that perfect pint.

The three variations on the stout that comprise the heart of the Guinness portfolio contain essentially the same ingredients, although Foreign Extra Stout is higher in alcohol. This is because its ancestor originated with a requirement for a beer with higher alcohol to withstand the rigors of being exported over great distances in conditions such as existed in sailing ships in the nineteenth century. It contains about 7.5 percent alcohol by volume, although that varies slightly depending on which market in which it is found. The other two variants have 4.2 percent alcohol by volume.

Foreign Extra Stout is found throughout Africa, the Caribbean, and the Far East, but rarely elsewhere. Guinness Draught is found in Ireland, the United Kingdom, North America, Australia, Europe, and Japan, but rarely in the same markets as Foreign Extra Stout. Extra Stout is sold in Ireland, the United Kingdom, and North America.

"Before 1959, it may not have happened in exactly the same way, but great pubs and great bartenders have always been creating great rituals and great ceremonies," the master brewer continues as he contemplates the carefully crafted pint of Guinness Draught and reflects on its two dozen decades of family heritage. "There has always been an art to drafting beer. Getting beer out of a cask and into a glass with the right consistency, the right temperature, and the right look, was an art, it is why people went to a specific pub. Being a draught publican was a real trade."

Turning to a bottle of Extra Stout—for it is available only in bottles, as was the custom with nearly all Guinness for many years.

He explains that "there is a ritual to pouring from a bottle of Guinness Extra Stout, but a different ritual. In Ireland, a publican will not pour a bottle of Extra Stout into a glass for you. He'll give *you* the bottle *and* the glass. It may be a pint glass, a half pint or a tankard. Then *you* get the excitement of continuously topping it off yourself, of continuously creating a new head every time. You get the excitement of the explosion of the carbonation, and the lovely brown head. The bartender will never replace the glass. The bartender will just drop you the bottle. He knows that it's your glass, and that you're creating your own ritual. He'll just give you a new bottle and there you are. This was a ritual in its own respect before Guinness Draught, and it's something that we're proud of."

Far from Ireland's shore, Foreign Extra Stout has also come to enjoy an identity of its own. "I've talked to Nigerians who think of Guinness as their national beer," said Murray, who worked as a Guinness brewer in that West African country for more than three years. "They wonder why Guinness is sold in Ireland. You can talk to Nigerians in Lagos who will tell you as many stories about their perfect pint as an Irishman will. They'll tell about how they've had a perfect bottle of Foreign Extra Stout at a particular bar on their way home from work."

Yet, Guinness, in its various forms, is enjoyed in nearly every nation on earth because of the Irish, the people from that tiny green island in the North Atlantic. That, as they say, is part of both the history and the folklore of Guinness.

"The brand has been fundamentally associated with Ireland since 1759," the master brewer tells me. "As Irish people have traveled around the world, they want to hold onto that piece of Ireland, they want to hold onto something tangible. Guinness is a great connection with home. When an Irishman travels, he'll always sniff out an Irish bar somewhere. We know that we can be among our own and watch a rugby match."

Indeed, it is the *craic*, the Irish term for good times, that causes everyone else to seek out a good Irish pub.

"We're very proud that people will always gravitate to an Irish pub because of the fun aspect," Murray smiles. "I was in Australia recently and had a fascinating night on my own in Melbourne. There was a medical conference going on in the hotel where I was staying, and the people were gathering in the lobby to go out for a social night and they were asking for the nearest Irish bar. That defines what it means. They were stuck at a convention in Melbourne and they wanted to go somewhere for a bit of fun. Their view was that to find that fun, they had to find an *Irish* bar. That sums it up. That's why this feeling transcends boundaries. When they turn up at the Irish bar, the Guinness is the celebrated choice with which to enjoy the evening."

Whether in Dublin, or in a pub called The Dubliner in Melbourne or Mombasa, the essence of Guinness is that which we seek, and this is what leads us through their doors—or through that big black gate at the place called St. James's Gate.

"It's a bit of craft, and it's a bit of theater. It's a ritual," Murray says of the Irish pub, and of the pouring of the pint. "If you get the bartenders doing this in a passionate way, they'll enjoy themselves commercially and they'll be proud of what they do. Consumers will recognize this and they'll enjoy their pint even more as well. Once it's done correctly, it delivers an extraordinary experience to the customer. You get what is probably the most attractive beer product in the world. We say you drink Guinness with your eyes first. And the bonus is in the complexity and balance of the flavor."

Today, millions of people visit Ireland to enjoy the rolling green hills and the *craic*. Of them, nearly a million visitors come to St. James's Gate each year to touch a piece of Guinness history and to enjoy a pint of the most attractive beer product in the world—at the source, of course.

Will their pint be the elusive perfect pint?

As Fergal Murray has assured us, the perfect pint is dependant on the hand of the publican and the perfect pour. Beyond that, it is the perfect ambiance, the crafting of the perfect pub. This is one part the job of the publican—and one part that intangible something within us that reacts to the *craic* to produce that perfect smile, just as the nitrogen reacts within the Guinness to produce the perfect visual manifestation within the black liquidation with the froth on the top.

As the mysterious and enigmatic author B. Traven masterfully relates in *The Treasure of the Sierra Madre,* and as countless others convey in countless tales of quests for buried treasure and Holy Grails, the quest is as much about the quest *itself* as it is about the pot of gold at the end of the proverbial rainbow. It is the search that inflames the mind and fires the spirit. In large measure, the perfect pint is made perfect by the adventures and the myriad of pints along the road that have led us to the mythic perfect pub.

"That's why people look for that Holy Grail of the perfect pint," Murray muses. "They come to Ireland looking for the best pint. People are always looking for that. Even *I'm* looking for that perfect pint. That's why Guinness is such a legend."

The perfect pint is, after all, a state of mind that you and I and countless others have created within ourselves as we have walked that long and winding road. You and I walk this road alone, just as we walk it in the company and the footsteps of others.

Long ago, before all of us, and before there were all of those pubs and pints and footsteps, there was a single set of footsteps on that road to the perfect pint. They were those of one Arthur Guinness, and therein begins our tale.

Origins

Brewing has been part of civilization since antiquity. Professor Solomon Katz at the University of Pennsylvania has found Sumerian recipes for beer that date back four millennia, and beer is mentioned often in ancient Egyptian literature. As H. F. Lutz points out in *Vitaculture and Brewing in the Ancient Orient*, published in 1922, Middle Kingdom texts from Beni Hasan "enumerate quite a number of different beers." Among these a "garnished beer" and a "dark beer." As David Ryder points out in the *Newsletter of the American Society of Brewing Chemists*, Egyptian beer "was also used as a medicine, a tonic for building strength . . . a universal cure for coughs and colds, shortness of breath, problems of the stomach and lungs, and a guard against indigestion."

It has been suggested that the brewing of beer is at least as old as the baking of bread, and certainly both have been practiced since the dawn of recorded history. Indeed, the art and science of the brewer and those of the baker are quite similar, both involving grain, water, and yeast. In fact, the Sumerians baked barley loaves called *bappir* that could be stored in the dry climate and either eaten as bread of mixed with malted barley to form a mash for brewing.

Beer, by definition, is a beverage originating with grain, in which the flavor of the grain is balanced through the addition of other flavorings. Since the Middle Ages, those other flavorings have principally been hops. Today, a brewer typically starts the process with cereal grains—usually, but not exclusively, barley. The grains are malted, meaning that they are germinated and quickly dried. The extent to which malted grain is then roasted imparts a specific color to the beer, a step in the process that is obviously important to making Guinness what it is. The malt is then mashed, meaning that it is soaked long enough for enzymes to convert starch into fermentable sugar. The mashing takes place in a vessel that is generally called a *mash tun*, although the old Irish term *kieve* has always been the word favored at Guinness.

Next, water is added to the mash to dissolve the sugars, resulting in a thick, sweet liquid called *wort*. The wort is then boiled in what brewers call a brew kettle. At this point, most brewers add hops, the intensely flavored flower of the *humulus lupulus* plant. Originally a preservative as much as a flavoring, hops have been used by brewers for centuries. Throughout history, brewers have occasionally added seasonings other than hops to their beer. The Egyptians added flavorings such as fruit and honey, and certain modern beers contain fruit and spices.

Finally, the yeast is added to the cooled, hopped wort and the mixture is set aside to ferment into beer. During the fermentation process, the yeast converts the sugars into alcohol and carbon dioxide.

Having been brewed at the birth of civilization in the regions surrounding the Mediterranean, the beverage grew up with that civilization. Beer is mentioned by Xenophon and Aristotle (as quoted by Athenaeus). Among others, the Roman consul and scholar Pliny the Younger estimated that nearly 200 types of beer were being brewed in Europe by the first century. The Latin texts refer to the barley beverages as *cerevisia* or *cerevisium*, root words that are still with us in the Spanish and Portuguese words for beer—*cerveza* and *cerveja*—as well as in the latin name for brewer's yeast, *saccharomyces cerevisiae*.

Brewing, like wine making, was practiced in the lands whose shores were washed by the Mediterranean, but it was also practiced in Europe's northern latitudes. Here, cereal grains and brewing flourished, while grapes and viticulture usually did not.

In the British Isles, brewing existed in the misty distant past, long predating the Roman occupation. In the first century, Pedanius Dioscorides, the Greek pharmacologist and botanist traveled extensively throughout the Roman Empire collecting various substances with medicinal properties. He observed that the Britons and the Hiberi, as the Romans called the Irish, used a liquor variously known as "cuirim," "courm," or "courmi," an ale made from barley. Meanwhile, cuirim is also mentioned in the first century, the *Táin Bó Cúailnge* (The Cattle Raid of Cooley), the central tale in the Ulster Cycle, one of the four great cycles that make up the core of Irish mythology. In these stories, the Irish king Conchobar (Conor) MacNessa spends his day drinking cuirim "until he falls asleep therefrom."

The beer brewed in the Middle Ages was similar to modern ale, which is fermented at cellar temperatures using *saccharomyces cerevisiae*, a top-fermenting yeast. Today, such beer styles include porter and stout, as well as ale. These beers are distinct from lager beer, which is fermented at much colder temperatures using *saccharomyces carlsbergensis*, a bottom-fermenting yeast. Lager, whose cultural importance is described in more detail later, is also fermented for a longer time than top-fermented beers. Perfected in Germany early in the nineteenth century, lager is named for the German word meaning "to store," a reference to the longer fermentation.

The use of hops to flavor the beer, which is now the universally accepted standard, originated in central Europe, while in the British Isles, bayberries and ivy berries, as well as the flowers of the heath and other bitter herbs, rather than hops, were used as seasonings up through the Middle Ages.

In the fifth century *Senchus Mor,* the well-known book of the ancient laws of Ireland, there are abundant references to the growing of barley for malt, and to the enjoyment of ale. Later in the fifth century, a man named Mescan is widely described as having been the brewmaster of St. Patrick's household. In the ancient texts on the life of St. Patrick that were translated by Whitley Stokes in the 1880s, we learn that while the saint was dining with the King of Tara, "The wizard Lucatmael put a drop of poison into Patrick's cruse, and gave it into Patrick's hand: but Patrick blessed the cruse and inverted the vessel, and the poison fell thereout, and not even a little of the ale fell. And Patrick afterwards drank the ale."

Thomas Messingham, the seventeenth century Irish hagiologist who published biographies of many Irish saints, made note of the fact that the celebrated St. Brigid of Kildare (451–525) was, herself, a brewer. Translations from Rawlinson Manuscript B512 in the Bodleian Library at Oxford explain that Brigid was extremely diligent about brewing high quality ale that was filled with nutrients. The Rawlinson papers also note that she once supplied 17 churches with an Easter Ale that she brewed from one sack of malt.

At the beginning of the seventh century, when Irish monks set out to revitalize classical scholarship in Europe by founding monasteries as centers of learning, at least two of them brought the brewer's art. Saint Columbanus (543–615) and Saint Gall (550–646) traveled into the Frankish and Italian duchys, setting up a number of such cloisters, and legend has it that these places had breweries. This probably contributed to the tradition of European monastic brewing that survives—especially in Belgium—into the twenty-first century. A biography of Columbanus notes that "When the hour of refreshment approached, the minister of the refectory endeavored to serve the ale, which is bruised from the juice of wheat and barley, and which all the nations of the earth—except the Scordiscae and Dardans, who inhabit the borders of the ocean—Gaul, Britain, Ireland and Germany and others who are not unlike them in manners use."

In Europe during the Middle Ages, each town had numerous breweries and a great deal of beer was consumed. As graphically portrayed in the scenes of daily life painted by Peiter Brueghel, beer was a routine part of life in Northern Europe's villages and towns. Indeed, beer was a major element in the medieval diet. Boiled during the brewing process, beer was essentially germ-free, which meant that it was a good alternative for the typically unsanitary drinking water. Beer was also high in nutrients and food value.

During the Middle Ages, beer, like bread, was produced at home. The peasant housewife brewed for her family, the baron's servants brewed in the kitchen of his castle and the monks brewed in their monastery. As taverns and inns sprang up in the towns and along major roads, many of these establishments brewed their own, much in the manner of modern brewpubs. Gradually, small commercial brewers came into being, brewing larger quantities for sale to taverns and individuals. Such establishments remained small by later standards, with a relatively confined distribution radius.

By the end of the twelfth century, a number of breweries existed in Ireland along the Poddle River, which flows into the Liffey in Dublin. In the tradition of St. Brigid, many of the brewers were women. Indeed, female brewers—known in Old English as "brewsters"—were common throughout Northern Europe in the Middle Ages. Barnaby Rich in his *New Description of Ireland*, published in 1610, gives an account of the brewing industry in Dublin during the reign of James I and Charles II. By that time, he estimated that there were more than 1,100 alehouses and nearly 100 breweries and brewpubs in the city of Dublin, whose population was only 4,000 families. Rich also describes at length the tradition of a certain celebrated Holy Well near St. James's Gate, where an annual summer festival took place. St. James's Gate was the ancient entrance to the

city from the suburbs to the west. It took its name from the Church
and Parish of St. James, which date back to the twelfth century. The
gate is mentioned in the thirteenth century, and shown both on
Speed's 1610 map of Dublin and on Brooking's 1728 map of the city.
It was here, more than a century later, that Arthur Guinness would
lease his Dublin brewery. The original medieval St. James's Gate
itself deteriorated over time and was pulled down in 1734.

"On the west part of Dublin they have St. James, his Well,"
wrote Rich, "And his feast is celebrated the 25th of July, and upon
that day, a great mart or fair is kept fast by the Well. The commodity that is there to be vended, is nothing else but ale, no other
merchandise but only ale."

The fair or festival of St. James was also described by Richard
Stanihurst in his 1577 "Description of Dublin," in which he mentioned booths and ale-poles pitched at St. James's Gate in connection
with the event.

Though brewing certainly existed in the vicinity of St. James's
Gate in the sixteenth century, it is not known when the first brewery was established here. We do know that in 1670, a brewer named
Giles Mee obtained a lease from the Municipal Corporation that
included water rights described as the "Ground called the Pipes in
the parish of St. James." These rights eventually passed into the
ownership of Sir Mark Rainsford, a brewer and alderman. Documents preserved in the Public Registry of Deeds in Dublin record
that in 1693, Rainsford had a brewhouse at St. James's Gate where
"beer and fine ales" were made. In November 1715, Rainsford leased
his brewery to Paul Espinasse for 99 years.

By the turn of the eighteenth century, the brewing of beer in
European cities such as Dublin was gradually passing from the hands
of small pub brewers and home brewers to those of larger commercial brewers, who had first been incorporated in Dublin by Royal
Charter in 1696. Soon there would be an industry consolidation
that saw the rise of larger commercial breweries both in Ireland and
England.

Among these commercial breweries in Ireland was the St. Francis Abbey Brewery in Kilkenny, which was founded by John Smithwick in 1710 on the site of a Franciscan abbey where monks had brewed ale since the fourteenth century. This brewery is worth singling out because today it survives as Ireland's oldest operating brewery—and because the brewery, as well as the Smithwick's brand, have been part of the Guinness portfolio since 1956.

By the eighteenth century, as John Smithwick was brewing his first commercial batch of ale, the culture and economies of England and Ireland had long been inextricably intertwined. English rule had been firmly established in Ireland for centuries. With this, a class system had been imposed which favored Protestants over Catholics, and people with English, rather than Celtic lineage. Had Arthur Guinness not been Protestant, he never would have had the opportunity to buy a brewery in eighteenth century Ireland.

The Gaels, the ancient Celtic people who had lived in Ireland for thousands of years, converted to Christianity around the fifth century, ruled the island politically until the twelfth century except for occasional raids and inroads made by the Vikings after about the ninth century. In 1172, King Henry II of England invaded Ireland. Though England claimed all of Ireland for over five hundred years, the English occupation was mainly confined to a few east coast cities such as Waterford, and the Pale, the area surrounding Dublin. As this foothold expanded in the sixteenth century, it led to the gradual collapse of the old Gaelic social and political structure, and also to the Protestant Ascendancy, the rise of a new English ruling class. Being Protestant (since King Henry VIII had replaced the Catholic church in England with the Protestant Anglican church in 1534), this ruling class was distinct from the Catholic indigenous Irish majority. Catholics, despite their constituting 90 percent of the population, owned less than 10 percent of Irish land, and were barred from the Irish Parliament.

Beginning in the seventeenth century—aside from the decade that England was ruled as a republic—there was a de facto unified monarchy throughout the British Isles. Monarchs were considered to be of England, Scotland, and Ireland. The latter had no monarch of its own, but the two separate kingdoms of Scotland and England had shared the same monarch since James VI, King of Scots, became James I of England in 1603. (In Ireland, the English-dominated Irish Parliament had, in 1542, voted to make the sitting English monarch automatically the monarch of Ireland.) In 1707, the kingdoms of England and Scotland officially merged as the Kingdom of Great Britain, with a single parliament and government, based in Westminster in London, controlled the new kingdom. The Kingdom of Great Britain was superseded by the United Kingdom of Great Britain and Ireland in 1801 when the Kingdom of Ireland was absorbed after the English put down the Irish Rebellion of 1798.

It was against this backdrop of political and social events that Arthur Guinness was born in Celbridge, County Kildare, in 1725. Arthur's father is known to have been a man named Richard Guinness, but little is known of who he was or where he came from. By various accounts, Richard Guinness was probably born in or around 1690. The names of his parents are not known, although he is believed to have had a brother named William who later became a gunsmith in Dublin.

If true, his having been born in 1690 places Richard's origin in the same year as one of the milestone moments of Irish history, the Battle of the Boyne. Fought near Drogheda on the River Boyne on July 1, 1690, it was the turning point in the war between the Jacobite armies of the deposed Catholic King James II of England (who had also ruled as James VII of Scotland) and the Williamite armies of his Protestant son-in-law and successor, William III (William of Orange) who had deposed James from his English and Scottish thrones in the previous year. The outcome of the Battle of the Boyne was that William ruled and James ran. For Ireland, this outcome ensured continued English and Protestant rule that would last more than two centuries.

The Battle of the Boyne figures prominently in the various tales of Richard Guinness's ancestry. One of the more colorful and improbable stories casts Richard Guinness as the illegitimate son of an Irish girl and an English soldier named Gennys, who was stranded in Ireland after the battle.

A more likely story, and one that Arthur Guinness himself believed to be accurate, was that his father was descended from or related to Bryan Viscount Magennis of Iveagh (Uibh Eachach) in County Down. Magennis was a Catholic nobleman who supported James II before and during his failed fight on the Boyne. In the aftermath, Bryan was one of those who fled Ireland as part of the "Flight of the Wild Geese," the exit of Irish Jacobites from Ireland to France. The story continues that a wing of the Magennis clan dropped the prefix "Ma" (short for Mac, meaning "the family") from their surname and converted from Catholicism to Protestantism.

What *is* known for sure about Richard Guinness includes his marriage to a woman named Elizabeth Read, and the fact that he was an administrator and land custodian in the employ of Reverend Dr. Arthur Price, the affluent Protestant vicar of Celbridge in County Kildare. A romantic legend has it that Richard had earlier been a groom for Elizabeth's father near Oughter Ard, and that he had eloped with her. In fact, their nuptials probably involved much less drama because the vicar would not have hired someone involved in something as scandalous as an elopement, and an eloping couple from Oughter Ard would have traveled farther than the few miles to Celbridge.

As Reverend Price's career flourished, Richard and Elizabeth Guinness prospered and eventually bought property of their own. The reverend's fast track to success often took him to Dublin or London, and while he was away, Richard was in charge of his lands and property.

In 1725, when young Arthur Guinness was born, Reverend Price became his godfather and namesake. Arthur was the first of six, the others being Frances, Elizabeth, Benjamin, Richard, and Samuel.

Though numerous sources refer to the year of Arthur's birth, we do not know the day. Records of his birth, such as a birth certificate or church records, have not survived.

Among his other duties in the employ of the vicar, Richard Guinness served as the house brewer at the Price estate. It is recalled that he brewed a delectable dark beer that was said to be immensely popular with the reverend and his guests. Almost certainly, young Arthur and his siblings were familiar with this beer and would possibly have helped in the brewing process.

In 1744, Reverend Price reached the apogee of his career with an appointment as Archbishop of Cashel, one of the most important offices in the Protestant Church of Ireland. At this time, young Arthur is listed as having been on Price's payroll along with his father. Eight years later, however, the old cleric passed away. In his will, he generously left £100 to Richard, and another £100 to his godson and namesake, Arthur Guinness. In those days, £100 was real money, considering that Richard, who was well paid, earned about a quarter of that sum annually. With his inheritance, Richard, a widower since his wife died in 1742, remarried, this time to a woman named Elizabeth Clare. They opened a roadhouse inn, where Richard almost certainly continued to brew his famous and well-loved dark beer.

As for the young Arthur Guinness, he started his own business nearby. Then, having done this for a few years, he did as ambitious young men have done throughout history—he headed for the big city to seek his fortune.

2

Arthur Guinness, Brewer

In 1756, Arthur Guinness joined the ranks of Irish commercial brewers. He used £100 left to him in the will of Archbishop Price to lease a small brewery in Leixlip, County Kildare. By this time, brewing as a commercial enterprise in the British Isles—mainly in England—had grown beyond the status of the localized craft that it had been since the Middle Ages. Some Irish brewers had grown larger, but Ireland was still a tiny market compared to England. Being a mere colony, Ireland was dominated by England, which was vastly larger both in population and economic power.

Economic dominance included not only massive exports of English goods to Ireland, but the passage of tariffs in Parliament that favored English exporters. For example, English revenue laws allowed

English beer to be imported into Ireland on such favorable terms that it could be sold at a lower price than Irish brewers had to charge. Arthur Guinness entered the trade against this backdrop and amid a decline in the Irish brewing industry brought about by the revenue laws. This is not to say that Irish brewers rolled over and played dead, although for a time they continued to brew brown ale rather than competing directly with the imported English porter, which was the most popular beer style in England and Ireland during the mid-eighteenth century.

Porter is a dark, sweet style of beer that is brewed in a manner similar to ale, and which, like ale, is produced with top-fermenting *saccharomyces cerevisiae* yeast. It originated in England in 1722 and was invented—according to the commonly believed account—by a brewer named Ralph Harwood who operated in Shoreditch, a place within the London borough of Hackney. His original name for his beer was the unappetizing term *entire butt*. A butt was the largest barrel in common usage, and the term implied that the entire barrel contained the same type of beer, unblended with other types. Darker and richer than the ales then available, it became instantly popular with working class people, especially the porters who worked on the Thames River docks. Hence, entire butt earned the more agreeable name *porter*.

One of the first references to porter brewing in Ireland is in a petition presented in 1763 to the Irish House of Commons by Joseph and Ephraim Thwaites, who were Dublin brewers. They requested that Ireland encourage them in the brewing of Irish porter, which they claimed to have brought to perfection after what they described as repeated and expensive attempts. However, English porter dominated the Irish market and the Irish brewing industry continued to suffer.

Arthur Guinness, though, was an optimistic young entrepreneur who found opportunity in the gradual decline in Irish brewing. In 1759, he made the leap from rural Leixlip to the Irish capital. Here, he cut an incredible deal for a shuttered brewery property overlooking the Liffey River near where Dublin's St. James's Gate had stood until 1734.

As noted in the previous chapter, the origins of brewing at the site dated back to 1670, and to the brewery that was owned by Giles Mee. Sir Mark Rainsford had acquired the property in 1693 and had leased it to Paul Espinasse in 1715. When Espinasse died in 1750, the lease reverted back to the Rainsford family.

On December 31, 1759, the premises were formally leased by Mark Rainsford's son to Arthur Guinness for £100 down and £45 a year. This was not exceptional, but the term of the lease was an incredible *nine thousand years*! The lease is still preserved in a vault at St. James's Gate, with a facsimile on display in the Guinness visitor center. With an 89-foot frontage facing north onto the busy thoroughfare where James's Street and Thomas Street merge, the four-acre site contained a brewhouse, a grist mill, two malt houses, and stables to accommodate a dozen brewery horses. It was also reasonably close to the River Liffey, which led to the port of Dublin for access to the sea. A popular and long-repeated legend suggests that water drawn from the Liffey goes directly into Guinness beer, but this has never been the case.

Also worth noting is that two years before Guinness made his acquisition, work had begun on Ireland's Grand Canal, which would link Dublin with the River Shannon and with Limerick. In Dublin, the canal's terminus was at James's Street, practically at Arthur Guinness's front door. Through the years, this canal would allow Guinness direct access to transportation for both raw materials and finished product.

"The Grand Canal automatically gave Arthur Guinness access to trade routes down into the country for his porter," Guinness Archivist Eibhlin Roche explains. "And as importantly, grain came up from the farmers to the city through the canal."

Because of the dominance of English-brewed porter in the Dublin market, the young entrepreneur probably brewed ale, and did not jump immediately nor exclusively into porter brewing.

Guinness may have brewed porter in addition to ale during his early years at St. James's Gate, but Guinness kept ale as part of his product portfolio practically until the end of the century.

By this time, two of Arthur's brothers had also made the move from Kildare to Dublin. Richard, who had assisted Arthur at his Leixlip brewery, remained there, but Benjamin came to the city to become a grocer, and young Samuel became a Dublin goldsmith. Samuel would also become the patriarch of a family that would later distinguish itself in banking, politics, and the legal profession.

On June 17, 1761, two years after setting up shop in Dublin, 36-year-old Arthur Guinness married 19-year-old Olivia Whitmore, a most eligible young woman. The daughter of a wealthy and successful Dublin businessman who had died a few years before, she brought to their marriage an inheritance that amounted to tenfold that which Arthur had inherited from Reverend Price. Olivia also brought to the union a series of connections to Dublin society that would put Guinness and his business activities in good company. Olivia was related to the Darleys and to the LeTouche banking dynasty, as well as to the Smyths, whose lineage included archbishops and at least one lord mayor. Olivia's mother was a member of the prominent Grattan family, and her cousin Henry Grattan was a rising star in Irish politics. Later in the century, as a member of the Irish Parliament, Henry was an outspoken advocate of Catholic emancipation and of Irish legislative independence from Britain.

Arthur brought a touch of class to the union. By now, he officially recognized his lineage as including the Magennis clan. At the wedding, his inlaws presented him and Olivia with a silver cup that bore their names as well as the crest of the Magennises, a rampant golden boar beneath the red hand symbolic of Ulster, the province containing County Down, from which the Magennises hailed.

Arthur and Olivia would have 10 children, but poor Olivia would also suffer 11 miscarriages. It is a testament to her solid constitution that she survived 21 pregnancies in an era when so many women died in childbirth. The children, four girls and six boys, were

Elizabeth, Hosea, Arthur, Edward, Olivia, Benjamin, Louisa, John Grattan, William Lunell, and Mary Anne. Of these, Olivia died in childhood, but the others outlived their father. Elizabeth, their first daughter, was born in 1763, and Hosea, their first son, was born in 1765. Mary Anne, the youngest daughter, was born in 1787 when her mother was in her late forties and her eldest sister was already married.

Despite becoming a steadfast member of the gentry, Arthur Guinness would become an outspoken advocate of the rights of the Catholic majority underclass. Like Henry Grattan, he questioned the wisdom of excluding Catholics from professional jobs and joined with those who advocated overturning restrictive laws. He was an early member of the Dublin Society, an organization that promoted the improvement of domestic industry and agriculture to the benefit of the oppressed majority. Though he was a strict member of the Protestant Church of Ireland, he is recalled as having been fair and respectful of his mainly Catholic workforce at St. James's Gate. He developed a keen interest in Gaelic arts and culture, promoting and encouraging indigenous music and poetry. Arthur was well known as a philanthropist, and in 1786, he founded Ireland's first Sunday School. A deeply religious man, he adopted the motto "Spes Mea in Deo," meaning "My Hope is in God."

Meanwhile, business at Guinness's St. James's Gate brewery was growing, providing Arthur with profits that befitted a man of his newly acquired social standing. His beer was popular throughout Dublin. So popular, in fact, that in 1779 Guinness became the official purveyor of beer to Dublin Castle, the seat of the British government in Ireland. Guinness would use his profits to acquire property, including a home on Dublin's Gardiner Street, and Beaumont, his expansive country estate north of Dublin Bay. He also became a partner, along with his brother Samuel, in the Hibernian Insurance Company, and he bought the Hibernian flour mills at Kilmainham, which would remain an important family asset well into the nineteenth century.

Arthur joined the Dublin Corporation of Brewers, the local trade organization, serving as warden in 1763 and as master four years later. In this role, Arthur Guinness would spend the next quarter century testifying in the Irish Parliament on behalf of the Irish brewing industry.

By 1773, Arthur Guinness, along with George Thwaites, Master of the Corporation of Brewers, were part of the committee of brewers who went to the Irish House of Commons to formally draw the lawmakers' attention to the fact that imported porter was taxed at less than a shilling per barrel, while Irish brewers paid more than five shillings. In the preceding decade, the importation of English porter into Dublin had risen from 28,935 barrels to 58,675, while it was observed that the taxes collected on beer brewed in Ireland hardly amounted to the cost of collection. It should be noted that it was also during the 1770s that George III's taxation policies were about to get him into very big trouble across the Atlantic.

This might also be a good place to mention that two of King George's most notable American antagonists, George Washington and Thomas Jefferson, were very big fans of porter—specifically Philadelphia porter. Their references to this love of porter are documented by handwritten memoranda preserved in the Library of Congress. It is well known that Washington patronized a Philadelphia brewer named Benjamin Morris, and that he also favored the porter brewed by Robert Hare, also of Philadelphia. An expatriate Englishman, Hare is believed to have been the first American brewer to produce this smooth dark style of beer.

Washington had certainly become acquainted with Hare's porter by 1788 because, on July 20 of that year, he wrote to his friend, Clement Biddle, "I beg you will send me a gross of Mr. Hare's best bottled porter if the price is not much enhanced by the copious droughts you took of it at the late procession."

Back in Ireland, in his role as a member of the Corporation of Brewers, Arthur Guinness managed to convince his majesty's tax collectors that it was to their financial advantage to *encourage,* rather than penalize, the Irish brewing industry. It was in 1777, a year after King George was given that rude wake-up call issued in Philadelphia, that the English-controlled Irish House of Commons officially changed the tax code that had previously subsidized the importation of English porter into Ireland. Arthur Guinness, as a master in the Dublin Corporation of Brewers, had played a pivotal role in this change.

The swing of the pendulum would soon be manifest in an increasing popularity of Irish porter in England! The tables were turned, and Ireland became a beer exporter. The output of Irish brewers, which had declined in the early eighteenth century, hit its nadir in the early 1770s, then rebounded nicely. Thanks to favorable trade legislation passed in the 1790s, Irish brewers could now compete with the English in England as well as in Ireland. The Irish brewing industry soon experienced a renaissance, and Arthur Guinness undertook a major brewery expansion.

Dublin in the eighteenth century was coming into its own as a prosperous commercial port within the United Kingdom. Much has been written about the thriving maritime trade, the important network of routes that linked the cities on both sides of the Irish Sea—such as Dublin, Waterford, and Cork on the west, to Liverpool and Bristol on the east. Commercially, Dublin had closer ties to England and the English economy than to rural subsistence economy in the west and the interior of Ireland. Dublin, and to a lesser extent Cork, with their Georgian architecture and growing middle class, began to look and feel more like English cities.

With their large populations and growing middle class, Dublin and Cork were among the few Irish cities to have industries, and one of the largest and most robust of these was the brewing industry. Having gradually superseded brewpubs in these cities, the commercial breweries were evolving into a major economic force.

Dublin and Cork had easy access not only to the maritime trading economy, but to the barley-growing regions of eastern Ireland as well. Most of the hops still needed to be imported—from England

and Flanders—but by weight, they were a far less bulky item in beer production than barley, so the shipping costs were less than what it would have been if grain was the commodity that needed importing.

In addition to the market in England, there was a strong domestic demand for the produce of the Dublin and Cork brewers in the growing and increasingly affluent Irish east coast. Elsewhere in Ireland, however, there was little market for the east coast beer. Because it was a subsistence economy that relied on barter rather than money, the rural people could not afford commercial beer. Here, they either brewed their own, or more commonly, they distilled homemade spirits.

In addition to Guinness, the major breweries in Dublin in the late eighteenth century were the Phoenix Brewery and Robert Mander, both of which were neighbors of St. James's Gate, as well as the Anchor Brewery on Usher Street and Sweetman's Brewery on Francis Street. By this time, the largest and possibly the oldest continuously operating brewery in Dublin was the Ardee Street Brewery that had been brewing since the middle of the sixteenth century.

Cork was home to Beamish & Crawford, the largest brewery in Ireland at the end of the eighteenth century. Founded in 1792 by William Beamish and William Crawford, this brewery, like St. James's Gate, was located on a site where brewing dated back to the middle of the seventeenth century. Another important brewer in Cork was James J. Murphy & Company, founded in 1856 at Lady's Well by the four Murphy brothers, James, William, Jerome, and Francis. Located on the hill opposite the brewery, the celebrated Lady's Well was dedicated to the Virgin Mary, and it was believed to possess miraculous properties. Both Beamish & Crawford and Murphy continue to operate in the twenty-first century, but the former was acquired by Scottish & Newcastle in 1995, and Heineken now owns Murphy.

Brewing was a craft that was uniquely suited to being enlarged into a major operation in the years before the technological innovations of the Industrial Revolution. Essentially, all that was needed to transform a craft brewery into an industrial scale brewery was to scale it up. As Patrick Lynch and John Vaizey have pointed out, as the more successful brewers expanded the scope of their operations and gradually began to absorb their less enterprising competitors, they discovered that "there were advantages in enlarging the scale of their production within a single plant; for brewing, unlike other industries, did not have to await the application of steam before large-scale production was possible. . . . No single new invention was necessary to enable the brewers to cater for the expanding market."

In a gravity brewhouse, once all the materials were hoisted to the top, gravity carried everything through the whole "assembly line" of the brewing process. As Lynch and Vaizey put it, "It was possible in the brewing industry, as in no other, to achieve industrialized manufacture on a large scale by harnessing the forces of gravity. And since specialization is limited by the extent of the market, the growth of the market was vital. An increase in the scale of production realized economies which could not readily be secured in the production of solid goods until the adoption of steam power."

Meanwhile, despite his social standing and his position as a captain of a growing industry, Arthur Guinness was no stranger to controversy and confrontation. Between 1773 and 1775, along with two factory owners, Foster and Greene, whose plants adjoined the St. James's Gate Brewery, Guinness was involved in a particularly contentious dispute over water rights. The Dublin City Corporation claimed that Guinness was using more water than that to which he was entitled by his lease from Rainsford. The Dublin City Corporation claimed that the water was theirs to parcel out to users, and that it was not included in the St. James's Gate lease. Arthur Guinness strenuously disagreed, pointing out that in his lease, he had been granted the water "free of tax or pipe money."

Finally, in 1775, backed by the sheriff, the other parties attempted to physically cut off the St. James's Gate water entirely.

This brought Arthur Guinness himself out to the scene brandishing a pick. He said that if they took his water, he'd redig his channel. The sheriff and the others backed down, preferring to let the courts decide rather than to face an angry, pick-wielding Guinness. The case was settled 10 years later with Guinness leasing the needed water from the City of Dublin for £10 annually.

In retrospect, the showdown over the water rights, including the colorful image Arthur Guinness with the pick, is seen as one of the pivotal moments in Guinness history. Indeed, a brewery with no water, or with water too expensive to use, cannot survive. Had he not stood his ground that day, history would have been quite different, and we might live today in a world without the black liquidation with the froth on the top.

As we have seen, in his early years at St. James's Gate, Arthur Guinness concentrated on brewing Irish ale rather than competing for price with English porter, but he was keen to change this situation. It is not known exactly when Arthur Guinness started brewing porter as well as ale, but it was certainly before 1783.

The earliest references to the specific beers that Arthur Guinness brewed at St. James's Gate are contained in his brewery memoranda book of 1796 that is still preserved at St. James's Gate. In it, we find that Guinness was then brewing both ale and porter, and it is safe to assume that Guinness had been brewing both ale and porter for some time. We also see that he was brewing much more porter than ale.

What we know about Arthur Guinness's business in the eighteenth century comes to us as a collage, gathered in bits and pieces from a variety of sources. Just as we know about what he brewed from the memoranda books at St. James's Gate, we know about his commitment to quality and to porter from Volume IX of the *Journals of the Irish House of Commons*. In 1783, Guinness told a parliamentary committee that "a porter brewer buys none but the best, as none else will answer!"

In 1799, the popularity of Irish porter had evolved to the point where Guinness made the historic decision to completely discontinue brewing ale at St. James's Gate and to focus exclusively on porter. On March 14 of that year, Arthur wrote in his memoranda book that he combined 14 barrels of pale malt with 6 of brown malt, added hops and brewed 43 barrels of ale. He then wrote that this was his last brewing of ale. This was, in turn, crossed out and replaced with a notation referring to the reverse of the page. Here, there is a single entry recording Arthur's having brewed 40 barrels of ale on April 22, 1799, marking the end to his ale brewing career.

By this time, porter had indeed eclipsed ale in the product line at St. James's Gate. In this same notebook, we see that Arthur had been brewing porter on average about 10 times a month, with these brews averaging between 50 and 60 barrels, while ale was brewed just a couple of times monthly and in smaller quantities. The handwriting was, if not on the wall, clearly spelled out for posterity in Arthur Guinness's own hand in his notebook. St. James's Gate was now a porter brewery.

As for *types* of porter, the records contained within the Guinness brewery notebooks tell us that these included Town Porter, Country Porter, Keeping Porter, and Superior Porter. Town Porter was brewed for sale in and near Dublin, while the Country Porter was obviously brewed for sale farther afield within Ireland. The Keeping Porter was brewed for blending with other beers, especially during the summer months. Superior Porter was a stronger beer available throughout the market.

On December 14, 1801, Arthur Guinness—or possibly his son—jotted in the brewery notebook the first known reference to a beer that was called West Indies Porter. High in hops and alcohol, this beer was designed specifically for export to the Caribbean, an area that is still an important market for Guinness. Like the India Pale Ale produced by the British brewers for export to India, West Indies Porter was highly hopped and higher in alcohol to preserve in on the long overseas voyage.

The recipe for the West Indies Porter called for 75 parts black malt to 55 parts pale malt and 20 parts brown malt. This, and other aspects of his notes on ingredients and brewing technique, lead scholars to call West Indies Porter a true precursor to Guinness Foreign Extra Stout, a beer that is still brewed today at St. James's Gate. Beginning with the 145 barrels of West Indies Porter brewed in 1801, this lineage of brewing makes today's Foreign Extra Stout perhaps the oldest continuously brewed beer in the world.

Jonathan Bryan Guinness, the 3rd Baron Moyne and a seventh generation descendant of Arthur Guinness, wrote in his memoir of the family business:

> In Arthur's day brewing was still an art, not a science; Louis Pasteur was as yet unborn and there were no laboratories to analyze samples of barley and hops; the brewer's eye was the only measuring tool. As to yeast, it is a living organism, and a quick-breeding one; and even now with strict scientific control it can develop a genetic mutation so inconvenient as to require the destruction of an entire batch. Arthur must have mastered all these problems better than most. In particular, he was among the first Irishmen to become really good at producing the black porter. There was money in this. . . . Once Arthur Guinness and the other Irish brewers— he had competitors—had cracked the technical problem and produced a porter as good as that which came from London, it was worth their while to concentrate on it. Soon the Irish product not only equaled the London porter, but surpassed it. After conquering the Dublin market, Irish porter became in demand in Britain.

Meanwhile, Ireland was enjoying a brief period of autonomy from the mother country. In 1782, Ireland achieved legislative independence from his majesty's privy council—thanks in part to both the American Revolution and the crusading efforts of Irish legislator Henry Grattan, the cousin of Mrs. Arthur Guinness. Through the series of legal changes that comprised the Constitution of 1782, the Parliament of Ireland was freed from restrictions that had been imposed since medieval times by successive English and British governments. Beginning in 1782, Ireland would enjoy 17 years of unprecedented legislative freedom, an era that came to be known as Grattan's Parliament after Henry Grattan's role in its creation.

It is worth noting this turn of events because Grattan was also an enthusiastic supporter of the Irish brewing industry and of Irish porter. In a letter to his inlaw, Arthur Guinness, Grattan described the Irish brewing industry as "the natural nurse of the people and entitled to every encouragement, favor and exemption."

Grattan's support of the brewing industry echoed that of many people in the Irish society of the day, who saw beer as a healthy alternative to higher alcohol—and hence more intoxicating—spirits such as whiskey.

Though Ireland, or at least its locally born Protestant elite, enjoyed some measure of self-determination during the latter decades of the eighteenth century, there was an emerging contingent who wanted more. Inspired by the ideals of the American and French Revolutions that were taking place in this time period, they wanted complete independence. Led by a revolutionary group known as the United Irishmen, the Irish Rebellion of 1798 flared up in the counties surrounding Dublin and soon spread. Despite the intervention of French forces, and some surprising rebel victories, the rebellion was crushed by British troops.

Instead of being a step forward in the cause of Irish independence, the rebellion resulted in the British curtailment of autonomy rights already granted to Ireland and dissolution of the Irish Parliament—after only 17 years of the autonomy that had been granted by the Constitution of 1782. The Act of Union passed by the British Parliament took effect on the first day of 1801, abolishing self-government and merging the Kingdom of Ireland and the Kingdom of Great Britain—created by the earlier merger of the Kingdoms of England and Scotland—to form the United Kingdom of GreatBritain and Ireland. Catholic Emancipation was intended to be part of the plan, but King George III—the same stubborn monarch whose inflexibility cost Britain its American colonies—reneged. Catholic Emancipation would eventually come to Ireland, but not until 1829. The last words spoken in the Irish Parliament in 1800 by Henry Grattan were in favor of Irish freedom and against the Act of Union.

By the late 1780s, it had come time for the oldest of the Guinness boys to think about careers and about how they felt about the issues of the day. Arthur's oldest son, Hosea, had chosen to become a Protestant minister, but both Arthur Guinness II and Benjamin would join their father at St. James's Gate. During the Rebellion of 1798, the sons found themselves at odds. By now, 33-year-old Hosea was a minister, and ostensibly a man of peace, but his brothers Edward and William Lunell joined the Protestant paramilitary organizations that actively opposed the revolt. Even young John, still a teenager, was caught up in the Protestant cause.

For Arthur and Benjamin, regardless their sympathies in the rebellion, the focus was on St. James's Gate and the management of what was now one of the most successful brewing companies in Ireland. Soon, they would be on their own.

A little more than a year after the first brew of West Indies Porter, Arthur Guinness passed away on January 23, 1803, at Beaumont, his country estate. His funeral was presided over by his eldest son, the Reverend Hosea Guinness. He was buried next to his mother, not far away at Oughter Ard, borne to this site in County Kildare by a carriage draped with a cloth bearing the Magennis family crest.

In the graveyard, the inscription states: "In the adjoining Vault are deposited the mortal remains of Arthur Guinness late of James's Gate in the city and of Beaumont in the County of Dublin Esquire who departed his life on the 23rd of January AD 1803 aged 78 years."

The man, who had arrived in Dublin three decades earlier with scarcely more than his original nest egg of £100, had died one of the city's most prosperous businessmen. He had made ample provisions for his wife, who lived comfortably at their home in Dublin until her death in 1814. Arthur Guinness was generous with his children, leaving Beaumont to Hosea and his wife Jane Hart Guinness, and substantial cash sums to his other children. To Arthur, his second son and namesake, the founder left the proprietorship of the family business at St. James's Gate.

A Family Business

When the 35-year-old Arthur Guinness II, still known around St. James's Gate as "the Second Arthur," took up the reins of the brewery management in 1803, he already had more than a decade of experience in the business. During young Arthur's period of apprenticeship to his father, the enterprise had flourished. Annual output had continued to increase to the point where St. James's Gate was Dublin's largest brewing company. In 1800, the brewery sold 10,026 36-gallon barrels. By 1803, sales had more than doubled to 22,479 barrels. During their years of working together, the two Arthurs had presided over a major plant expansion, and the decision to cease brewing ale in 1799 in order to concentrate on porter.

According to the *Dublin Directory*, the Second Arthur was taken into the business by his father in 1794. In 1793, the firm was known as "Arthur Guinness, brewer and flour dealer." In 1794, this entry reappears, with the phrase "Guinness, Arthur and Son, brewers." Between 1795 and 1807, the entry reads "Guinness, Arthur and Son, brewer and flour merchant." The Guinnesses still considered their Hibernian flour mills at Kilmainham to be a business venture whose importance was on par with the family brewery.

Company records show that upon his father's death, the Second Arthur not only inherited the proprietorship of the business, but the all-important title of head brewer at St. James's Gate. Over the coming years, he would be successful in solidly expanding the market reach of the family business. He inherited a brewery that sold most of its beer within a day's ride of Dublin, with the English trade being a minimal part of its business. By 1816, records show that bottled Guinness porter from St. James's Gate "successfully rivaled the London product even in the English metropolis."

Under the Second Arthur, Guinness expanded its trade with England, but looked even farther. Beginning with West Indies Porter—the brewery's first product especially brewed for the export market—Guinness products were being shipped not only to Caribbean destinations such as Barbados and Trinidad, but to the British Crown Colony of Sierra Leone in West Africa.

Throughout the nineteenth century, the era when "the sun never set on the British Empire," casks of Guinness were shipped to wherever British troops were serving, and to wherever British expatriates were living. During the Napoleonic Wars—an era that coincided generally with the Second Arthur's tenure as head brewer—the beer from St. James's Gate was made available to grateful British troops in Europe. One of the greatest triumphs of the British Army in the nineteenth century was the 1815 victory over Napoleon by Arthur Wellesley, the Duke of Wellington at Waterloo, but it was also a victory for Guinness's porter.

In *Long Forgotten Days*, Ethel M. Richardson writes of a British cavalry officer, wounded at Waterloo, who confided in his diary as he lay in the hospital: "When I was sufficiently recovered to be permitted to take some nourishment I felt the most extraordinary desire for a glass of Guinness. . . . I shall never forget how much I enjoyed it. I thought I had never tasted anything so delightful."

Victory at Waterloo, though greatly celebrated, also turned an unwelcome page in the evolution of the United Kingdom's economy. The interest on the national debt, increased by the expenses of the war years, combined with the military pensions, sucked up the government's revenues. The House of Commons refused in 1816 to continue the wartime income tax, forcing His Majesty's government to borrow heavily to meet its commitments. In turn, this led to recession by 1817.

Against the backdrop of the economic downturn throughout Great Britain and Ireland, all businesses suffered, brewers included. Up from 39,790 barrels sold in 1808, Guinness had a record year in 1815, with an all-time (to date) peak production of 66,672 barrels in 1815. From there, business declined, hitting a low of just 27,185 barrels in 1823, the company's worst year since 1804. It would take a decade of hard work and shifting economic winds to pull Guinness back up to prerecession levels.

In the meantime, as the young Second Arthur Guinness was taking his place among Ireland's elite, several of his siblings also moved into positions of importance. Elizabeth Guinness became Dublin's first lady in 1809 when her husband, Frederick Darley, became the lord mayor. Reverend Hosea Guinness became the rector of St. Werburgh's Church, one of the most important churches to Dublin's upper crust. Louisa and Mary Anne Guinness both married well-connected young clergymen. Respectively, they were William Dean Hoare, a member of a successful banking family, who later became vicar general of Limerick, and John Burke, a young nobleman from County Galway. John Grattan Guinness, the youngest brother, joined the East India Company and sought his fortune in faraway India. He returned many years later a war hero with the rank of captain.

At St. James's Gate, Arthur was aided by his brothers Benjamin and William Lunell Guinness, who had both joined him by around

1808. We see this in the *Dublin Directory* for 1808. Through 1807, the entry for the family business had read "Guinness, Arthur and Son, brewer and flour merchant." In 1808, the entry becomes "Guinness (A., Ben., and W. L.) brewer." Their fourth brother, Edward, meanwhile, attempted to make it on his own as a businessman, but his ventures failed.

As the second generation Guinnesses were making their way in the world, the Second Arthur had begun a family of his own from which would be drawn the third generation management of the family brewery. He married Anne Lee in 1793, the daughter of Benjamin Lee of Merrion, and the couple had three sons. Born in 1795, William followed his Uncle Hosea into the clergy. Arthur Lee Guinness, born in 1797, and Benjamin Lee Guinness, born the following year, would both have future roles at St. James's Gate.

By the 1820s, the Second Arthur was officially moving away from day-to-day management at the brewery to pursue banking interests. However, he still apparently kept an interest in brewing activities because, in 1821, he wrote explicit instructions for the brewing of a beer then known as Guinness Extra Superior Porter, considered to be the precursor of today's Guinness Extra Stout. A true patriarch of the brand as it exists today, Arthur had also been present at the birth in 1801 of West Indies Porter, the precursor of today's Foreign Extra Stout.

We say precursor because the two beers are extremely close to the modern analog, but not exactly. Brewing methods have changed many times in two centuries. So too has the ability of the brewer to measure nuances in the brewing process.

"Brewing in the nineteenth century and before was definitely more of an art than a science, but there was science in it, just as there is in a Michelin star restaurant," Master Brewer Fergal Murray explains. "There was an art and a passion, but because they had that passion, they had rules. They had developed a way that worked, and they repeated the process, doing it the same way, which is the scientific method. In the nineteenth century, the alcohol content was probably in the 7 to 8 percent range, but nobody knew precisely. Nobody measured it. By 1900, Guinness would be measuring the specific gravity. While it wasn't possible to control production to the specification standards we have today, they got the best they could out of the quality of the grain, fermented it, and got a product that tasted quite good."

Judging by sales figures, it apparently tasted very good. In 1821, Guinness sold 30,519 barrels, and in 1828, the number increased to a total of 42,384 barrels. Extra Superior Porter quickly became the signature beer being produced at St. James's Gate. By 1828, it accounted from 28 percent of all Guinness trade, but in just seven years, its share of the Guinness product line had increased to 59 percent. In 1840, it accounted for 82 percent of the 79,924 barrels sold by Guinness.

What is the origin of the term *stout?* When it was introduced, Extra Superior Porter was considered to be a "stouter" variant of porter that was referred to generically as "stout porter." At that time, the term stout was an adjective describing the strength—in density and character as much as alcohol content—of the porter, but gradually the term became a noun. Eventually, "stout porter" became simply "stout." Extra Superior Porter became Guinness Double Stout, and later Guinness Extra Stout.

Calculating the exact "stoutness" of mid-nineteenth century beers is a moving target because the gravity—and hence the alcohol content—fluctuated frequently. The fluctuation had to do with a myriad of factors ranging from raw materials to market conditions to government mandate. During the Napoleonic wars (as again during the world wars) the British government would require brewers to produce lower gravity beers. Recorded using a hydrometer, original gravity refers to the density of unfermented wort relative to the density of water as a prediction of the probable alcohol content of the finished beer. For example, an original gravity of 1.050 (written as 1050 degrees) predicts an alcohol content of 5.4 percent by volume.

As Guinness Extra Superior Porter evolved into Double Stout, and later into Guinness Extra Stout, a weaker variant called Guinness Porter continued to be brewed simultaneously. It would continue as a major product variant until the early twentieth century. Though its importance in the English and Irish market waned, it would remain part of the product portfolio until 1974. As previously noted, Foreign Extra Stout, the product variant that was stronger than Guinness Extra Stout, was—and still is—brewed for overseas markets.

Guinness Archivist Eibhlin Roche points out that "throughout the nineteenth century, you had effectively two types of stout being brewed at St. James's Gate. Foreign Extra Stout was purely for far-flung markets, and Guinness Extra Stout was for domestic markets in Ireland and Great Britain." As noted previously, the higher alcohol and higher hop rate in the Foreign Extra Stout served as a preservative on long overseas voyages.

A big part of the story of Guinness during this period was the expansion of its distribution network within the massive beer market in England. This included the relationship that Guinness forged in the 1820s with the Samuel Waring shipping company of Bristol. Considered to be England's "second city" during the early nineteenth century, Bristol was the major port city on the west coast, and it was half the distance by sea from Dublin as was London. From here, intra-England transportation was facilitated by an excellent network of canals, and later by railroads.

Guinness also opened a door into northwest England in 1821 when Henry Antisell set up a Guinness distribution agency in the big port city of Liverpool. An agency here facilitated not only access to the market within the British Midlands, but because of Liverpool's growing status as a key port for international trade, it was also a convenient avenue for exporting beer to the increasingly important West Indies and North American markets.

In London, Guinness used a variety of agents during this era. These included Henry Tuckett, with whom the Second Arthur had a tempestuous (and eventually terminated) relationship, and Sparks Moline, with whom Guinness would still being doing business well into the twentieth century. During the second half of the nineteenth century, the number of Liverpool and London agents distributing Guinness would grow enormously.

In 1824, Captain John Grattan Guinness returned from two decades abroad and was given a job at the brewery. He showed little interest in being part of a management team, so he was assigned to take a lead role in working with the partnership of Bewley & Nevill, a distribution agency for Guinness that the company was set up in Liverpool in 1824. John lasted only a couple of years in this job, and returned to Ireland around the time that his wife Susanna died after a long illness. Back in Ireland, John married Jane d'Esterre, the widow of a Protestant activist who had been killed in a gentleman's dual with Irish nationalist Daniel O'Connell.

It was in the early years of the recession that the Second Arthur gradually moved from brewing into banking. It has been said that some of his contemporaries eventually came to think of him as a banker first and a brewer second. Patrick Lynch and John Vaizey believe that the Second Arthur's banking interests may have led him to lessen his investment in the family business. "The period of Arthur Guinness's high office at the Bank coincides with a decline in the brewery's trade," they point out. "The Bank of Ireland took up a great deal of his time and money, and it would have been against his own interests to sink more money into a declining trade like brewing. . . . Many thousands had been invested in government stock which they were unable to realize because of its low prices. . . . For these reasons therefore it is possible that Guinness's may have given harder terms to their customers than their competitors did, and they may have in consequence lost some of their share of the Dublin trade."

Indeed, a banker he had become. After a couple of years in commercial banking, Arthur became deputy governor of the Bank of Ireland—the central bank responsible for backing currency—in

1818 and governor two years later. It was in this role that Arthur was part of the welcoming committee when King George IV became the first reigning English monarch to visit Ireland in four centuries.

Despite such royalist trappings, Arthur shared his father's belief in Catholic emancipation, and he was very vocal in calling for reforms. He was a supporter of Daniel O'Connell, the leading Catholic political leader and nationalist who won election to Parliament from County Clare despite the fact that Catholics were barred from taking office. In response to the O'Connell conundrum, the British passed the Catholic Relief Act of 1829, which, among other things, permitted Catholics to hold public office.

Arthur Guinness, speaking at a meeting in Dublin, said "I am much joyed at the final adjustment of the 'Catholic Question,' as it is wont to be called—but more properly the Irish Question—for hitherto although always a sincere advocate for Catholic freedom, I never could look my Catholic neighbor confidently in the face. I felt that I was placed in an unjust unnatural elevation above him; and I considered how I would have felt if placed in a different position myself. Sorrow was always excited in my mind by such a contemplation, and I longed much to have the cause removed. That consummation, so devoutly to be wished for, is now at hand. My Catholic brother is a freeman. We shall henceforth meet as equals."

Unfortunately, Arthur Guinness and Daniel O'Connell had a falling out two years later. One of O'Connell's sons had opened a brewery not far from St. James's Gate. An unfounded rumor whispered that the Guinnesses had played a role in this brewery's subsequent failure.

From being the largest brewery in Dublin at the turn of the century, St. James's Gate became the largest in Ireland by 1833, as its annual output now exceeded the Beamish & Crawford Brewery in Cork. At the beginning of the nineteenth century, Beamish & Crawford was brewing 44,000 barrels annually compared to 10,026 brewed by Guinness. Between 1806 and 1815, annual production of this Cork mega-brewer topped 100,000 barrels annually, putting it on par with the big British brewers and roughly double the output at Guinness. During the postwar recession, though, Beamish & Crawford slumped to an annual average of 61,000. As the recession waned, Guinness experienced a much more robust recovery. In 1833, Beamish & Crawford brewed 65,570 barrels, eclipsed by Guinness with 68,357 barrels. This, at last put Guinness in the lead in Ireland, as it has remained.

The importance of Guinness's beer to lives of people from all walks of life was underscored in a letter that Benjamin Disraeli, the future Prime Minister of England, wrote to his sister Sarah on November 21, 1837: "There was a division on the Address in Queen Victoria's first Parliament, 509 to 20. I then left the House at ten o'clock, none of us having dined. . . . I supped at the Carlton, with a large party, off oysters and Guinness, and got to bed at half-past twelve o'clock. Thus, ended the most remarkable day hitherto of my life."

Generations and
Dynasties

When the first Arthur Guinness died in 1803, the Second Arthur, as the eldest son to enter the family business, became the patriarch and head brewer at St. James's Gate. In 1820, when the Second Arthur withdrew from his management role to focus his attention on banking and shed the mantle of head brewer, the next step in the succession was a great deal more complicated.

The Second Arthur's brothers, Benjamin Guinness and William Lunell Guinness had joined him in the management at the family business early in the century, and they were still involved in 1820. Meanwhile, the Second Arthur's sons, Arthur Lee Guinness, age 23, and Benjamin Lee Guinness, age 22, were also coming of age and interested in the brewery.

Thus, as the Second Arthur stepped aside, brother Benjamin took over as the head man at St. James's Gate, but he would have his brother William Lunell, as well as his two nephews as partners. (The Second Arthur remained a partner, although he had no active management role.) In turn, the two generations of Guinnesses would have two additional partners—albeit not equal partners.

The first family of the family business was certainly the Guinnesses. However, during most of the nineteenth century, there was a second family at St. James's Gate whose importance to the management of the brewery and the brand was nearly on par with that of the Guinnesses. These were the Pursers.

John Purser, an English porter brewer from Tewkesbury had come to Dublin in 1776, where he found work with James Farrell's brewing company, and with whom he became a celebrated brewmaster. He may or may not have also worked for Arthur Guinness, but in either case, Guinness certainly knew him. In 1799, Purser's son and grandson both went to work at St. James's Gate. His son, John Purser Sr., was employed as chief clerk, while John Purser Jr. became an apprentice brewer. This began an association between the St. James's Gate Brewery and successive generations of Pursers would continue through most of the nineteenth century.

In 1820, the Second Arthur Guinness relinquished his title as head brewer, passing the title John Purser. Meanwhile, both John Purser Sr. and John Purser Jr. became partners at St. James's Gate. The latter's son, John Tertius Purser, would join the company as an apprentice in 1825 at the age of 16. He served as head brewer himself from 1840 to 1867, and remained with the company until 1886.

Among the Guinness family, both Benjamin and William Lunell deferred to their nephews, Arthur Lee and Benjamin Lee. They, in turn, deferred to the older and more experienced Pursers when it came to the technical aspects of brewing and the hands-on management of operations. When Benjamin Guinness died in 1826 and John Purser Sr. died in 1830, the role of John Purser Jr. increased dramatically. For the next decade, he ran St. James's Gate, functioning not only as head brewer, but as the de facto managing director, hiring, firing, signing memos, and controlling brewing operations.

Gradually, as Arthur Lee Guinness lost interest in the routine executive management of the business, Benjamin Lee assumed a lead role second only to their father, Second Arthur Guinness, who continued as titular head of the firm until he passed full control to Benjamin Lee in 1839. The following year, John Purser Jr. passed his management role and his title as head brewer—although not his partnership in the company—to his son, John Tertius Purser. Benjamin Lee continued to depend on John Tertius as his father and uncles had depended on John Jr. In turn, John Tertius taught the brewer's trade to Benjamin Lee Guinness's sons.

Arthur Guinness passed away in June 1855 at the age of 87. Though Benjamin Lee Guinness had headed the company since 1839, he did so in the shadow of his father. He had even acquiesced to his father's desire that he marry his cousin—and Arthur's favorite niece—Elizabeth "Bessie" Guinness in 1837. The daughter of Arthur's brother Edward, Bessie bore four children, among whom were the fourth generation of managers for St. James's Gate.

When the Second Arthur Guinness died, Benjamin Lee stepped out from the shadow of the patriarch. At last, he could run the company as his own, and so he did, adding additional space to the St. James's Gate campus and increasing brewery output. At the age of 57, he moved with the energy of a young man with a lot to prove.

He moved out of the family home at Number 1 Thomas Street, immediately adjacent to the brewery gate—where every generation since the first Arthur Guinness had lived—and turned it into offices, as it remains to this day. He eventually settled in an elegant town-house at 80-81 St. Stephen's Green. He entered politics as a Tory, and was elected as Lord Mayor of Dublin in 1851. His political ambitions later took him to Parliament. Beginning in 1865, he went to London to serve as Dublin's representative.

No discussion of the Guinness family in the transition from second to third generation is complete without a mention of two other young men. These were Edward and John Burke, the sons of the Second Arthur's youngest sister Mary Anne and her clergyman husband John. The Burke brothers saw great opportunities overseas, especially in America, and they set up an international distribution agency that yielded excellent results. In his drive to expand distribution of St. James's Gate products, Benjamin Lee Guinness called on the services of his cousins and, by 1860, they had extended distribution to Australia and South Africa. The story of the firm of E. & J. Burke would be intertwined with that of the Guinness Brewery for more than a century. As we will see in the following chapter, the company became one of the world's most important bottlers and distributors of Guinness products until well into the twentieth century.

Perhaps one of Benjamin Lee's most important business decisions was to look inward and to tap the market within Ireland itself. By the 1860s, a number of factors had come together to make this the right time for such a move. For one thing, transportation had improved dramatically with the development of canals and a rapidly expanding railway network. Under Benjamin Lee's leadership, Guinness experienced a 400 percent increase in market share within Ireland.

Benjamin Lee Guinness was responsible for beginning the process of making the brand an integral part of Irish life and culture. It might even be said that he "invented" the "Irishness" of the Guinness brand. In my opinion, the greatest single marketing choice that Benjamin Lee Guinness made was the selection of a logo for the company. In keeping with his policy of anchoring the brand to its Irish roots, he chose to use the Irish harp as the company emblem.

Adopted in 1862, the graphic representation of the Irish harp was not just any harp, but the most revered harp—and arguably the most revered inanimate object—in Ireland. The specific harp that Benjamin Lee chose to be pictured on the labels of Guinness bottles is the famous Brian Boru harp, which is preserved at Trinity College. The oldest surviving Irish harp, it dates from the late fourteenth century, making it somewhat younger than its namesake, Brian Boru (in Gaelic, Bórumha), the great High King of Ireland who died in 1014. Nevertheless, this harp is greatly prized as a symbol of Ireland, and it appears in Ireland's current coat of arms (facing in the opposite direction of the Guinness harp). By choosing this cherished symbol, Benjamin Lee linked Guinness with Ireland at a time when the country was experiencing a revival of interest in Gaelic art and music. At the same time, the harp also benefited the brand in England, where the myriad of Irish workmen who toiled in England's expansive Victorian economy, chose to drink it because it was a link to their homeland.

In 1875, when the English Parliament passed the Trademarks Registration Act permitting the registry of trademarks, the first registered trademark in the United Kingdom went to a brewer—Bass of Burton-on-Trent registered the red triangle that is still a well-known trademark. The Guinness harp was registered shortly thereafter.

As Benjamin Lee's political ambitions took him to Parliament in 1865, he found himself dividing his time between Dublin and London. This led to his taking a house on Park Lane, thus beginning a Guinness family tradition of maintaining a second home in the British capital. He also became the first of several members of the Guinness brewing family to receive a knighthood.

At home, Sir Benjamin Lee was said to be the richest man in Ireland. He became a philanthropist, and the most important benefactor to the efforts to restore the crumbling thirteenth-century, formerly Catholic, now Protestant, St. Patrick's Cathedral in Dublin. For this, he was made Baronet Ardilaun in 1867, the first Guinness to receive a title. (In the hierarchy of British nobility, a baronet is the rank beneath a baron and above a knight.) His role in restoring a Protestant cathedral has been called into question as a contradiction to his efforts to engrain the Guinness brand into the culture of a predominately Catholic country. However, without his £150,000, St. Patrick's may not have survived as it has, and Dublin would be a lesser place without it.

As he was supervising the rebuilding of the cathedral, Sir Benjamin Lee was also building the foundations for the next generation at St. James's Gate. His oldest child and only daughter, Anne, married the Reverend William Conyngham, a nobleman turned clergyman who would later serve as Archbishop of Dublin. His second son and namesake, Benjamin Lee, opted out of the business, leaving eldest son Arthur Edward and youngest son Edward Cecil Guinness as the heirs apparent. Their father carefully constructed a two-way partnership agreement between them that he designed to keep the family business intact after his death.

When Sir Benjamin Lee Guinness died at his Park Lane home in London on May 19, 1868, his Trinity College-educated heirs were still quite young. Arthur Edward was 28, and Edward Cecil was just 21. Despite their youth, the boys soon proved themselves to be their father's sons. Both were good in business and both became prominent in Dublin civic and social life.

In contrast to the succession from the second to third generations, the transition to the fourth was very straightforward. Since the death of John Purser Jr. in 1858, Benjamin Lee had been the sole owner, and he had made no new partnership agreements. As Patrick Lynch and John Vaizey point out, "The two sons inherited the fortune and the business, while John Tertius Purser had a considerable bequest from his own father, John Purser Jr., a salary and a 'centage' on all the sales of beer. There was great hazard in leaving the brewery in the hands of the two young men alone, but Purser was a guarantee that responsibility and experience would remain at the helm."

In 1871, Arthur Edward, who inherited his father's title to become the 2nd Baronet Ardilaun, married Olivia Hedges-White, the daughter of the Earl of Bantry, one of the movers and shakers in Cork. Edward Cecil, meanwhile, married their second cousin, Adelaide "Dodo" Guinness, in 1873. She was the daughter of Richard Samuel Guinness. Known inside the family as "old Pelican" or "Old Pel." Richard was the son of the first Arthur Guinness's goldsmith brother Samuel.

Dodo, who had been raised in Paris by the brother-in-law of her widowed mother, brought to the marriage a level of continental sophistication in art and music that was in contrast to the Gaelic cultural interests that had inspired the previous Guinness generation. Beginning late in the 1880s, two of Dodo's brothers, Reginald Robert Guinness and Claude H. C. Guinness, would have management roles at St. James's Gate. Claude would serve as managing director, and Reginald would serve both as managing director and as chairman.

Gradually, Arthur Edward's interests drifted away from the work at St. James's Gate. Like his father, he entered politics as a Tory, and in 1868 he followed in his father's footsteps with his election to Parliament. He served just one year, but was reelected in 1874. In Parliament, he fell into line with Prime Minister Benjamin Disraeli's point of view that Ireland derived more benefit from its union with Great Britain than it could alone, and therefore it should always remain a British colony.

Benjamin Lee Guinness had anticipated this turn, foreseeing that one of his sons—like his own brother Arthur Lee—might choose to withdraw from the management of the company. In his will, Benjamin Lee said that he earnestly hoped his sons would continue to carry "at the same place by their Ancestors for so many years." In the case that one of them did not, he directed that "Brewery concerns shall not be divided or broken up but shall remain as they now are," and that the son retiring from the business should "make over his moiety of . . . the said Brewery Concerns . . . to his brother so continuing in said business and to no other person whatsoever."

Lynch and Vaizey credit Benjamin Lee Guinness with a great deal of foresight. "He was typical of many Victorian industrialists," they wrote. "But more far-seeing than most, in his awareness of the temptations which great wealth offered the next generation. The terms of his will sought to ensure that the family fortune should remain concentrated in the brewery and that in no circumstances should it be dispersed among his heirs for use outside the business."

In 1876, Arthur Edward formally withdrew from the brewery, selling his half interest to Edward Cecil for £600,000. Like their father, Arthur Edward went on to a life of philanthropy. He was a benefactor for the restoration of a number of buildings in Ireland, and he gave St. Stephen's Green to Dublin as a public park. For all this he was awarded an upgrade to his title. In 1880, he was made Baron Ardilaun, a title that died with him, for he and Lady Olivia—known within the family as Olive—remained childless.

Bottlers and the
Export Trade

It always comes as a surprise when you tell someone that Guinness did not bottle its own beer in its own plants until the second half of the twentieth century.

"It's really quite incredible that throughout the history from the eighteenth, nineteenth and into the twentieth century, Guinness brewed beer and that's all," Guinness Archivist Eibhlin Roche explains. "They didn't bottle it, they didn't market it, they didn't really sell it. The company was run by brewers. The concept of marketing is something with which we are very familiar now, but it wouldn't have been a common concept at St. James's Gate before the twentieth century. The trade department fell under the company secretary who looked after a huge number of other things."

Today, we take it for granted that major breweries have bottling facilities, but in the nineteenth century, it was customary for brewers in the United Kingdom and Ireland to ship their beer in bulk—especially that which was destined for export—to independent bottlers. Though Guinness adopted a label design in 1862, most of the Guinness sold in bottles for nearly a century thereafter was sold under other labels. Indeed, the Guinness trademark label was mainly for export products, and was not even used in Ireland until 1896.

Packaged by various bottlers, Guinness had been sold in both glass and stoneware bottles with paper labels since at least the early nineteenth century. After the 1840s, the use of glass bottles increased as a tax on them in the United Kingdom was repealed in 1845 and as the technology to mass produce them improved. By the late nineteenth century, beer, including Guinness, was widely available around the world in quart, pint, and half-pint glass bottles. Just as with brewing, there was a skill to the bottler's craft. He had to know not only how to bottle, but when in the maturation life of the living, fermenting beer, was the right time to "put it into glass." As with brewers, those with the right skills flourished.

British brewers found it advantageous to utilize the services of firms that specialized in bottling, of which there were many. The bottlers, in turn, often bottled for several competing brewers. Indeed, Guinness Stout and Bass Pale Ale were not only bottled by many of the same bottlers, they were often marketed in the same piece of advertising literature or point-of-sale sign. The major bottlers also doubled as export agents and distributors, getting the beer to market after it had been packaged. Many bottlers of beer also packaged other products, such as mineral water and whisky, and a few became brewers themselves.

From the middle of the nineteenth to the middle of the twentieth century, Guinness used a complex network of more than 40 major export bottlers and traders to package and distribute its beer. This is not to mention smaller retail level bottlers—from pubs to grocers to wine merchants—as well as unauthorized packagers of the product.

Of the bigger firms doing the most business with Guinness, the three largest and most important historically were Read Brothers, founded in 1871; Robert Porter & Company, founded in 1848; and the firm of E. & J. Burke, founded in 1849. As we have seen, Edward and John Burke were the first cousins of Benjamin Lee Guinness, and like him, were grandsons of the first Arthur Guinness. In the United Kingdom, the major centers of bottling included London, as well as major ports such as Liverpool and Southampton. Of the big three, Read and Porter were both headquartered in London. Burke was based in Liverpool, although they also maintained offices in New York and Dublin.

Some bottlers used the Guinness trademark on their labels, but most did not. Guinness was strict about letting bottlers use the trademark unless they agreed not to bottle "brown beer" from other brewers. Most brewers, whether they used the Guinness Harp logo, mentioned the name "Guinness" on their labels, although others did not.

Until the twentieth century, most of the bottlers used labels with their own trademark, and most of these depicted animals. Read Brothers used a bulldog's head, while Robert Porter used the whole bulldog, and E. & J. Burke used a cat. Other notable members of the menagerie included the beaver and pelican brands of Machen & Hudson, the boar's head brand of T. B. Hall, the red bull brand of Ihlers & Bell, the kangaroo brand of C. G. Hibbert, the monkey brand of Sparks Moline, and the pig brand of William Edmonds. Blood, Wolfe & Company of Liverpool naturally used a wolf's head, although they also used a bear, as well as the Guinness trademark harp.

Among bottlers who used emblems other that animals were Mackie & Gladstone, who used a Union Jack among other logos; and J. P. O'Brien, who used numerous logos from a dagger to the jack of hearts. Johnson & Company of Liverpool used a compass as well as an elephant. Famous for their lightship brand, Alexander Macfee of Liverpool also used a flamingo.

As Eibhlin Roche points out, "In many overseas countries, Guinness would be known only by the animal that was the trademark of the distributor."

The story of Guinness labeling is sufficiently long and complex to warrant a book length discussion of its own. In fact, such book does exist. David Hughes's *A Bottle of Guinness Please* is an excellent and extremely colorful telling of this tale, complete with more than a thousand reproductions of Guinness labels in full color, many dating back more than a century.

It was under this vast array of labels that the world knew Guinness, as the various bottlers competed to sell their brand of Guinness to Africa, the Far East, Australasia, North America, and elsewhere. Other companies, notably Mackie & Gladstone, concentrated on the lucrative and more easily accessible market within the United Kingdom itself.

Most bottlers specialized in specific regions of the world, and many had Bass, as well as Guinness in their product portfolios. Read Brothers were strong in Australia and the Far East, although they eventually expanded into South Africa, the Caribbean, and continental Europe. Read's simultaneous business with both Guinness and Bass is recalled in numerous old posters where one is advised to "Ask for Dog's Head [the Read logo] Bass and Guinness."

Like Read, Robert Porter also exported to Australia and the Far East, as well as doing business in South America and India. The largest market for E. & J. Burke was the United States, to which they also exported Bass Ale, and where they dominated the Guinness trade until the early twentieth century. Indeed, between 1864 and 1874, Burke had the exclusive rights to use the Guinness trademark label in the United States (although others could sell Guinness in the United States). Burke also did business in Australia, Canada, and other places around the world. Another major player in the U.S. trade was Thomas McMullen & Company in New York, who imported both Guinness Stout and Bass Ale.

The other bottlers with a smaller share of the Guinness trade had worldwide distribution, but concentrated on specific target markets. Most did some business in Australia and South Africa, which were large markets for Guinness. For Machen & Hudson, this included Egypt, as well as Australia. T. B. Hall's strength with their Guinness business was Australia and the Far East. Ihlers & Bell was the biggest player in Brazil and West Africa before being overtaken by Blood, Wolfe in 1887. Blood, Wolfe themselves did the majority of their business in Australia and South Africa. The Parisian firms of L. Gillet and Felix Potin, meanwhile, did Guinness bottling in France.

C. G. Hibbert was active in Australia, South Africa, and the Caribbean. For Sparks Moline (later just Moline), it was South Africa, India, and the Far East. William Edmonds did a great deal of Guinness business in Australia, and they were also active in South America. J. P. O'Brien was active in the Guinness trade worldwide until the end of the nineteenth century, when their business declined. Thereafter, they concentrated on West Africa and the Far East. Because it was based in the busy port of Liverpool, Alexander Macfee could specialize mainly in the business of supplying ships stores, although the company also sold into the British market and did a little export business in Australia.

These snapshot views of a few of the principal export bottlers of Guinness provides a glimpse of an idea of the great complexity of the business of distributing the brand around the globe from the mid-nineteenth century to the mid-twentieth century.

6

Building Sales While Building Rails

When Benjamin Lee Guinness died in 1868, the family business at St. James's Gate had been the largest brewery in Ireland for a generation and it was one of the half dozen largest in the world. In less than another generation, his son would turn it into the largest brewery in the world. During the eight years of the partnership between Edward Cecil and Arthur Edward Guinness, the annual output of 350,411 barrels in 1868 more than doubled to 778,597 barrels in 1876. Beginning in 1876, the output grew 5 percent annually, topping 1.2 million barrels by 1886.

Much of this was due to the efforts of Edward Cecil, as well as to John Tertius Purser, the stern hands-on manager at St. James's Gate. Both men had literally grown up inside its walls. When Edward

Cecil assumed full control of the brewery in 1876, he and Purser had the benefit of a new generation of excellent managers within the company, many of them related to the Guinnesses and Pursers. These included Edmund and George Waller, grandsons of the Second Arthur's older brother Hosea. George Waller even served as head brewer from 1867 to 1880 as John Tertius Purser moved into higher management. Waller was, in turn, succeeded by John Tertius Purser's nephew William Purser Geoghegan, who served as head brewer until 1897. Two other John Tertius nephews, Edward Purser and Samuel Geoghegan, also held important positions at St. James's Gate. Beginning in 1873, Samuel served for many years as the engineer-in-chief for the brewery. Prior to this, he had worked as an engineer with the British Army in India.

In the 10 years of Edward Cecil's sole proprietorship, he and Purser, along with their able team of nephews and cousins, transformed St. James's Gate. New offices were constructed, as were new storage facilities for hops and grain. Between 1877 and 1879, Guinness built an all-new Brewhouse No.2 at St. James's Gate. It had four mash tuns or kieves, compared to eight at the existing Brewhouse No.1, but it would double to eight by 1886.

As the output of the brewery increased, so too did the physical size. In the 1870s, Guinness purchased the land that lay between James's Street and the River Liffey, providing access on company-owned property to the quays, and from there to the Port of Dublin. In 1877, Edward Cecil issued contracts for the first of a fleet of barges that would be named for Irish rivers.

As head brewer D. Owen Williams wrote in his 1957 *Notes on the St. James's Gate Brewery:*

> The expansion of trade during the 1800s continued to leave Guinness short of plant and buildings to contain it. Between 1870 and 1876 the Brewhouse was mostly reconstructed. A new building containing bins, elevators, mills, and hoppers, necessary for the receipt and storage of malt and preparing it for brewing, was

erected. The four existing kieves were increased to eight in 1865. The additional plant required for brewing and fermentation was also correspondingly increased, including the addition of new tuns and skimmers and five new vathouses, containing 72 vats, making a total of 134 vats. Most of this expansion was done in existing premises but the space available was already too small. By 1872, new ground had been acquired to the south of the main brewery east of Robert Street and new stables and an additional vathouse, No.8, containing 32 vats, erected there. A large tract of land to the North between James's Street and the Liffey was bought in 1873, almost doubling the area of the brewery, and by 1874 a large maltings, a new cooperage, and new cask cleansing and racking sheds were being erected there. The new arrangements set the pattern that was to last for over a hundred years whereby the beer was brewed and fermented around the original premises to the south of James's Street and racked and dispatched to the north.

The area between James's Street and the river allowed the company to relocate nonbrewing activities such as its cooperage and kegging operation away from the crowded brewhouse area. As the brewery spread out, however, the need arose for an efficient means of hauling material between the upper level at the brewery and the lower level near the river. The solution was obvious—Guinness should have a railway!

Sam Geoghegan, the new chief engineer had his work cut out for him. To fit in with existing brewery buildings, the Guinness railway would have to be narrow gauge. However, if the company was going to the expense of building it, the railway should also be able to interchange with the standard gauge of the Great Southern & Western Railway at Kingsbridge Station, which was just outside the new property that Guinness had acquired. Geoghegan solved the problem by using two intersecting track layouts, a 22-inch narrow gauge system and a standard gauge one that tied into the Irish rail network.

The other engineering challenge that Geoghegan faced was the 50-foot elevation difference between the river and the uppermost parts of the brewery complex. Initially, there was an idea of using an hydraulic elevator to raise and lower locomotives and freight cars, but this was obviously cumbersome and it would have been prohibitively slow in operation. A strait tunnel was also considered impractical because it would be too steep. Samuel Geoghegan went to the drawing board, and came up with an alternative.

"He created a spiral tunnel that goes two and a half revolutions underneath James's Street to get from one end of the brewery to the other," Eibhlin Roche explains. He knew that railway engineers had used on a larger scale to solve a similar problem in the Alps, and decided that it would work in Dublin as well.

Completed in 1877, the spiral tunnel was the centerpiece of Geoghegan's Guinness railway. A touch of engineering brilliance, the spiral had a diameter of 122.5 feet. The spiral allowed the trains to be in continuous motion, whereas with an elevator, the whole system would have backed up, having to stop for each section of a train to be raised and lowered.

Among Geohegan's other accomplishments as chief engineer was a system that did away with dangerous ether as a refrigerant in the cooling plant. Installed in 1890, Geohegan's process replaced the ether with carbon dioxide, which was a by-product of the brewery's own fermentation.

Between 1875 and 1878, Guinness acquired five steam-powered, narrow-gauge locomotives for its railway, including two five-ton engines that were nicknamed "Hops" and "Malt." A sixth locomotive was designed by Sam Guinness himself to incorporated a dirt protection feature, eliminating a problem that had been encountered when running the first five. Manufactured by the Avonside Engine Company, it entered service in 1882. Geoghegan's design proved so effective, that an additional 17 locomotives of his design were built in Dublin by William Spence at the Cork Street Foundry between 1887 and 1921. These remained in service until the 1940s, and one is still on display at St. James's Gate. Two others can still be seen at the Narrow Gauge Railway Museum in Wales and at the Amberley Working Museum in West Sussex.

Rather than recommending that Guinness acquire standard gauge locomotives for the interchange at Kingsbridge, Geoghegan designed what he called "haulage wagons," so that the narrow gauge engines could operate on the wider track. This worked reasonably well, and Guinness would not have to buy a standard gauge engine until 1912. In that year, Guinness bought a four-wheel, gasoline-powered locomotive from Straker & Squire of London. In 1914, and 1919, two 0-4-0 saddle tank locomotives made by Hudswell Clarke were added to the fleet.

As Edward Cecil was building the company into a much larger entity than it had been in earlier generations, he and Dodo had produced the next generation to control the Guinness family business. Their eldest, Rupert Edward Cecil Lee Guinness was born in London on March 29, 1874. They had two more children, both sons, Walter Edward Guinness and Arthur Ernest Guinness. Of these fifth generation Guinnesses, only Ernest (as he was called by the family) took an operational role in the company. He served as assistant managing director from 1902 to 1912, and as vice chairman until 1947. Rupert remained uninvolved in the company until he stepped in as chairman after Edward Cecil's death in 1927.

Edward Cecil also kept pace with his brother's social climbing. He was named to the ceremonial post of Sheriff—later High Sheriff—of Dublin, and in 1885, when Edward, Prince of Wales, visited Ireland, he made High Sheriff Edward Cecil Guinness a baronet. The seat of the prominent Dubliner's baronetcy was Iveagh (Uibh Eachach) in County Down, the ancient home of the Magennis clan from whom Edward Cecil's great grandfather felt the Guinnesses were descended. Edward Cecil's Iveagh title would be upgraded to baron in 1891, to viscount in 1905, and to earl in 1919.

In the meantime, Edward Cecil Guinness had big plans for the company that his great grandfather had founded at St. James's Gate, big plans that would make the already wealthy Baronet Iveagh a very, very rich man.

A Public Company

In 1886, after a decade as the sole proprietor at St. James's Gate, Sir Edward Cecil Guinness decided to take the Guinness company public, making it the first major brewing firm to be traded on the London Stock Exchange. By now, the company was producing more than a million barrels of beer annually, making it not only the largest brewer in Ireland, but the largest brewing company in the United Kingdom. In his 10 years as sole proprietor, Edward Cecil had grown the company by 56 percent, and in the 18 that he had been with the company, production had grown fourfold. This made the company an attractive candidate for a public stock offering.

Edward Cecil had probably discussed the idea of a public offering with Lord Rothschild of the Rothschild banking family as early as 1880, but finally decided to work with Edward Baring (Lord Revelstoke after 1885) of the Baring Brothers banking firm.

The share capital in the prospectus issued by Baring on October 21, 1886, consisted of 250,000 ordinary shares at £10, another 200,000, 6 percent cumulative preferred shares at £10 and 150,000 5 percent debenture shares redeemable at the company's option in 20 years. One third of the ordinary shares were reserved for Edward Cecil Guinness, who would become the Chairman of the new company to be known as Arthur Guinness, Son & Company, Limited. Edward Cecil's second cousin (and his wife's younger brother), Claude Guinness, would serve as managing director. The corporate headquarters would be in London, rather than Dublin, to be close to the financial center of the United Kingdom.

The response to the prospectus was considerable. "Nothing within the memory of living man had been quite like it," gushed the *Daily News*. "On Saturday morning Baring's place was literally besieged. Special policemen kept back the pushing crowd of clerks, agents, messengers and City men, and pains were taken to have one of the swing doors only partly open, notwithstanding (or because of) whim one of the outer doors of Messrs. Barings's office was broken." The *Times of London*, meanwhile, called the response "extraordinary."

The *Economist,* was a good deal more reserved in its careful analysis, observing on October 23, that "If instead of one year, take the average of say 10 years, and also calculate the present market value of the £6 millions of capital asked for, the calculation works out that £8.5 millions (of which £6 millions represents nothing more solid than goodwill) is being paid for a concern whose profits during the past decade have not averaged more than £380,000 per annum, which possesses no monopoly of any kind, and which is engaged in a branch of manufacture that, taken as a whole, has for many years been declining. The bargain, as we have said, seems to be a very dubious one, and it would not be at all surprising to find before many years are over those who have been so eager to embark on it lamenting their imprudence."

The subscription to the offering outlined in the Baring prospectus opened on Monday, October 25, and was scheduled to close before 4:00 P.M. the following day. On that day, the offering sold out within an hour in London, much to the disappointment of potential customers in Dublin. Estimates of the oversubscription of the issue ranged from 10 to 30 times the £6 million offered. In fact, the amount applied for was £130 million. The £10 shared soared to nearly double and the debentures to £117.

At St. James's Gate, the brewing staff received shares from Edward Cecil's personal allotment, and other employees received cash bonuses. John Tertius Purser, on the eve of retirement, declined the shares offered him and took a retirement package totaling £217,196.

Now the richest man in Ireland and one of the richest men in the United Kingdom, Edward Cecil acquired a grand home at Grosvenor Place in London and began furnishing it with antique furniture and great works of art. On the philanthropic side, he provided £250,000 to jumpstart the Guinness Trust for housing of the poor and slum clearance in London's East End. In Ireland, he founded the Iveagh Trust that funded the largest piece of urban renewal in Dublin, providing housing and amenities for the poor people in the city.

The success of the Arthur Guinness, Son & Company, Limited offering inspired a number of other public offerings by major British brewing companies. Within three years, Allsopp, Bass, and Whitbread had all gone public, although they were only among the first of nearly a hundred brewers to follow suit. The London financial community's interest in brewers extended across the Atlantic. In 1889, a consortium of British financiers, doing business as Milwaukee & Chicago Breweries Limited, proposed a take-over and consolidation of the big three brewers in Milwaukee, the brewing capital of the United States. Captain Frederick Pabst and Joseph Schlitz, the largest two brewers, rejected the solicitation, but Valentin Blatz, another prominent name in Milwaukee brewing, parted with a share in his company. That same year, a British holding company also succeeded in consolidating no fewer than 18 breweries in St. Louis, Missouri, into an entity that would be called the St. Louis Brewing Association.

In Dublin, meanwhile, Chairman Edward Cecil Guinness was putting together his corporate board of directors, which included Claude Guinness, who succeeded John Tertius Purser as managing director. William Purser Geoghegan, the head brewer since 1880, who was Purser's nephew and heir apparent, remained on the staff as head brewer. According to S. R. Dennison and Oliver MacDonagh's Cork University Press study of the company in this era, he resented being passed over for managing director and resigned in 1897.

With the corporate headquarters in London, and with corporate chairman Edward Cecil Guinness resident there, the powerful role of the head brewer in Dublin became even more so. For all of the first two centuries of its operations, the person who held the title of head brewer held the most important post within St. James's Gate. For the first 61 years, it was one of the two Arthur Guinnesses, and for nearly half a century thereafter, it was a Purser. As the center of gravity for the Guinness family moved to London, especially after incorporation, the power and authority of the head brewer only increased. He was *the* man in charge because he was on site at the brewery every day.

As Eibhlin Roche points out, "From Arthur Guinness's time onward, the head brewer was 'god' in brewery. Each of the brewery departments, such as malt house, hops, brewhouse, fermentation and so on, had a brewer in charge, whose authority derived directly from that of the head brewer."

In rare instances, when the head brewer was not on duty, the final authority lay with whomever he designated, with whichever brewer, or "gentleman," was on duty. And gentleman he was, for the upper echelons of management were drawn from the upper echelons of society. The deification that Ms. Roche ascribes to the head brewer was actually not far from reality. In his book, *A Bottle of Guinness Please*, David Hughes quotes a pre-1939 foreman's manual that states, "at crucial points in the process [the brewery staff] were to seek the authority of the Gentleman On Duty to proceed." The manual, and presumably signs posted at the factory, used the initials for "Gentleman On Duty," which carried the appropriate acronym: GOD.

This system of the head brewer as the omnipotent figure in brewery operations continued up through the middle of the twentieth century when disciplines other than brewing, such as sales and marketing, became just as important.

With Edward Cecil and Claude on the board were Reginald Robert Guinness, Claude's older brother, and James R. Stewart, Guinness's Dublin attorney. Edward Cecil had intended to retire in 1890, and he wanted the skilled and energetic Claude, then only 38 years old, to succeed him as chairman. However, Claude proposed that his older brother take the top job. When Claude resigned because of ill health in 1895, Reginald became both managing director and chairman until his own retirement in 1902 at the age of 60. Edward Cecil Guinness, now 55 and without a family member who wanted the job, resumed the chairmanship. C. D. LaTouche came in as managing director, and Edward Cecil's younger son Ernest was named as assistant managing director.

One of Claude's most important initiatives was the introduction of scientific brewing techniques. Phrased so colorfully by Dennison and MacDonagh, "At the time of incorporation, the brewery was virtually innocent of scientific knowledge of brewing, and remained so until 1893 when the recruitment of science graduates as brewers started."

This isn't to say, however, that a chemistry degree was an obvious essential for a brewer. The art had been mastered by thousands of brew masters through the centuries who intuitively comprehended the craft well enough to produce excellent beer. The basic chemistry and biology of brewing and fermentation had been well understood since the dawn of civilization. Though this chemistry and biology was not articulated in modern scientific terms, brewers had always followed the scientific method. They developed and documented a procedure by which they could achieve a desired result, and they repeated the same procedure to achieve the same desired result again and again. In the late nineteenth century, modern science had been applied to brewing science by only in a handful of laboratories in places such as Copenhagen and Munich.

The first modern scientist whom Claude brought on board was the Oxford-educated chemist, Thomas Bennett (T.B.) Case, who was sent to Copenhagen to study brewing science. Meanwhile, a second Guinness chemist, Alexander Forbes-Watson, developed a method of recovering beer at the bottom of vats that had previously been wasted. He also undertook studies ranging from drying methods for yeast to understanding the color imparted by malt roasting.

In 1901, Forbes-Watson established the first Guinness research laboratory, an experimental brewhouse, and an experimental malting facility. An important member of his staff was young Alan McMullen, who would head the Guinness research department after World War I. Forbes-Watson, more than anyone else, was responsible for the transformation of St. James's Gate into a state-of-the-art twentieth-century brewery. He remained an essential part of the team until an accident caused his death in 1909 at the age of 37. One important result of the scientific work early in the century was in the area of malt wastage. While beer production increased 92 percent, malt consumption increased by just 85 percent.

Another important scientific project undertaken shortly after the turn of the century was to work with the Irish agricultural community to develop a strain of domestic barley that would be ideal for Guinness maltings. At this time, half the barley was imported from England, up from 30 percent in the 1880s. From a logistical point of view, Guinness wanted to use Irish barley, but English barley was of a higher quality while barley was a relatively negligible crop in Ireland. Only 8 percent of the acreage devoted to barley in the United Kingdom was in Ireland. To address the barley issue, Guinness consulted with and supported the Irish Agricultural Organization Society, a scientific think tank created in 1894 to promote Irish agriculture. In the end, new strains were developed that revolutionized barley farming in Ireland and reversed the downward trend in Guinness's purchasing of domestic grain.

By the turn of the century, Guinness directly employed more than 3,000 people, with an additional 10,000 persons indirectly dependent on the St. James's Gate Brewery. Meanwhile, Guinness was well ahead of other large U.K. industrial firms in terms of wages and benefits. Indeed, salaries were always 10 percent to 20 percent higher than the Dublin average. Among the benefits were a company-sponsored medical plan—there had been a free medical dispensary at St. James's Gate since 1870—and pensions for widows and orphans. The medical plan was extraordinarily well administered by Dr. John Lumsden for half a century.

During this period, Arthur Guinness, Son & Company, Limited eclipsed all others to become the largest brewing company in the world. Annual output increased to 1.58 million barrels in 1888 and to 2.08 million in 1899. By 1909, the volume was up to 2.77 million, and in 1914, on the eve of World War I, it stood at 3.54 million barrels.

Also during the first quarter century after incorporation, the relative market share of Guinness Extra Stout versus Guinness Porter was increasing. In 1888, Guinness Extra Stout amounted to 42.1 percent of total volume, but by 1900, it topped 50 percent for the first time, reaching 56.8 percent in 1910 and 63 percent in 1914. Around the turn of the century, the market share for Foreign Extra Stout remained between three and 7 percent, a third of which was shipped to Australia and a third to the United States.

In Ireland, meanwhile, a third of Guinness Extra Stout and more than 80 percent of Porter were sold as draught beer, while in England, most Guinness beer sold was in bottles. The largest bottler of Guinness within the English market, Mackie & Gladstone in Birmingham, did nearly £40,000 of business with the company in 1897, more than twice any other English firm and more than four times that of any Irish bottler.

In Britain, Guinness had a unique advantage at the pub level that it would continue to enjoy for more than a century. Most pubs in Britain, were and would continue to be, brewery-owned "tied houses," meaning that they were "tied" to a specific brewery and sold only the beer brewed by that firm. Guinness had no tied houses of its own in Britain, and therefore it could be a "guest" beer at the tied houses of many different brewers, as well as at "free" houses that were not tied to a brewery. This allowed Guinness to expand to more pubs than other beers, and it could be done without the company having to bother with the business of operating pubs.

After the turn of the century, Guinness exports rose steadily. In 1888, 70.3 percent of Guinness production was still sold in Ireland, but this dropped to 66 percent in 1905 and less than 62 percent in 1910. By 1914, only 57.3 percent of the beer brewed at St. James's Gate remained to be consumed in Ireland. This was despite the fact that the Guinness market share in Ireland rose from 65 percent to 80 percent during this same period. Meanwhile, Guinness share of the total U.K. trade increased from 5.7 percent to 10.3 percent.

One of the changes made in Guinness marketing after incorporation was the move toward using company-owned stores rather than agents in key markets. This had always been the case in the Dublin metropolitan area (a 10-mile radius from the General Post Office), and John Tertius Purser had long advocated doing it elsewhere. Stores were opened to replace agencies in Cork in 1891, Belfast and Carlow in 1893. The following year a store opened in Glasgow, Scotland, followed by one in Cardiff, Wales in 1896. In the English market, stores in Manchester and Newcastle were opened in 1898.

It is important to note that the growth of the brand during the years after incorporation was accomplished without advertising. Through the nineteenth century, Guinness advertisements had appeared only rarely, and Edward Cecil Guinness staunchly resisted the notion that Guinness *needed* to advertise. Aside from point-of-sale cards, it was company policy not to advertise in the core markets in the British Isles, and rarely elsewhere.

It would not be until the second quarter of the twentieth century that the company would fully embrace the concept of vigorous self-promotion. As we see in the following chapter, many of the export bottlers of Guinness beer filled the void in Guinness advertising by promoting their own brands, rather than the brewer who actually produced the beer.

The Guinness
World Travellers

The enormous boom in exports that helped turn Guinness into the world's largest brewing company in the latter decades of the nineteenth century brought with it the problem of quality control. Indeed, this became an issue for many breweries as the successful ones grew larger and larger during this era. How could the brewery monitor the condition of its products being sold in England, much less in far-flung markets across the globe?

To address such concerns, major breweries had started hiring "travellers," men who would literally travel to places where the product was being sold to check on the quality. In the United Kingdom and Ireland, Guinness had employed several such men, including J. C. Haines, himself a former brewer, who traveled the

London region for Guinness in the 1890s. Haines also became a Guinness "World Traveller," making trips to Europe and the Middle East, as well as to Australia. Perhaps the most famous Guinness World Traveller was Arthur T. Shand, a former World Traveller for British ale brewer Allsopp, who was hired by Guinness in 1898.

For the next 15 years, until the eve of World War I, the tireless Shand traveled throughout the United States and Canada, and also made visits to Latin America, South Africa, and Australia, which was the largest market for Foreign Extra Stout until eclipsed by the United States in 1910.

In the preface to his report of his 1904 travels to South Africa, Shand summarizes that the role of the World Traveller was: "To obtain information as to the general conditions of trade; to gain knowledge of the most important of our bottlers doing business there; condition of stout after undergoing the severe climatic test, inseparable to sending the articles so far; the price at which it is vended; size and style of bottle popular there; as to whether we have competition; as to whether there was any trace of fraud or imitation of our trademark or label, and the prospects of our trade in the future."

To this, Shand added that when the Guinness Board sent him on his way, "it was also suggested I should obtain and send to Dublin bottles of our stout in the different parts of the country I visited; report on the conditions under which the Stout was stored, as to temperature, etc.; period of storage; the temperature at which the stout was served, and a general idea of the hops and malt used in the production of the colonial [domestically produced] article."

The Travellers' primary task was to check on the condition of Guinness in far away places. The effects of long ocean voyages through hot and cold weather often took its toll. So too did the way bottles were corked and packed. The minutes of the Guinness Board meeting in August 1980 are indicative: "Mr. Shand stated that nine percent of our Stout sent to Messrs. Robert Porter & Son was lost through blowage. Apart from explosive beer blowage may arise from inferior corking. Thus, a bottler who wired the bottles properly would escape but on the other hand a good bottler might not escape from complaints of excessive condition at the counter, and if the beer were really in explosive condition, repacking would not be any remedy."

The memos written by Haines and Shand, still preserved in the Guinness Archives in Dublin, often read as great travel literature—particularly for those of us interested in the history of beer. We learn a great deal, not only about Guinness, but about other beers and beer marketing as they existed in various places around the world. For example, we learn from Haines that domestic ale brewed in Australia in 1900—which he calls "Colonial" to distinguish it from English ale—was noticeably sweeter than the imported variety. The reason? Shend tells us with a nearly audible shrug, "The people are accustomed to it."

We can't be present for a tasting in Sydney at the turn of the last century, but we can live vicariously through the World Traveller. It should also be mentioned that both Haines and Shand routinely tasted both competitive English products and local beers as they traveled, and these commentaries read like a conversation that we might have with a fellow beer lover. From Shand and Haines, we are also treated to wonderful stories of ordering beer in hotels from South Africa to South America, and in the dining salons of transoceanic steamships. We also can enjoy wonderful descriptions of casks of stout being loaded aboard camels, bound for the outback.

In Grahamstown, South Africa, Shand reported his drinking experiences with colorful flair, writing: "The half pints [bottles, that is] are beginning to go well, as private families find where stout is ordered by a doctor, it is much easier and pleasanter to use the half pint than to open a pint, drink half of it and cork it up again for the next meal. There are two clubs in town and they use half pints nearly entirely. Machen & Hudson's is the bottling and it is in fine order. The trade here for [Guinness] Stout is nearly three times greater than for Bass, the claim being that they can drink Stout even in hot weather but that Bass makes them bilious. Colonial stout does not interfere with our stout. People who buy it are the poorer classes who cannot afford to pay for Guinness."

Haines reported from Egypt in 1907 that "I made careful inquiries into the report that the Arabs had taken to drinking stout, and found that such is the case. The population in Cairo and Alexandria is very cosmopolitan. . . . I must say, however, that the coffee and water still seem to hold premier place, followed by draught lager. During my sampling I occasionally, even in the daytime . . . saw three or four Arabs sitting with a quart of Guinness before them. This generally means a quart apiece. The peculiar habit exists of serving small pieces of bread, biscuit, cheese, meat, etc., with each bottle. In one case I saw three Arabs thus engaged, one was eating an orange between sips of stout, and the others little morsels of cheese."

On this expedition, Haines was pleased with the condition of the Guinness that he sampled. He observed that "[N]early all the good class bars, cafes, epiceries (grocers), and hotels keep Guinness. I examined about 40 samples at Cairo, 25 Alexandria, 10 each Tantah and Zagazig, and 15 in Port Said, and although a few may have been a year or more in bottle . . . in no case did I find beer which I would think required withdrawing from the market. I found the stout at all the railway station buffets which it was possible for me to try. Messrs. Wills & Company of the Eastern Exchange Hotel, Port Said, supply the dining cars on the express trains. Cook's Nile Steamers and the express Nile Steamers Limited both get supplies of Johnson's Compass brand. Refrigerators are not uncommon, and in many instances the beer was served to me in nice cool condition."

On his way home from this trip, however, Haines met disappointment in Marseilles: "I tried all the best cafes, bars, hotels and grocers at Marseilles, but only met with two samples [of Guinness], and they were at the two best hotels. . . . Both are supplied by Gillet, from Paris. Bass & Company have an agent, S. Serene & Cie, who bottle their ale and stout. The latter was offered to me on several occasions at cafes and epiceries, including the 'Bodega,' and at some hotels. There is little demand for it, and the bottles seemed aged.

In one case I was offered Allsopp's stout, and in another an ancient bottle of Reid's was fished out for me."

Haines discovered that the scarcity of Guinness routinely led to thievery between steamships that made Marseilles a port of call. He went on to say that "as Guinness cannot be had at Marseilles, it is customary for pursers to wire in advance from homeward bound steamers run out of stout to rob an outgoing vessel."

And then there are the statistics, which provide interesting glimpses into the beer market at the turn of the last century. Shand reports that 211,773 cases of bottled Guinness were distributed in Australia in 1907, up from 169,710 three years earlier. We see the relative fortunes of the Big Three bottlers. Robert Porter is up from 55,000 cases to 61,558, while Burke is up from 24,615 to 40,891—but Read Brothers had fallen from 35,000 to 26,440. At the same time, Haines reports from Egypt on the relative importance of stout versus English lager. In 1906, 8,400 cases of lager (mainly in quart bottles) reached Egypt from the United Kingdom. At the same time, 10,590 cases of stout were imported. Of this, Guinness had a 68 percent market share.

Among the observations that Arthur Shand made were those about advertising. Because various bottlers sold Guinness under their own label, they advertised themselves, rather than Guinness. In Australia in 1908, Shand complained about Machen & Hudson advertising and got an earful in return.

"Mr. Greig [the agent for Machen & Hudson] has a feeling that we are singling out his Company in regard to the bottlers subordinating the name Guinness," wrote Shand. "And so far as Australia is concerned, he is quite right. On the wagons employed by the Agents for Read Bros., the sign reads 'Dog's Head' Stout, and in fact, now, the E. & J. Burke Company with the possible exception of W.E. Johnson & Company are the only people who publish our name with their own in advertising."

Shand encountered the same situation with the same bottlers in Buenos Aires in 1907, when he traveled to Argentina to assess the market for *cerveza negra* (black beer, as stout was called). "So far as

Guinness Stout is concerned, we are not known at all as it is all sold under the Mark of the bottler," Shand exclaimed in frustration. "The most prominent Mark is Cerveza Negra Marca Chancho, which interpreted means Black Beer, Mark of the Pig [the William Edmonds & Company bottling of Guinness]. Then there is Cerveza Negra Boar's Head Marca [T. B. Hall], Cat Marca [Burke], Bull Dog Marca [Robert Porter], and so on, but no Guinness. I venture to say that were Edmonds & Company to leave off our label or were to bottle some other stout with only his own label on the bottle, trusting to his mark only as Cerveza Negra Marca Chancho, he would sell just as much Stout as he is doing at present."

Haines, meanwhile, encountered the identical phenomenon in Egypt, where Blood, Wolfe & Company advertised Guinness as "Blood Wolfe Stout." In their signage, the word "Guinness" did not appear at all.

"The Guinness trademark label holds a very minor position," Haines observed, "The absence of 'Guinness' would in no way perturb the majority of the Arabs drinking that brand in particular. . . . Blood, Wolfe & Company brand their cases 'Blood's renowned Foreign Export Stout.' It may have been quite unpremeditated, but the fact remains that a demand has been created by the means alluded to, for Wolfe brand Stout more than for Guinness. Steps should, I think, be taken to remedy this without delay."

Not only were the World Travellers concerned about people selling Guinness under their own name, Shand was concerned about people selling inferior "colonial" stout and pretending that it was Guinness. In 1904, he wrote from Adelaide in South Australia, "I am sure there are many frauds perpetrated on the people in the way of serving Colonial Stout for Guinness over the counter. If you challenge the server, he or she has a bottle of the genuine article open and is prepared to swear that that is the bottle your glass was poured from, and it is difficult to prove that it is not so before a crowd."

In his 1907 report to the Guinness Board concerning his South American trip, Shand described a similar experience: "I will give you two examples of how unknown the name of Guinness is in the Argentine. While lunching on the river boat on my journey to Rosario, a gentleman sitting by me asked the steward to bring him a bottle of Cerveza Negra Chancho [Edmonds's Mark of the Pig Guinness Stout], and instead of this was brought a bottle of bock beer. He expostulated, but was told they did not have what he asked for. Shortly afterwards, I introduced myself, expressing my surprise that Guinness should not be carried, and asked him to come with me to the Major Domo, and we would investigate. We did so, with the result that we found they had Guinness, but it happened to be the Toro [Bull] Brand [bottled by] Ihlers & Bell. At the principal Restaurant in Corrientes. I asked for a bottle of Cerveza Negra Guinness, but so far as understanding me, I might as well have asked for anything else. I had to go to the place where the beers were kept and point out what I wanted."

Arthur Shand spent a great deal of time in the United States during the first decade of the twentieth century. At that time, the price of a bottle of Guinness in New York was 30 cents, when domestic stout sold for half that price. Much of that had to do with the beer being bottled in Britain and shipped as such. Shand suggested that Guinness could improve its position in this fast-growing market by increasing the volume of Foreign Extra Stout that was bottled in the United States. Shand further suggested that Guinness begin marketing draught beer in the United States. He also recommended that the company begin a major newspaper advertising campaign in New York and Chicago to heighten brand awareness.

Shand lined up bottlers that included Hudson Distributors, who had no product of their own, so were exclusive to Guinness. They were able to compete so well on price that they earned market share. This effort by Shand was so successful that E.& J. Burke opened a bottling plant in New York to expand their Guinness American trade.

The U.S. market was always high on the agenda for the Guinness Board during this period. In 1913, after Shand's last visit before World War I changed the American market, an internal memorandum grappled with the technical problems of shipping casks of beer to New York.

"Is there any means of getting the Foreign Extra Stout in summer to New York under cooler conditions than at present?" The memo asked rhetorically: "Would it be possible for instance, to ship in smaller consignments and by this means obtain the use of the White Star [Steamship Line] "meat boxes?" It is very desirable, if possible, that arrangements should be made for our New York bottlers to bottle our Foreign Extra Stout in summer in order that their plant and equipment might not remain idle. This can only be accomplished successfully if we can arrange to land the beer in New York at a proper temperature. It is considered that it must be detrimental to the Stout that it should undergo a temperature higher than 60 degrees between leaving Dublin and being placed in bottle. At the present time in Summer weather it is very likely to reach a temperature of 70 degrees before it is bottled, through lying at Victoria Quay after racking, exposure to the sun in transit down the river, heat on board the Liverpool steamers, exposure on the Quays in Liverpool, and, worst of all, exposure on the Quays in New York for one or two days after the ocean steamer arrives. The Head Brewer [Edward Phillips] gave it as his opinion that if we ship Foreign Extra Stout during July and August it should not be subjected to higher temperature than 50 degrees before arrival in New York, if it is to be exposed to the sun on landing at that port. If it could be arranged that immediate delivery, was taken in New York, and that the beer was placed in proper cellars, the Head Brewer would not raise any, objection to the beer reaching a temperature of 60 degrees between Dublin and its destination."

Arthur Shand also traveled the length of the West Coast on several occasions, visiting Seattle, Portland, San Francisco, and Los Angeles. In early 1908, when he stopped over in San Francisco, he discovered that things were getting back to normal in the wake of the earthquake and fire that had destroyed much of the city in April 1906. "I have spent a full week here and have been much interested in noting how much progress has been made in the way of building up since the great fire of nearly two years ago," he wrote. "Many firms are still doing business in temporary shacks, but only waiting for the finishing of the many permanent buildings which are going up on every side. I am pleased to be able to report that so far as our business is concerned all the agents of the several bottlers say that the consumption of Guinness Stout is on the increase."

He returned to San Francisco numerous times, each time finding that it was a robust beer market, but that competition was stiff from more than two dozen local brewing companies. Indeed, America's Western metropolis was also a major brewing center. Some of the leading breweries in town at this time included John Wieland Brewing, which was one of the West's most important breweries by the turn of the century, and the National Brewery, established by John Glueck and Charles Hansen near city hall. The legendary Anchor Brewing Company, today San Francisco's best known, had just been acquired by Ernst Baruth and his son-in-law Otto Schinkel in 1896. Shand probably had the opportunity to taste the brewery's famous Anchor Steam Beer during his visits.

While traveling in the United States, Shand was especially fond of Boston. "There is a great Irish element in Boston, which is most influential politically and largely interested in the liquor business, so that it always has been a good city for our manufacture," he wrote enthusiastically in 1911. "The general public there are destined to be I think, very large consumers of draught stout. . . . There are at present over seventy places drawing Extra Stout in this city, and a great majority of these are all first-class, thirteen of them being hotels. I am pleased to say that it was a treat to see the condition in which the Stout is drawn, all from iceboxes at a temperature which made the article exceedingly palatable."

In the United States, Shand also initiated litigation when he observed trademark infringement by counterfeit bottlers who bottled domestic stout under a Guinness label. When these cases were won, sales figures increased. Sales of Foreign Extra Stout in the United

States, while modest, grew steadily, from 10,400 barrels in 1900 to 14,000 in 1904 and 26,000 a decade later. As a proportion of total sales of Foreign Extra Stout, the United States market increased from less than 30 percent when Shand started to more than 40 percent in 1914. This was, however, the end of an era. World War I would dramatically interrupt trade with the United States, and thereafter, Prohibition would end it entirely for more than a decade.

As we can see, advertising was one of the key issues present in the reports of the World Travellers. Wherever the Travellers went, brand identity was seen as a major and obvious issue. However, it would take time—more than a decade after Arthur Shand's last pre-World War I report—for the Guinness Board of Directors, and Chairman Edward Cecil Guinness, to finally come around to the idea that advertising was almost as necessary to supporting the brand as quality control. In the meantime, sales were growing, but when they slowed, there would be other issues with which to grapple.

To the Ends of the Earth, and Manchester, Too

During the first dozen years of the twentieth century, the largest brewery in the world experienced a great deal of growth, not only in its home markets in Ireland and Britain, but around the world. This meant not only the markets visited on the itineraries of the busy World Travellers, but in remote places that even Arthur Shand never visited. Guinness was being enjoyed farther from the beaten track than Arthur Guinness could have imagined in his wildest dreams.

Indeed, Guinness had traveled literally to the ends of the earth. Sir Douglas Mawson, the great Australian Antarctic explorer and geologist, carried the black liquidation with him on his 1911 expedition. He and his companions had it as they wintered at Cape Denison, experiencing nearly the constant blizzards. In 1929, Mawson led a joint British, Australian, and New Zealand expedition back to the same area of Antarctica. A member of this team explained in a 1933 interview with the *Belfast Telegraph:* "The stores [left by Mawson's earlier expedition of 1911] were in good condition after 18 years; cocoa, salt, flour and matches from these stores were actually used afterwards. . . . There were also four bottles of Guinness on a shelf, which, although frozen, were put to excellent use."

Meanwhile, Ralph Patteson Cobbold, the British explorer, found Guinness on sale deep in the Pamir Mountains near the Hindu Kush range in Central Asia during the late nineteenth century. In his *Innermost Asia: Travel and Sport in the Pamirs,* published in London in 1900, Cobbold wrote: "I directed my attention to a wine and spirit store where I spied, gently to my delight, the magic harp of Guinness inscribed on imperial pints of stout. The price was stiff—eight shillings a bottle—but it didn't seem exorbitant when one considered the distance it had travelled from its native land. The stout was excellent."

The first 14 years of the twentieth century capped a magnificent era in Guinness history. As witnessed by the World Travellers, global market penetration was at hand, Guinness was exporting to continental Europe and the fast-growing United States was increasing into a significant consumer of Foreign Extra Stout. All of this led to a mood of expansiveness in which Guinness acquired its own merchant fleet and seriously planned a second brewery.

Throughout the nineteenth century, Guinness had very limited market penetration in continental Europe. In 1910, however, the company rediscovered the continent. Charles J. "Ben" Newbold, the young Cambridge-educated analyst whom Guinness sent to study the market, suggested that Paris might be a good market, but that Belgium could be an *excellent* market. He recommended that the company go into this tiny country—where beer drinking is as much a part of life as wine is in Italy—with a strong marketing push. He recommended that rather than Foreign Extra Stout, the company should send in Guinness Extra Stout, just as it did into the British market. Further, he recommended an aggressive advertising campaign. Edward Cecil Guinness, who was always cool to the idea of advertising, reluctantly agreed.

To meet the growing demand for Guinness Extra Stout and Guinness Porter, the company also undertook two major expansion projects at St. James's Gate in 1901 and 1907. To meet the need of getting the bulk beer from Dublin to the bottlers in England, mainly in Liverpool, Guinness made the decision to acquire its own steamships. Purchased in 1913, the first was the *W.M. Barkley,* a collier built by John Kelly & Sons of Belfast. Three months later, Guinness acquired a second vessel from Kelly, the *Carrowdore,* and sent her on her maiden voyage to London in March 1914. Guinness commissioned two additional ships, *Clareisland* and *Clarecastle* to be built to company specifications and launched in 1915.

Meanwhile, with market share in England growing as rapidly as it was, the topic of building a second brewery in England cropped up from time to time. In addition to the growing sales in England, there was the fact that Guinness was importing barley and malt from England, and it was theoretically a cheaper proposition to use it in England rather than bringing it across the Irish Sea as grain and sending it back across as beer.

In August 1913, Edward Cecil informed the board of directors that he had taken an option on a 100-acre plot adjacent to the Manchester Ship Canal. He stated publicly that the issue of building an expansion brewery had been "considered in all its aspect, and especially in view of the developments of our trade in England and Scotland, and the large increase which is taking place in the cost of freight."

The chairman went on to say that he didn't intend for there to be any reduction in operations at St. James's Gate, but the Irish press wondered how moving all the production work that supplied the British market to Manchester would *not* impact production at St. James's Gate. After all, two of every five barrels brewed in Dublin were exported to England. Meanwhile, even though Guinness market share was increasing in Britain, overall per capita consumption of beer was actually declining.

The size of the Guinness Manchester brewery was to have been immense. As S. R. Dennison and Oliver MacDonagh point out in their study of the company, "the first plans were for huge breweries of 48 and 64 kieves, respectively. The site would have accommodated the larger size, but even a 48-kieve brewery could have produced nearly four times as much as St. James's Gate (still the 'largest brewery in the world') had done in 1912."

Architects and engineers apparently drew up preliminary plans for than a dozen configurations, which by January 1914 were boiled down to four alternative plant sizes, ranging from 6 to 24 kieves. The phase one plan was for six kieves but it would probably start working with only four. Phase two would have brought a 16-kieve brewery online, but apparently the ultimate goal was s 48-kieve plant. On April 7, 1914, the board officially decided that the Manchester facility should be run at its fullest capacity and that market fluctuations "would be met by increasing or decreasing the amount of Stout sent from Dublin."

Four months later, plans would change as the United Kingdom suddenly found itself at war. The dominoes that sent Europe tumbling into what would become World War I—then known as the Great War—began to fall in June when a Serbian named Gavrilo Princip shot and killed Archduke Franz Ferdinand, heir to the throne of the Austro-Hungarian Empire. The latter, with Germany's encouragement, declared war on Serbia, whose ally, Russia, mobilized for war against the Austro-Hungarians. Germany then declared war on Russia, angering France. On August 2, Germany occupied

Luxembourg and demanded free passage through Belgium to invade France. On August 3, Germany declared war on France, and the next day invaded Belgium. This violation of Belgian neutrality brought the United Kingdom into the war. As the dominos tumbled, most people predicted that the war would be over in a few weeks. However, virtually all of Europe had been sucked into a cataclysm that would last four years with the terrible cost of 10 million dead and twice that many wounded.

With the United Kingdom at war, plans for the Manchester expansion brewery, which were well underway in August 1914, were shelved for the duration of the war. They would never be unshelved. A great many plans would change over the next four years.

War at Home and Abroad

When World War I began in August 1914, Arthur Guinness, Son & Company, Limited responded to the crisis by promising to hold the job of any man who enlisted in the armed forces of the United Kingdom, of which Ireland was still a part, and to pay him half his salary while he was in the service. A hundred men volunteered immediately as the St. James's Gate Division of the St. John's Ambulance Brigade. Eventually another 500 left the brewery to enlist, costing the company nearly 20 percent of the St. James's Gate workforce.

For the first two years of the war, there were slight declines of less than 10 percent in sales, but 1917 sales dropped to half the 1914 level. Problems in getting raw materials were a growing part of the problem. Grain was necessary both for food and for industrial alcohol, and as availability declined, prices rose. Barley was in short supply because the government insisted that grain fields be used for wheat instead. As Ernest Guinness wrote, "It would be noting short of a calamity if after all our efforts for sowing in Ireland with suitable seed it should again lapse into the condition of 20 years ago."

Another part of the raw materials issue—as well as of exports—was the growing danger of German submarines to ocean shipping. The new steamships of the Guinness fleet, meanwhile, were commandeered by the British Admiralty as auxiliary vessels for the duration of the war and used to haul cargo. Completed in 1915, the brand new *Clareisland* and *Clarecastle* were pressed into service carrying coal to the Royal Navy's fleet in the Atlantic, and later for ferrying hay for the horses being used by the British army in France.

The *W.M. Barkley*, Guinness's first company-owned steamship, was used for several years to haul supplies to France, but was returned to the company in 1917 because she needed to stop for coal too often. On October 12 of that year, she was torpedoed by a German U-Boat off Kish Lightship while carrying hogsheads of stout. The captain and four men were lost, but others survived.

"We rowed away from the *Barkley* so as not to get dragged under," crewman Thomas McGlue recalled in an interview many years later. "Then we saw the U-boat lying astern. I thought she was a collier, she looked so big. There were seven Germans in the conning tower, all looking down at us through binoculars. We hailed the captain and asked him to pick us up. He called us alongside and then he asked us the name of our boat, the cargo she was carrying, who the owners were and where she was registered, and where she was bound to. He spoke better English than we did. We answered his questions and then asked if we could go. He told us to wait a minute while he went below and checked the name on the register. Then he came up again and said 'can't find her.' He went back three times altogether. Then he came back and said 'All right, we've found her and ticked her off.' He said could we go, but there were two colliers going into Dublin and he told us to wait until they were to windward and couldn't hear our shouts. Then he pointed out the shore lights and told us to steer for them. The submarine slipped away and we were left alone, with hogsheads of stout bobbing all around us. The *Barkley* had broken and gone down very quietly.

"We tried to row for the Kish, but it might have been America for all the way we made. We put out the sea anchor and sat there shouting all night. . . . At last, we saw a black shape coming up. She was the *Donnet Head*, a collier bound for Dublin. She took us aboard and tied the lifeboat alongside. We got into Dublin at 5 A.M. and an official put us in the Custom House at the point of the Wall, where there was a big fire. That was welcome, because we were wet through and I'd spent the night in my shirtsleeves. But we weren't very pleased to be kept there three hours. Then a man came in and asked 'Are you aliens?' I said, 'Yes, we're aliens from Dublin.' He seemed to lose interest then, so we walked out and got back in the lifeboat and rowed it up to Custom House Quay. The Guinness superintendent produced a bottle of brandy and some dry clothes."

Meanwhile, to finance the war, the British government raised taxes, including the excise duty on beer. In the autumn of 1914, they increased this sum from 7 to 23 shillings per barrel, adding another shilling in April 1916 and April 1917. An even higher duty on beers such as stout, with a higher original gravity than ale, was defeated in 1915 thanks to Guinness lobbying. The government did, however mandate a reduction in the original gravity of beer marketed in the United Kingdom.

The prewar gravities of Guinness Extra Stout and Guinness Porter were 1073 and 1058 degrees, respectively, higher than many British ales. Reductions were mandated in 1917 and 1918, ending up with the government ordering an average gravity of 1030 for British brewers and 1045 for brewers in Ireland. Thus, Guinness Extra Stout was reduced to 1049 and Porter to 1039 to meet a 1045 average. This reduction had the side effect of degrading the stability of the beer by opening the way for increased spoilage. To overcome this problem, additional hops were used, but there were complaints about the increased bitterness. The gravity restitutions would remain on the books until the early 1920s.

Another controversial dictum adopted by the U.K. parliament was the requirement that pubs close at 11 P.M. This decree, originally considered a temporary wartime measure to keep war workers from tippling too late, persisted until after the turn of the twenty-first century.

Just as these wartime measures survived past the Armistice on November 11, 1918, any illusion that things would immediately go back to normal after the war were soon dashed. There was no longer a "normal" by prewar standards. The United Kingdom had suffered more than 700,000 battle deaths and 1.6 million soldiers came home wounded. Edward Cecil's middle son, Walter Guinness, had fought on the Western Front and in the difficult action at Gallipoli, but he had come home in one piece. The war that everyone thought would conclude by Christmas 1914 would irrevocably change the United Kingdom forever. Old class structures began to crumble, and the optimism of the prewar years faded as a whole generation was gutted by the conflict. Events during the war years would also accelerate the United Kingdom's loss of Ireland from the realm.

In the midst of it all, Ireland—or most of it—had begun the road toward independence. In September 1914, just as the war began, the U.K. parliament passed the Third Home Rule Act. It was intended to establish self-government for Ireland, but it was not implemented because of the war and because of disagreements in Ireland over the status of the mainly Protestant counties in the north of Ireland. In 1916, through an insurrection in Dublin known as the "Easter Rising," an attempt was made by a small number of revolutionaries to force the issue and compel His Majesty's government to grant independence. Though there was little direct support for the radicals, there was less support for Britain's violent suppression of the Rising. More than 500 people were killed and much of central Dublin was in ruins. The columns of smoke and the gunfire could easily be seen and heard from St. James's Gate. Dr. John Lumsden, the company doctor, set up a first aid station where injured from both sides were treated.

Changes in public opinion after the Rising led to a declaration of independence in January 1919 and continued violence. In 1922, British and Irish negotiators agreed to the creation of the Irish Free State, a self-governing Dominion of the British Empire such as were Canada and Australia. Six of Ireland's 32 counties chose to remain part of the United Kingdom as Northern Ireland. In 1949, the 26 counties in the south formally declared themselves the Republic of Ireland and left the British Commonwealth.

Trouble, Triumph, and the Toucan

The market for Guinness products, which had grown steadily and predictably before 1914, changed drastically when the dust of World War I and Irish independence began to clear. After the wartime declines, annual sales of Guinness products in 1920 nearly recovered to their prewar level, and they increased 10 percent in 1921, but this was a short-lived silver lining in the clouds that were gathering after the war. The increase was due mainly to a resurgence of sales in Britain. After 1922, sales fell again, hovering at just over 80 percent of the 1914 levels through the early 1920s and falling slightly in the late 1920s. Prior to 1922, Guinness sales in Britain had been part of its intra-United Kingdom trade. Now that Ireland was independent, they were exports.

The wartime-mandated reduction of gravity of the Guinness products probably had an impact on Guinness sales in the immediate postwar years. So too did taxes. While the British now provided a measure of relief to its own brewing industry in the form of a 20-shilling-per-barrel rebate (on the condition that it be passed along to the consumer), the Irish Free State retained a 100-shilling duty, the same amount that had previously been imposed by the United Kingdom during the war.

Not to be ignored in assessing the decline in sales during the 1920s was the U.S. market. A prewar growth area that had been becoming one of the company's most important markets for Foreign Extra Stout, the United States simply ceased to exist for legitimate foreign brewers in 1920. After decades of lobbying by radical temperance organizations, the United States entered into the dark era of Prohibition. Ratified as the 18th Amendment, a total prohibition of alcoholic beverages became law in January 1920. It was enforced by the draconian Volstead Act of 1919. Under Prohibition, it became illegal to manufacture, transport, or sell alcoholic beverages—including beer and wine—in the United States. While forcing many family businesses—from the breweries of Wisconsin to the vineyards and wineries of California—out of business, the 18th Amendment and Volstead Act served to unleash a wave of organized crime, the likes of which had never been seen. For exporters who depended on the U.S. market, it was a major loss of revenue. E. & J. Burke, who had earlier opened a bottling plant in New York to be close to the action, were stuck with nearly a million bottles of unsalable inventory of Foreign Extra Stout.

Meanwhile, sales also slumped in Australia and South Africa— the other most important markets for Foreign Extra Stout—as the domestic brewing industries expanded in these countries.

The issue of quality and stability in lower gravity beers—and a remedy for the situation that didn't involve additional hops—was one of the challenges taken up by Alan McMullen, the Forbes-Watson protege who now headed the Guinness research department. Thomas B. Case, Guinness's first "scientist," became assistant managing director in 1919, and later served as managing director from 1927 to 1941.

Because St. James's Gate was not running at full capacity due to the drop off in sales, McMullen had the opportunity to take over a section and use a full-size production kieve and all its associated equipment as a laboratory. His experiments led to the development of continuous sterilization to remove contaminants. Though his conclusions were supported by head brewer Edward L. Phillips, there was a great deal of concern among the traditionalists in upper management that the sterilization might have a detrimental effect on organisms present in the wort that might be necessary for the established taste of the beer.

Additional research done by McMullen also identified a correlation between the stability of the beer and the nitrogen content in the barley. In 1924, he concluded that low nitrogen added to stability, and that Guinness could test for this factor when buying grain.

Such measures, in addition to a generally lower cost of raw materials during the 1920s, meant that profits remained good despite a decrease in sales. At the same time, the price of a pint of Guinness in English pubs had increased faster than that of a pint of English ale. Based on an analysis prepared by board member and marketing master Ben Newbold, Chairman Edward Cecil Guinness asked the board to mandate a reduction in the price of a barrel at the brewery. Unfortunately, the cost cutting did not have the desired effect on sales, and it reduced profits through the end of the decade.

In retrospect, the exercise had the positive result of initiating a mechanism within the company of more carefully tracking retail prices and the wholesale bottlers in England on whom Guinness depended. This began with Newbold spending two months at the end of 1926, traveling around England interviewing bottlers, retailers, and consumers in an effort to understand all the nuances of the distribution issue. His conclusion was that St. James's Gate needed to be in closer touch with the customers.

Newbold laid out a far-reaching program by which the marketing of Guinness could overcome its postwar stagnation. In his report, he told the board that:

> Apart from the "selling" organizations of our customers (the bottlers) we have relied on our stout selling itself. It is obviously financially impossible for us for many years to come to get Guinness back to the position of selling itself (as it did in prewar days) by being apart from its 'character' the best value for money to the consumer. Until it sells itself again it would seem that we must take steps to sell it ourselves, either by offering extra inducements to those handling it, or by creating a public demand by gravity or price, or by advertising, or by a much stronger selling organization of our own, or perhaps by a little of all of them.

He proposed that Guinness establish a new English trade department, with authority delegated from St. James's Gate to what he called a "coordinating official" who would be based in Britain. He also submitted that the gravity of Guinness Extra Stout exported to Britain and Northern Ireland be increased by two degrees annually to 1060.

Newbold also urgently suggested that Guinness itself get into the bottling business, possibly by buying into an existing British bottler. This was done, although not for several years. In 1932, Guinness acquired Alexander Macfee & Company of Liverpool. Founded in 1856 on Norfolk Street, the company had bottled Guinness under the flamingo logo for a time, and later under the better-known Lightship brand. Macfee bottled for the home trade in England, but had made a name for itself supplying Guinness Stout to ocean liners that called at Liverpool. This included all the famous name companies, including Cunard and Dominion, as well as the White Star Line, owners of the legendary and ill-fated HMS *Titanic*.

These great liners, coming and going between Liverpool and the North Atlantic, often passed the vessels of Guinness's fleet bringing the bulk beer from St. James's Gate to be bottled in Liverpool. The ships were essential to Newbold's plans. His marketing efforts were directed to the British market, and the ability to get the beer to Britain was vital. Britain was the largest market for Guinness, and with a population nearly 20 times that of the Irish Free State, it had a far greater growth potential.

Just as he had when he surveyed the Belgian market before World War I, Newbold understood that Guinness needed to advertise in Britain. He pointed out that competitors such as Bass and Worthington advertised, and called this medium "the quickest and cheapest means of increasing our trade in England."

His goal, as Newbold put it, was for Guinness was "to try to slowly regain the position of being, apart from its quality, the best value for money on the market." He added that the company should move quickly, noting that "it is easier for us (and much less expensive) to retain ground we have captured than to regain ground when it has been lost."

To get his advertising plan off the ground, Newbold first had to convince the chairman, who was staunchly predisposed *against* the idea of advertising. As Eibhlin Roche puts it, "Lord Iveagh felt that if you needed to advertise a product this meant that you had an inferior product, but Ben Newbold eventually convinced him that Guinness should advertise. Newbold was the first Guinness marketeer. I'd definitely consider him as one of the greats."

Edward Cecil Guinness finally agreed that the company should place a toe in the water of advertising. At the August 30, 1927, board meeting, the chairman approved the budget for a targeted advertising campaign in Glasgow. This was a big switch for a dedicated nonadvertiser who had just the year before refused a proposal to run a single ad in the *Times of London*. The Scottish city was singled out because there was a large concentration of free houses and because the loss of market share for Guinness since 1914 had been greater here than elsewhere—despite the presence of a large Irish minority population.

Presiding over this meeting, a turning point in Guinness marketing, was virtually Edward Cecil's last act as chairman. He died in London two months later, on October 27, 1927, at the age of 80.

A widower since Dodo's death in 1916, he had lived out his later years in England, holding court at his palatial residences and at the official corporate headquarters in London. Having become Viscount Iveagh in 1905, Edward Cecil was upgraded to Earl of Iveagh in 1919. He also added the title of Viscount Elveden—the seat of which was Elveden in England's County of Suffolk, which was to be his final resting place.

His brother, Arthur Edward Guinness—who had sold his share in the business in 1876—had remained in Ireland, and served as president of the Royal Dublin Society from 1892 to 1913. He died in 1915, without an heir to his titles, near his birthplace in Clontarf and was buried at All Saints in Raheny, County Dublin.

Edward Cecil's estate was valued for probate at £13.5 million—a record in Britain up to that time. He bequeathed his manor house at Kenwood in Hampstead and his art collection—that he purchased in Italy, Spain, and elsewhere with the proceeds of sales of Irish stout—to England.

At his request, Edward Cecil was succeeded as chairman by his 53-year-old eldest son, Rupert Edward Cecil Lee Guinness, though the younger man had not previously been involved in brewery operations. Rupert also received his father's title, becoming the 2nd Lord Iveagh. He inherited Iveagh House, the family's Dublin townhouse at 80-81 St. Stephen's Green, which was acquired in 1862 by Benjamin Lee Guinness. In 1939, he donated this property to the Irish government, who turned the building into its Department of Foreign Affairs. He retained the estate at Elveden, which he turned into an experimental farm, fulfilling a personal interest in scientific agriculture.

Rupert's younger brother Ernest, who had served as assistant managing director from 1902 to 1912, remained on the board. Edward Cecil's middle son, Walter Guinness, was also on the board but uninvolved in operations. Except for his time in the British Army during World War I, he represented a suburban London constituency in the British House of Commons from 1907 to 1931. In 1932, he received the title of Baron Moyne.

Thomas B. Case became managing director in 1927, succeeding Charles E. Sutton, who had been in the post since 1920. Ben Newbold remained on the board. He would succeed Case as managing director in 1941.

In 1927, as soon as authorized by Edward Cecil, Guinness had formally hired the British advertising agency S. H. Benson to come up with a slogan and an "experimental" campaign. At the first meeting in February 1928, Ben Newbold outlined what he expected of the campaign, and the agency put its nose to the grindstone with some market research to figure out *why* people enjoyed their pints of Guinness. To nobody's surprise, the almost universal finding was that people said they *felt good* after a pint of stout.

The initial campaign in Scotland got underway in April 1928, and by the end of the year, sales were up 7.3 percent in Scotland despite a 6.8 percent decline in Britain as a whole. In early 1929, sales in Scotland continued to rise, while they sagged in England. When advertising was introduced in England, this trend reversed. As Newbold had predicted, advertising worked. Advertising was focused on Britain rather than Ireland because of the much greater growth potential, and because Guinness already owned such a huge share of the Irish market that there was a fear that St. James's Gate might be seen as monopolistic.

The first national advertising campaign for Guinness Stout appeared in the British daily papers on February 6, 1929. Benson produced newspaper advertising and posters. Some featured parodies of Lewis Carroll's "The Walrus and the Carpenter," and others bragged about "the largest brewery in the world." However, the most outstanding slogan of them all was one of Benson's first. Still well remembered as one of the greatest slogans in the history of advertising, is the famous line, "Guinness Is Good for You."

Was Guinness actually "Good for You?" The slogan came against the backdrop of much anecdotal and media dialogue of implicit health benefits of Guinness stout, which is, in fact, high in iron and various other nutrients. Discussion of such advantages was considered acceptable then, but it no longer is. No alcoholic beverage maker would dare claim such a thing today, although the positive effects of red wine and Guinness are still spoken of extensively in the medical literature. Certainly Guinness in moderation affords a sense of well being. As Benson's market research showed long ago, most people *do* feel good after a pint of stout.

The slogan remains an enduring element of Guinness folklore. As Guinness Archivist Eibhlin Roche told me, "The slogan 'Guinness Is Good for You' is not a health claim that Guinness the brand nor Diageo the corporation can endorse. However, it is part of the history of the brand advertising, and it's not something we're ashamed of by any means."

The expansiveness of the company that was demonstrated by Edward Cecil's willingness to advertise was also seen in an aggressive upgrading of the fleet of vessels that Guinness used to ship its beer. As noted previously, the company commissioned had acquired a number of barges between 1877 and 1913. Beginning in 1928, the fleet was upgraded with a newer generation of barges.

By the 1930s, the Guinness property around St. James's Gate had increased from the original four acres to more than 60—all of it interconnected by Sam Geoghegan's eight-mile, narrow-gauge railway. The upper level of the world's largest brewery, near the main gate itself, included the two breweries, the fermenting rooms, the vat houses, and the stables. Also located here were the hop and malt storerooms—including the one that would be converted into the popular Guinness visitor center later in the century.

The malt house was located between the upper level of the brewery campus and the River Liffey quayside area. It was here that up to 120,000 barrels of germinated barley were toasted each year to the rich chocolate brown that gives Guinness Stout its distinctive color, texture, and flavor. Guinness still purchased 85 percent of its malt from outside suppliers. At the lower level of the Guinness plant, along Victoria Quay, there was a vat house and other buildings, including cooperage shops, cask-washing sheds, racking and filling facilities, and loading docks accessed by trucks and horse-drawn wagons. At this point, outside railroad tracks connected Guinness to the entire Irish railway network.

Within the sprawling campus of the world's largest brewery, the inhouse printing department was producing up to 1.8 million labels each day during the early 1930s—all of them used by the export bottlers rather than by Guinness, who did not bottle beer at St. James's Gate. Indeed, the company reckoned that the total number of labels printed in 1930 alone would have stretched nearly the circumference of the earth. In 1931, the company launched the steamship S.S. *Guinness*, the first ocean-going vessel of its kind to have been built expressly for bulk shipments of Guinness stout. In turn, Guinness soon sold the ship *Clareisland* that had been launched in 1915. Her sister ships *Clarecastle* and *Carrowdore*, would operate alongside the *Guinness* until after World War II. *Carrowdore*, the oldest of the Guinness fleet, would be retained by the company until she was sold in 1953.

Just when the advertising campaign bumped up sales in the British market, and as the new ships were coming online to transport stout from Victoria Quay to the world, the ship of the global economy struck an iceberg of disaster whose effects were to be longer lasting and arguably as devastating as World War I.

On October 29, 1929, known as Black Tuesday, share prices on the New York Stock Exchange collapsed, sending world financial markets into panic. Though prices recovered early in 1930, they slumped again, sliding to disastrous lows in 1932, carrying the world's economy into the Great Depression.

For the British brewing industry, which produced 25 million barrels in 1929 to 1930, the Depression meant a decline of 20 percent by 1923 to 1933. In Northern Ireland, hardest hit by the Depression of any place in the United Kingdom, sales of Guinness products in 1932 fell to half the 1927 level.

Nevertheless, Guinness continued to improve in terms of market share in the United Kingdom. Though the brewery's sales fell by

8 percent through 1931 in Britain, Guinness's share of the shrinking market increased from 4.6 to 5.5 percent.

Calculated in hogsheads that Guinness estimated to hold 52 imperial gallons, sales in 1929 were 1.36 million, or 89 percent of 1914 levels. At the depths of the Depression in 1933, they amounted to 1.2 million, or 79 percent of prewar levels. In 1939, sales had climbed back to 1.33 million, or 87 percent of the 1914 figure. Profits, meanwhile, were reported in 1929, 1933, and 1939 at 228 percent, 185 percent, and 200 percent of 1914, respectively.

Positive news came at the depths of the Great Depression, when the United States, dry for more than a decade, legalized alcohol sales again. In 1932, a plank in Franklin D. Roosevelt's presidential campaign platform called for "Repeal." He won in a landslide. Within a month of his inauguration in March 1933, he signed emergency legislation legalizing beer. Though Repeal was not fully implemented until the 21st Amendment took effect in December 1933, Roosevelt "got the *beer* flowing" in April. However, while some sales did return, the U.S. market was, for Guinness, literally like Rip Van Winkle waking up after 20 years' asleep. Because of World War I and Prohibition, it had been two decades since Foreign Extra Stout had been widely available and a generation of Americans were largely unfamiliar with the Guinness name. It would take another generation, and a great deal of work, to make Guinness popular once again in the United States.

Other markets were now gradually being opened for Foreign Extra Stout, but the pie was growing smaller, and a consolidation of bottlers was in the wind. The three largest bottlers of Guinness products—E. & J. Burke, Read Brothers, and Robert Porter—merged in 1935 to form Export Bottlers Limited. Many of the smaller bottlers—including Machen & Hudson—joined the Big Three's conglomerate over the next couple of years. The major exception was Alexander Macfee, which was controlled by Guinness itself. Macfee formed a rival conglomerate of its own in 1937. Among the important firms joining Macfee were T. B. Hall and Blood, Wolfe.

Like Macfee, both companies were headquartered in Liverpool and had their principal operations there.

The conditions were ripe for a trade war, but the two distribution firms entered into a civilized agreement to split the world of Guinness between them. Export Bottlers would market to the British overseas bastions in Egypt and India, while Macfee would take the South Atlantic rim—West Africa and South America. The remainder of the world would be split proportionally, with the larger Export Bottlers getting 77.5 percent of the Guinness pie. The two firms also came to a similar arrangement for the distribution of Bass Ale.

Another result of the consolidation of the export bottlers was a gradual discontinuation during the late 1930s of the use of the trademarks of the individual bottling companies. The name of the bottlers would continue to appear on the labels, but the labels themselves would be the standard oval with the Guinness harp logo.

For sales of Guinness Extra Stout and Porter in all-important Britain during the 1930s, Ben Newbold idea to commission an advertising campaign was clearly the right idea at the right time. Benson's famous line, "Guinness Is Good for You," could be easily paraphrased to say, "Advertising Was Good for Guinness."

At the same time, James Joyce, the Dublin-born writer and poet who is considered one of Ireland's greatest authors, had also submitted an idea for a slogan to the company. Joyce called Guinness "The free, the flow, the frothy freshener." The company stuck with "Guinness Is Good for You."

Nevertheless, Joyce made numerous references to Guinness stout, the St. James's Gate brewery, and the Guinness family in his work, especially his landmark novel *Ulysses* (1922) and in *Finnegan's Wake* (1939). In the latter, he writes, "Let us find that pint of porter place . . . Benjamin's Lea . . . and see the foamous homely brew, bebattled by bottle—then put a James's Gate in my hand." In the same book, Joyce even parodies the other slogan with the phrase "Genghis is ghoon for you."

Aside from the "Guinness Is Good for You" slogan, perhaps the greatest thing that S. H. Benson did as part of their advertising campaign was to hire the extraordinary artist John Thomas Young Gilroy—a graduate of London's Royal College of Art—to illustrate the advertisements. Throughout the 1930s and 1940s and beyond, his Guinness posters were seen far and wide, from the London Tube to Irish pubs, each one populated by creatures from Gilroy's imagination.

There were actually two Guinness campaigns with which Gilroy was associated, and the two ran concurrently for years. The first to appear was the "Guinness for Strength" campaign that pictured people performing feats of strength. Two of the most memorable showed a steel worker casually carrying an enormous girder over his head, and another in which a farmer is pulling a horse cart.

For the second campaign, Gilroy created a menagerie of cartoon characters that included such animals such as a bear, a crocodile, a giraffe, a gnu, a kangaroo, a kinkajou, a lion, an ostrich, a pelican, a penguin, a sea lion, and a tortoise—as well as a zookeeper who is a self-portrait of the artist. The poor zookeeper is often seen chasing a pilfered pint while exclaiming, "My Goodness, My Guinness!"

Gilroy recalled later that he got the idea for his menagerie while watching the Bertram Mills Circus. He was watching a sea lion balancing a ball on his nose and wondered what it would look like for the sea lion to be balancing a pint of stout on his nose. With brush in hand, Gilroy answered this rhetorical question, and the campaign was born.

In the ostrich poster, which appeared in 1936, the bird has swallowed the zookeeper's pint glass and it is seen in his neck right side up. This elicited a great deal of mail suggesting that the glass ought to be the other way around. The official reply is that "the ostrich had been imitating the seal lion and balancing the glass on its beak before flicking it into the air to swallow it."

When the same illustration reappeared in a 1952 advertisement, it was accompanied by a poem that read:

> The ostrich, travellers recall,
> enjoys his Guinness, glass and all.

How sad the Guinness takes so long
to get to where it makes him strong!

Gilroy also created posters with parodies of characters that included anthropomorphic pint glasses with the frothy heads sculpted as smiling faces.

In his famous posters, point-of-sale pieces, and print ads, Gilroy worked with copywriters such as Ronald Barton and Robert Bevan, who came up with the memorable slogans, including "Guinness for Strength," "It's a Lovely Day for a Guinness," "Guinness As Usual," and "My Goodness! My Guinness!"

Another copywriter with whom Gilroy collaborated was Dorothy Sayers, better remembered as the novelist and mystery writer who created the Lord Peter Wimsey stories, among others. She was employed by Benson from 1922 to 1931 and used an advertising agency as the setting for her 1933 novel *Murder Must Advertise*. She worked with Gilroy on the Colman's Mustard account as well as penning the copy for many Guinness ads featuring Gilroy's menagerie. His most famous Guinness creature is the toucan, and Dorothy's most famous Guinness jingle is the one that reads:

If he can say as you can
Guinness is good for you.
How grand to be a Toucan
Just think what Toucan do.

Another famous Toucan slogan reads:

Toucans in the nests agree
Guinness is good for you.
Open some today and see
What one or Toucan do.

Gilroy's illustration for this one, still widely reproduced, shows a jolly toucan with two pints on his bill. Just as Dorothy Sayers's works remain popular today, Gilroy's creations are still used occasionally by Guinness for point of sale and other applications, and the original posters are widely sought by collectors of Guinness memorabilia.

Perhaps the most famous slogan credited to Dorothy Sayers is the legendary line: "It pays to advertise." For Guinness, the 1930s certainly proved the truth of this statement.

Good for Girls, Too

"Guinness Is Good for You" say the advertisements that accompany drawings of fine, burly men carrying half-a-ton of steel girder on their ample backs. The inference is that Guinness is good for fine, burly men. I never heard such nonsense. Guinness is good for me.

When I was a handsome lassie in my late 'teens I went to the Gaeltacht to learn Irish. I fell in love with a man with a motor car. Now, that may not seem so unusual to you but, in those far-off days, a man with a motor car was a scarce enough commodity— especially to an eighteen-year-old whose previous boy friends hadn't as much as a bicycle. After six weeks my Irish showed little improvement but the romance blossomed under the sheltering hood of the car.

The day before I left for Dublin the man with the motor car proposed to me with these touching words: "I want to make you the Queen of Connemara." Nothing came of it all in the end. My vulnerable heart was given to a poet and that ended my possibility of ever becoming a queen.

Now, you might think that all this has very little bearing on theme in hand, which is that Guinness is good for me. But patience, and we'll get around to it. While I was being groomed for the Queenship of Connemara I was introduced to the delights of Benedictine. (The King was rich.) On my return home, I innocently told my father about this delicious concoction.

"Girl," he said, looking at me over his steel-rimmed spectacles, "if you're going to drink, have a bottle of stout. Put a bit of condition on you. Keep the roses in your cheeks."

My father drank a bottle of whiskey every day, and every night before going to bed he had for his supper two bottles of stout, a bunch of scallions and a lump of Stilton cheese. He retired never later than ten o'clock. He lived till he was 76. I have thirteen brothers and sisters. It is no wonder he thought Guinness was good for us.

I suspect that the taste was first developed in my early teens through secret sips from the paternal nightcap. After all, I was a growing girl and I new what was good for me. . . . In my tender twenties the fashion in my set was for Guinness and oysters, with home-baked brown bread. Very tasty and, we knew full well, very smart and sophisticated. . . . Now, in mature and reminiscent middle age, there is nothing I like better than a pint (or two pints) of draught stout, talking with the fishermen in some remote western pub, while the familiar tang of that dark nectar recalls a thousand memories of childhood and youth.

Note: Written by Monica Sheridan, excerpted from *The Guinness Harp*, the company magazine (1959).

Brewed in Britain and America, Too

Through 1933 and into 1934, there was a huge and mysterious construction project going on in an industrial area of the London Borough of Brent, about 25 miles northwest of central London. It was in a place that carried the somewhat pretentious appellation of Park Royal. It had been used by the Royal Agricultural Society as the exhibition site for the society's annual show, but that had only been for three years ending in 1905.

The mystery building was apparently a factory, but nobody seemed to know what kind of factory. The firms that were developing the site were Agricultural Processes Limited and the Park Royal Development Company. It was anybody's guess what sort of "agricultural processes" would be taking place here, and many people did guess. One of the most prevalent was that it was going to be a plant that would make alcohol out of potatoes. Another story held that the plant was going to be making explosives out of potatoes. There had even an amazing rumor one year earlier that the Park Royal site was to be a Guinness brewery, but this rumor was denied, and the denial was believed.

Then, on August 10, 1934, an announcement came. The Park Royal plant *was*, in fact, going to be an Arthur Guinness, Son & Company, Limited brewery after all.

The company had considered the idea of building a new brewery in Manchester before World War I, but put it on hold in 1914. The option was revisited again in the mid-1920s for a number of reasons, all of them having to do with the size and potential of the British market. The plan gained no traction during the 1920s, because unlike the prewar period, sales were down and not growing.

However, against the backdrop of the slow down in sales during the decade, England was seen as the key to growth. Ben Newbold kept the idea of a brewery in Britain alive. He was keen to have manufacturing close to the key market for ease of distribution. Manchester was revived as a possible venue for the hypothetical English brewery, but Newbold preferred thinking in terms of the south, nearer to the huge population concentration centered around London. The idea remained theoretical until 1932, when the issue of tariffs brought the subject to a head.

As the Irish Free State and the United Kingdom were bickering and sparring throughout the 1920s over a variety of trade issues, it was thought not impossible that the British would put prohibitively high protectionist duties on beer brewed in Ireland. This was especially probable after Eamon de Valera's Fianna Fáil party came to power in Ireland in 1932 amid promises (or threats, depending on one's perspective) that the Free State would revoke a deal previously stuck with the British government under which Irish farmers would pay an annuity to former British landlords whose property they had acquired before 1922. This opened the door for a full-fledged trade war. Guinness was more or less caught in the middle as a corporation with a London headquarters that produced its products in Ireland using English and Irish raw materials—as well as American hops.

In October 1932, the British government informed Rupert Guinness that the only way to avoid a high tariff would be to commit to brewing in England. With this, the decision had been made for Guinness, and plans got underway. The choice of London, preferred by Newbold for logistical reasons, was confirmed and Managing Director Thomas Case engaged the engineering firm of Sir Alexander Gibb & Partners as consultants.

A number of potential locations were investigated, including one on the Thames Dock that was seen as too pricey. Park Royal was finally selected because Guinness was able to acquire 134 acres for £132,000, less than a tenth the price of land in the London Docklands area.

The decision to keep this enormous undertaking a secret was backed by a variety of reasons. Obviously, English brewers would look askance at the coming of such an enormous rival into their own backyard, but on the other side of the Irish Sea, the de Valera government and Irish public opinion might take the move as a betrayal of sorts. Even though St. James's Gate would remain, the idea of Guinness beer with a non-Irish origin might be considered improper. The same might be construed by consumers in England. Guinness beers had a certain mystique, and there was a fear that drinkers would perceive beer not brewed at St. James's Gate to be somehow different, and therefore inferior in whatever qualities "Irishness" imparted to that mystique.

To address the latter issue, Case directed the new brewery to replicate the methods and equipment used at St. James's Gate as closely as possible. Alan McMullen, long a stanch advocate of modernization, proposed that a new facility at Park Royal was an ideal opportunity to build a state-of-the-art brewery from the ground up. However, Case felt that consistency was essential, and at Park Royal, the kieves would be made of wood, just like those at St. James's Gate, the most recent of which had been installed a generation earlier.

Work began in 1933, with Hugh Beaver of Gibb & Partners serving as project manager. The four-kieve Park Royal brewery was designed mainly by engineers, although an architect was brought in to design some of the more visible exterior features. The man chosen was Sir Giles Gilbert Scott, best remembered today as architect of Liverpool's Anglican cathedral and the Battersea Power Station in central London. Completed in 1933, the latter is still a prominent landmark on the bank of the River Thames.

To maintain the veil of secrecy, Beaver suggested the formation of the development companies with no obvious ties to Guinness. Rumors that Guinness was coming in were easier to deny when the entities developing the property were Agricultural Processes Limited and the Park Royal Development Company.

The formal public announcement lifting this shroud of obfuscation was made by Chairman Rupert Guinness on August 10, 1934, but Case had briefed Seán Lemass, Ireland's Minister for Industry and Commerce (and future prime minister) ahead of time. Case assured Lemass that Guinness remained committed to Dublin and to St. James's Gate and that Park Royal was not being viewed by the company as a replacement for the existing plant. As Case explained to the disappointed minister, the decision was made when "the proportion of our trade in England had increased from less than half to nearly two thirds of the whole, while our trade in London had almost trebled."

Case did assure Lemass that Foreign Extra Stout would continue to be brewed at St. James's Gate for export to areas beyond the British Isles. In his public announcement, the chairman added that, "We still hope to brew the stout for as much of our English trade, as may be possible in Dublin."

The chairman also assured those purists who might be concerned that "Park Royal is in the opinion of the board and of our Brewing Staff eminently suitable for the production of the same Guinness as we make in Dublin." By using the phrase "same Guinness," Rupert strived to finally put to bed the long supposed, and still widely believed, myth that water from Dublin's River Liffey went directly into Guinness's beers.

As Jonathan Guinness, Rupert's grandnephew pointed out in his memoirs, the myth of the Liffey water was always a sore point for Rupert. "He was wrong to get worked up," Jonathan observed. "For the story added, in a strange way, to the product's attraction [making it seem] more glamorous."

Just to be sure that the taste would be the same in both locations, Guinness planned to begin their marketing from Park Royal by mixing one part of the English-brewed stout with four parts of stout brewed at St. James's Gate. The first test batch of beer was brewed at Park Royal in February 1936 and sent to Dublin for mixing. After some initial problems with infected yeast, the company decided to bring the Dublin stout to Park Royal. By October, nearly two dozen of such blendings had been conducted, along with myriad tastings. The Park Royal stout was deemed indistinguishable from the St. James's Gate beer, so the proportions were reversed. By early 1937, London customers were receiving Guinness Extra Stout that was brewed entirely at Park Royal.

The importance of the new brewery grew rapidly. In 1937, it represented 12 percent of the company's total output and it brewed only 19 percent of the Guinness beer sold in Britain. By 1939, 28 percent of the total Guinness production and 46 percent of that for the British market came from Park Royal. After World War II, Park Royal would greatly exceed the production at St. James's Gate. This was only natural, given the fact that Great Britain boasted a population of nearly 50 million in the late 1930s, while the Irish Free State had just reached a population of 3 million. According to the *International Brewers' Directory*, the annual output at Park Royal grew to more than double that of St. James's Gate. Park Royal was the tail that wagged the dog for Guinness in the British Isles. Despite its early origins, Guinness was much a British beer as it was Irish.

While Park Royal was well known and will long be remembered, few people recall that Guinness was also, for a time, a beer brewed in the United States. The story goes back to Guinness's relationship with its agents in New York—and Arthur Guinness grandsons—Edward and John Burke, who had been given the exclusive distribution license for the largest metropolitan area in the United States in 1849. Until Prohibition brought down the curtain on beer sales in 1920, the E. & J. Burke firm had done good business in marketing Foreign Extra Stout among other products. Just before World War I, Burke hit its peak with sales of 54,000 barrels in 1912.

After Prohibition, Burke returned to the beer distribution business. The company also implemented plans to get into the brewing business itself. In 1934, within months of the end of Prohibition, the Burke Brewery, Inc. opened for business on a 1.4-acre site in the block bounded by 47th Avenue and 28th Street in Long Island City, within the New York City borough of Queens. The site was just south of Queens Boulevard and within sight of the skyscrapers of Manhattan. While continuing to distribute Foreign Extra Stout, Burke brewed its own ale and stout, using its trademark cat logo on labels and point of sale materials.

The Burke Brewery opened in an excellent location, but the timing was wrong. It was the bottom of the Great Depression, consumers were strapped for cash and there was a lot of competition in the New York City area from major regional brands such as Ballantine, Ruppert, Rheingold, and Schaefer. By 1943, Burke was teetering on the edge of bankruptcy when Guinness made the corporate decision to buy the Long Island City brewery.

The acquisition of the Burke Brewery actually fit into a long-range plan. With the Park Royal operation in motion, Guinness had been consciously considering a brewery in the United States. If the U.K. market was huge compared to that in Ireland, the U.S. market was gargantuan. Actually, before the Burke acquisition opportunity presented itself, Guinness had been eyeing the West Coast, rather than the East Coast. The target city was Seattle in the Pacific Northwest, where the market was dominated by brands such as Olympia of Tumwater and Rainier, produced in Seattle by colorful brewing tycoon Emil Sick. How different history might have been if Guinness would have located in the West, where the craft brewing movement took root a generation later.

The opportunity to take over an existing and relatively modern brewery in the largest market in North America was too good to pass up. Guinness acquired the Long Island City plant in 1943, but it was not until after World War II that the facility was converted for the production of stout to the true Guinness specifications.

World War II

Even as Park Royal was coming online in the late 1930s, and as the people of Britain and Ireland were crawling out of the depths of the Great Depression, the world was inching toward a second world war.

The clouds of war had been gathering over Europe throughout the 1930s. Adolf Hitler came to power as Germany's chancellor in 1933, and began the steps that led to the rearmament of Germany in violation of the terms of the Treaty of Versailles that had ended World War I. In 1936, his armies occupied the German Rhineland, again in direct violation of the Treaty of Versailles. The lack of active opposition by Britain and France encouraged him. In 1938, he annexed Austria and the Sudentenland region of Czechoslovakia, making them part of Germany. Britain and France complained, but at a summit conference in Munich, Hitler promised no further land grabs. To avoid war, Britain and France acquiesced, but in March 1939, Hitler's troops took control of all of Czechoslovakia. Again Britain and France complained loudly, but took no action.

Britain's Prime Minister Neville Chamberlain returned from Munich proudly claiming that his appeasement of Hitler meant "peace in our time." History would soon prove him dreadfully wrong. Indeed, to many observers, it was clear from Hitler's aggressiveness that war was virtually inevitable.

On September 1, 1939, Hitler's army launched a full-scale attack on Poland, and Britain and France finally acted, formally declared that a state of war now existed. World War II had begun.

With the coming of the war, Guinness was for the second time in the careers of many at the company, brewing beer for a nation involved in a world war. Ireland, now independent from the United Kingdom, remained neutral, but Park Royal and the Guinness corporate headquarters were in London, in the heart of Guinness's largest market. With Park Royal, Guinness became a British beer, but even before, Benson's brilliant advertising campaign—ubiquitous in Britain but unseen in Ireland—had created an identity that made it so.

Guinness would patriotically support the British war effort. John Gilroy's characters donned uniforms. One memorable poster had a formation of toucans—each with a pair of pints on his bill—overflying a British air base as two Royal Air Force officers look up hungrily. There was also a poster depicting a sea lion offering a pint to the zookeeper—now in military uniform—and another of a sailor escaping with his comrade's pint aboard a torpedo. Restrictions on paper usage meant that some posters were printed on the backs of earlier ones, and hence they were designed with black backgrounds. Apparently, there were no restrictions on printing ink.

During World War I, the British government had officially viewed beer as a detriment to the effectiveness of soldiers and war workers—but in World War II, beer was considered valuable in keeping up the spirits of the troops, as well as those of the people on the home front. Stout was provided at a discount or donated free of charge to convalescent hospitals so that injured soldiers could enjoy an occasional pint.

The prohibitionist tendencies in popular culture that reached their frenzied crescendo during World War I had long since run their course. The idea of a war worker enjoying a pint at the end of his or her shift was no longer frowned upon. Though the government again, as in 1914 to 1918, mandated that the breweries reduce the gravity of their beers, there was no effort to curtail the availability of beer. Quite the contrary, beer was now seen as essential to the morale of the troops, and Guinness was asked to set aside 5 percent of its production for those in uniform. It was considered so indispensable that the British Army *itself* insisted on the troops getting their bottle of Guinness.

One of the earliest and most unforgettable examples of Guinness supporting the war effort in this way came in December 1939, shortly after the German conquest of Poland. The war was in a lull as the German army reoriented itself from east to west for the expected invasion of France. As British troops went to France to prepare for this eventuality, the British Army decided that each soldier who was deployed to the front should be sent a bottle of Guinness to enjoy with his Christmas dinner. The bottling of this special consignment was handled by Alexander Macfee in Liverpool. The exact number of bottles was kept secret for security reasons, and it remains unknown.

As recalled later in the Guinness inhouse magazine, getting the tens of thousands of specially marked bottles delivered in time for Christmas called for cooperation from everyone concerned on a staff, "which was already depleted on account of war service. Much overtime was worked, and even competitors' staffs came in to help in their spare time and gave their earnings to the Red Cross."

Two decades later, a man named C. O. Brewster sent Guinness the original bottle he had received and related, in an accompanying letter, how it remained in his possession still unopened. When the war began, he was recalled to service with the Grenadier Guards and sent to France. In December 1939, he met with an accident and spent Christmas lying in a barn outside Rouen. It was here that he received his bottle of Guinness, but was unable to drink it. Early in January 1940, he rejoined his battalion after traveling 60 miles carrying 156 pounds of "kit" and his bottle of Guinness. He was then given seven days special leave, which he spent at home in London. His bottle went with him, and he left it with his mother.

After a winter of stalemate, Hitler launched an offensive in April that swallowed Denmark and Norway. On June 10, the German Army invaded Belgium, the Netherlands, and France. By this time, C. O. Brewster had returned to the front, and was present for the complete rout of the British forces. Between May 26 and June 4, more than 300,000 British and French troops were evacuated from the French port of Dunkirk, saving them from certain capture. Brewster was among them. He finally left France with the only 15 surviving members of his regiment. When Allied soldiers returned to the continent four years later on D-Day, Brewster was again among them.

In August 1959, as Brewster and his wife were clearing out his mother's home, he rediscovered his bottle of Guinness from Christmas 1939. "I can assure you that had I not been on the sick list when it was received the bottle would not have had such a long life and would never have come into your possession," he wrote in his letter to the brewery, "Never let it be said that a Grenadier refused a Guinness!"

France surrendered on June 22, shortly after Dunkirk, leaving Britain to face the onslaught of Germany's blitzkrieg alone. Hitler's Luftwaffe then launched the "Blitz," a full-scale air offensive against London and British industrial cites. Because of Ireland's neutrality, no German bombs fell on St. James's Gate during World War II, but Park Royal was hit several times. In October 1940, the Park Royal ice plant was destroyed and four Guinness workers were killed.

The German attacks also disrupted rail transportation within Britain making it harder to get the beer to market. Quite a lot of Guinness was lost when rail cars and warehouses were destroyed, but the three company-owned steamships operating between Dublin and Liverpool survived the war undamaged. In Liverpool, Macfee's bottling plant was bombed on May 3, 1941, and was largely destroyed. Because their work was considered vital to the war effort, Macfee was allowed to repair the facility, although the factory was not fully rebuilt and restored until 1957.

During World War II, as in the previous conflict, Guinness was carrying out its production in an environment where raw materials were more expensive and harder to get because the top priority for sea-going transport was materiel. Overseas trade was also dramatically reduced because of the war. Through the 1930s, exports of Foreign Extra Stout had stood at about 25,000 barrels annually, but quickly fell when the war started because of a shortage of shipping space, and because many of the traditional export markets in Europe and the Far East—including Malaya, Hong Kong, and Singapore— had been occupied by enemy troops.

Until 1944, the government did not interfere with the trickle of foreign trade that continued, but they then imposed a total ban on exports so that there would be an adequate supply of Guinness for military bases, troop ships, factory cafeterias, and the Navy, Army, and Air Force Institutes (NAAFI), the stores that supplied service personnel. This ban did not end when the war ended, although it was revised somewhat. It was not finally lifted until the middle of 1947.

As with the staff at St. James's Gate during World War I, many employees at Park Royal enlisted in the British Army during World War II. This time, the roster of those leaving the employ of the brewery to go into uniform reached all the way to the top—to the son of Guinness Chairman Sir Rupert Edward Cecil Lee Guinness. Born in 1912, Arthur Onslow Edward Guinness was the heir apparent to take over the chairmanship of the family business after the war. He held the title Viscount Elveden, and was in line to both head the company and to eventually assume the family title as the Earl of Iveagh. As Britain went to war, however, he was just Major Arthur Guinness of the Suffolk Yeomanry.

As the British, American, and Canadian soldiers went ashore in Normandy on D-Day—June 6, 1944—to push the Germans back into Germany, Guinness was behind them. After the breakout from the Normandy beachheads, it had seemed for a time as though the Allies would defeat Hitler by Christmas. However, their advance slowed as the combat troops literally outran the supply system. With the onset of winter, it was apparent that the Allies would not reach German soil by Christmas.

The last winter of World War II in Europe was a difficult one for the Allied troops on the Western Front. By Christmas Day 1944, the Allies found themselves on the defensive in the Battle of the Bulge. The "Bulge" was the large indentation in Allied lines that was cre-ated by a major German offensive in the Ardennes highlands of Belgium. Though the Allies were able to defeat this offensive, their counteroffensive was slow to start and the war did not finally end in Europe until the first week in May.

It was during the hard fighting that winter, as the Allies battled to regain the initiative, that the Guinness family—and the line of succession at the Brewery—suffered a serious tragedy. On February 8, 1945, Major Arthur Guinness was killed in action during the fight-ing at Nijmegen in the Netherlands. The 32-year-old son of the chairman was assigned to the 218th Battery of the 55th Anti-Tank Regiment at the time he was killed.

Major Guinness and his wife, Elizabeth, Viscountess Elveden, had two daughters and an eight-year old son, Arthur Francis Benjamin Guinness. With the death of his father, young Benjamin Guinness would now be groomed to eventually assume the chairmanship. His grandfather, Sir Rupert Guinness, however, would remain in the top post for two more decades, before finally turning over the leadership to Benjamin in 1962.

In the meantime, a second member of the family and of the Guinness board to die violently during World War II was Walter Edward Guinness, titled Baron Moyne. The younger brother of Sir Rupert, and the uncle of Arthur Onslow Edward Guinness, Walter was a prominent British politician and a confidant of Prime Minister

Winston Churchill. He had served as a Conservative member of the House of Commons from 1907 to 1931—except during World War I—and later in the House of Lords. During World War I, he had served with distinction in the Suffolk Yeomanry—the same unit with whom his nephew served during World War II—in Egypt and at Gallipoli. In 1917, he was awarded a DSO for his bravery under fire in the bloody fighting at Passchendaele.

During World War II, Walter Guinness served as Resident Minister of State in Egypt. During much of his tenure, his post was near the front lines of the fight against the German Afrika Korps. After the defeat of the German forces in North Africa in 1943, one of the issues with which Walter dealt was that of the resettlement of displaced European Jews in the area that eventually became the State of Israel. Because of his position as a minister of the government of the British Empire, Walter was perceived as being part of the opposition to a Jewish state, and this perception cost him his life. On November 6, 1944, he was assassinated in Cairo by members of a Jewish underground group. The killing was denounced by numerous Jewish leaders, including Chaim Weizmann, who became the first president of Israel.

At the Guinness breweries, problems of tardy shipments and labor shortages were small beer compared to the enormity of World War II and the coming decades of crisis in the Middle East. Though sales and profits dipped during the early years of the war, both rebounded after 1942.

During the war, Guinness had excellent leadership in the person of Ben Newbold, who became corporate managing director in 1941. Overseeing both St. James's Gate and Park Royal, he took the lead at a turbulent time in company history, but one in which growth occurred despite adversity. Under his leadership, the breweries were gradually modernized with wooden brewing vessels giving way, at last, to stainless steel.

In 1945, the year that the Allies finally defeated the Axis, Guinness total production topped two million hogsheads (of 52 imperial gallons each) for the first time since 1921. St. James's Gate produced 1.34 million of this total, and the 710,000 hogsheads brewed at Park

Royal were twice the expected annual output of this four-kieve facility.

The years between the world wars had been especially hard for the brewing industry worldwide. By comparison, the U.S. brewing industry, which suffered through a decade of Prohibition in the 1920s and a decade of Depression in the 1930s, would not recover to pre-World War I levels until the 1940s. The U.S. industry had its best year to date in 1914 with 66.2 million 31-gallon barrels, and then slid into a slump that lasted three decades. Reaching a trough of 2.8 million barrels of nonalcoholic beer in 1932, the U.S. industry did not top the 1914 production total until 1943. In that year, the Americans brewed 71 million barrels, and in 1945, they were up to 86.6 million.

Though the residual effects of wartime restrictions and shortages would be slow to clear in the United Kingdom, Guinness—like the Americans across the pond—faced a far rosier future after World War II than it had in the aftermath of the previous conflict.

The Postwar Years

In 1945, with Ben Newbold reaching retirement age after his many decades of service, Sir Rupert Guinness asked Sir Hugh Beaver, late of Gibb & Partners, to come aboard as Newbold's assistant and heir apparent. Beaver had remained as a partner at Gibb until 1942, when he joined the British government as Director General and Controller General of the Ministry of Works, a job for which he was knighted in 1943. Sir Hugh accepted the Guinness offer, and in 1946, when Newbold died suddenly, Beaver became managing director, a post he retained until he retired in 1960.

Among the management steps taken by Beaver was the reorganization of St. James's Gate and Park Royal into separate and freestanding corporate entities within Arthur Guinness, Son & Company Limited. He also proceeded to invest a great deal in converting both breweries for the type of continuous sterilization that Alan McMullen had advocated before Park Royal was built.

Another decision made immediately after the war as to supply the two breweries with barley entirely from the nations in which they were situated. By this time, total Irish barley production had quadrupled, so Guinness was now buying only a fifth of total Irish production instead of dominating the market with four fifths as it once had.

By the late 1940s, it was also time to start upgrading the fleet of steam locomotives that had been running on Samuel Geoghegan's remarkable Guinness railway since the late nineteenth century. The first of these, an enclosed cab "Planet" diesel built by F. C. Hibberd of London, entered service in 1947. An additional 11 Hibberd engines joined the Guinness railway through 1950, and they operated until 1975, when railway operations were discontinued. One of the Hibberd diesels is still on display at St. James's Gate.

As promoters of the Guinness brand, John Gilroy and his jolly menagerie returned in force after World War II. This time, they were seen not only in the familiar bus and tube posters, but also as promotional items that ranged from ceramic knickknacks to table lamps.

In 1953, Gilroy brought the whole menagerie together for the first time for an advertising campaign that celebrated the coronation of Queen Elizabeth II. Two years later, Guinness and Gilroy's creations starred in the first night of commercial television in the United Kingdom on September 22, 1955. This first-ever British beer commercial featured a live sea lion pirating the zookeeper's cap. Later commercials, featured in both movie theaters and on television, used puppets and animated characters as well as live animals.

One of the most memorable appearances by the animals was as part of the Guinness Festival Clocks. The first of these was constructed as the Guinness contribution to the Festival of Britain in 1951. The Festival was a national trade fair and science fair held in London and other cities, as well as including touring exhibitions. The idea was to promote postwar recovery and boost postwar morale using the centennial of London's Great Exhibition of 1851. As part of the Festival, a FunFair and Pleasure Garden were installed at London's Battersea

Park. Designed by the firm of Lewitt Him and built by the clockmakers Baume & Company Limited, the first Guinness Festival Clock was part of the Battersea installation.

At first glance, Gilroy's animals seemed merely as decorative elements on the clock, but on the quarter hour, the zookeeper would emerge, ring a bell, and the animals would begin to scamper about. With accompanying music, each animal in turn performed a dance of some sort. Finally, after about five minutes, the zookeeper again rang his bell and the animals suspended their performances.

In addition to the clock, Guinness also produced Festival Guinness, a special limited edition Double Extra Stout—based on its Guinness Export Stout—to commemorate the Festival of Britain. The abstract design on the labels had the look of fireworks. The idea was that it would be released during the last week of April 1951 and would remain on sale for 12 months. The beer was to debut in Liverpool rather than London, with distribution in other northern cities such as Blackpool, Edinburgh, and Glasgow. Plans to get it distributed into London fell apart, and it was not actually launched until May 1951. Sales in the limited distribution area were less than hoped, and Festival Guinness was discontinued in November 1951.

The Guinness Festival Clock on the other hand was a hit at Battersea. It was such a hit in fact, that the company received requests to borrow it for retail promotions. To meet the demand, Guinness built a total of 13 clocks in two sizes. These toured the United Kingdom and Ireland—appearing in venues such as the Phoenix Park Zoo in Dublin—and two of the clocks even traveled to the United States. The clocks remained on tour until 1966, when they were withdrawn from service. By this time, Gilroy's menagerie was also being retired—,a sign of changing times.

Gilroy himself continued his parallel career as a portrait painter— which he always insisted was his true calling. His subjects included Sir Harold Alexander, Sir Winston Churchill, Sir John Gielgud, Edward Heath, Louis Mountbatten, Pope John XXIII, and most members of the Royal Family.

In the United States, meanwhile, Guinness had acquired the relatively new Burke Brewery in New York's Long Island City in 1943, but waited until after World War II to begin brewing Guinness products there. The decision to begin brewing in the United States after World War II was an important one. In the wake of the war, the United States emerged as the world's largest economy by a large margin. European economies and infrastructure were still reeling from the effects of the war, but in the United States, the infrastructure was untouched and the economy was beginning to boom. Americans were discovering that they enjoyed a prosperity unprecedented in their history, and they were ready to spend money on leisure activities that included enjoying a glass of beer now and then.

Against this backdrop, Guinness was keen to be part of the postwar American economy. The official word was "Before any brewing of Guinness took place in the United States, we followed our traditional policy of considering long and acting quickly. Many and varied factors had to be explored: the difference in American malt and hops, the very different climatic conditions, variations in water, and so on. After all these had been taken into consideration, and months of experimental work had been undertaken, the decision was made."

That decision included sending a team of brewers, engineers, and chemists to "consider the modifications necessary to the existing plant and procedure" for the brewing of Guinness. Dr. C. J. Virden, M. W. Plumpton, and J. L. McCowen went from Park Royal, joined by J. C. Anderson and A. C. Kelly from St. James's Gate, as well as Dr. Arthur Hughes, who would later serve as managing director of Guinness.

The experience of building the Park Royal plant and bringing it up to speed to brew a product identical to that of St. James's Gate was of immeasurable benefit. So too was the fact that Guinness had many years of experience using American hops and barley. The Guinness team easily adapted to the fact that in the United States, grain is shipped in bulk, not in sacks. It was easy to get used to the fact that the malt reached the brewery in closed railcars and was moved by vacuum suction, reducing handling to a minimum. The exclusive yeast culture could be flown to New York from Dublin faster than it could be carried to London by ship. The New York City water supply was deemed "entirely suitable," although the myth of Guinness being made with Liffey River water was still hard to overcome.

However, the team faced new problems not encountered in London. The principal difference between Park Royal and New York was the climate. London and Dublin have generally the same weather most of the year. New York, on the other hand, experiences extremely hot and humid summers. Hops had to be kept in cold storage because they quickly began to mold in the heat and humidity. Meanwhile, the fermentation and maturation facilities required air conditioning to maintain constant year-round temperatures.

Guinness also inherited something at Long Island City that was common to all major American breweries, but not yet a routine part of Guinness culture—a bottling line. At home, Guinness still brewed in bulk and relied on outside bottlers.

March 1948 marked the first commercial release of American-made Guinness Extra Stout, although the brewery continued to be known as the Burke Brewery until the following year and production of the Burke's Ale and Burke's Stout brands continued. So too did Guinness's continued exports of Foreign Extra Stout to the United States.

The Guinness Extra Stout produced at Long Island City was originally brewed to the classic specifications of the pre-1914 era, when the beer was produced at a higher gravity than that mandated during World War I and retained as standard thereafter. This produced confusion in the marketplace when the American product was being sold side-by-side with imported Foreign Extra Stout, which had a very different flavor. During 1949, The Guinness team at Long Island City reduced the gravity of the beer and made changes in the malt to reduce sweetness. The company also discontinued importing Foreign Extra Stout into the U.S. market so that there was just a single Guinness stout available. The production of the Burke products continued at Long Island until 1950.

Officially known as Arthur Guinness & Son, incorporated after 1949, the Long Island City brewery was a bold effort, but ultimately it continued in operation for just six years. After having made a huge investment in the plant and spending a million dollars on national advertising, Guinness deemed the venture unsuccessful because of disappointing sales. The brewery shut its doors in August 1954.

It is important to put the Guinness New York experiment into context. During the 1946 to 1954 period, the era of the rapidly expanding postwar American economy, the brewers within the United States were also moving to exploit the growing market for beer. Major companies with broad distribution were now taking steps to establish themselves as truly national brands. Both Anheuser-Busch of St. Louis and the Joseph Schlitz Brewing Company of Milwaukee, America's top two brewers, invested in anchoring themselves on both coasts by establishing major brewing operations in both California and the New York metropolitan area. Pabst Brewing, also of Milwaukee and also in the top four American brewers, followed suit and all three were brewing on both coasts as well as in the heartland by 1954. Long an important fixture at the top end of the American brewing scene, Pabst had been the largest in the United States at the turn of the century when Guinness was the largest brewing company in the world. Meanwhile, the regional brewers within the New York area were also among the largest brewing companies in the United States. Ballantine and Schaefer were in third and fifth places nationally in the early 1950s.

Such was the competition that Guinness faced at it competed for market share in this era. All of the American brewing giants had what Guinness did not have. This included the experience of many decades in the marketplace, long-standing relationships with distributors, and the brand recognition that came from being household words in American households for several generations. In short, they had the marketing clout that comes from a long and successful presence in a market. All of these factors played a role in the failure of Guinness's strategy for a New York brewery. Even if Guinness would have tried for a regional, rather than national, launch, it would have faced stiff competition in the Northeast from Ballantine and Schaefer, not to mention from Ruppert and Rheingold, where these brands all had very loyal local followings. The experiment was ahead of its time. A broad market for specialty beers in the United States would not develop for another generation. When it did, Guinness would succeed as a specialty import.

Even as Guinness was making the painful decision to close up shop in New York, the company was making moves to expand its business in Ireland itself. The idea here was not to open new facilities to brew stout, but to acquire existing breweries that would continue, at lest for a time, to produce the beer they had previously brewed. In 1953, the company bought the Great Northern Brewery at Dundalk, north of Dublin, a stout brewery that dated back to 1897. That same year Guinness purchased Cherry's Brewery in New Ross. William Cherry had set up shop here in 1828 after moving from Waterford and closing two breweries there. In 1955, Guinness bought the Davis Strangman Brewery in Waterford, renamed it "Cherry's," and closed the New Ross premises. In 1956, Guinness began brewing the Cherry's Phoenix Ale brand at the Waterford plant.

Also in 1956, Guinness acquired the St. Francis Abbey Brewery in Kilkenny, which, at the venerable age of 246, was the oldest extant brewery in Ireland. Founded by John Smithwick, its flagship brand was Smithwick's Ale (pronounced "Smittick's"), a beer that continues to be part of the Guinness portfolio in the twenty-first century.

One major and quite fundamental change that Guinness made during the postwar years was in its distribution outside the United Kingdom and Ireland. As we have seen, Guinness exports were traditionally in the hands of distributors who bottled the stout under their own labels. Between 1935 and 1937, the myriad of distributors, large and small, consolidated into two firms—Export Bottlers Limited and the Guinness-controlled Alexander Macfee. These two companies then split the world between them for more than a decade. In May 1950, Guinness formally acquired Export Bottlers Limited, combining it with the Macfee assets and renaming the merged entity Guinness Exports Limited.

With this new subsidiary in place, Guinness moved to standard-ize labeling. Until this time, individual bottlers and distributors had continued to use their own trademarks on at least some of their labels. It was not until 1953 that other labels and trademarks were finally phased out entirely in favor of the buff-colored oval Guinness trademark label with the harp and Arthur Guinness's signature. The cats, bulldogs, monkeys, pelicans, and wolves had finally become extinct.

Each trademark label now also contains a racking number that is based on a series of complex mathematical formulations, which changed over time and some of which were never recorded. In deci-phering part of this complexity for us, Eibhlin Roche explained that "Until the late 1950s, the labels could be dated by reading the rack-ing number reads backward. For example, 521024 would identify a bottling on the 24th of October in 1952. The number is preceded by a letter whose meaning is not known for certain. The 'L' that appears on many labels may or may not have stood for Liverpool, where Guinness Exports Limited bottled the beer. By the 1960s, the num-bering system of reading the number backwards changed."

Eventually, the practice was discarded, and actual racking and bottling numbers were no longer used on the labels. However, up into the 1980s, some labels were printed with the letter "L" and the faux racking number "821212."

The relative importance of the specific Guinness product vari-ants was summarized by head brewer Owen Williams in his 1957 *Notes on the St. James's Gate Brewery*, when he wrote that "In Ireland, 50 percent of our Extra Stout is sold on draught, the remainder being sold in bottle. Porter is sold mainly on draught, with a small percent-age bottled in the North of Ireland. In Great Britain, however, a very big proportion of our Extra Stout is sold in bottle, about 8 percent being sold on draught. We sell no Porter in Great Britain. In Ireland we hold about 80 percent of the total beer trade, in Great Britain about 7 percent."

Once the company's principal draught beer, Guinness Porter declined rapidly in the postwar years. Though it continued to be brewed until 1974, a decade earlier H. S. Corran wrote in an update to Owen Williams's previous survey that Porter had "almost disappeared, except in Belfast." By the 1960s, Porter had a 22 percent market share in Northern Ireland, but a 1 percent market share in the Republic of Ireland.

The years immediately following World War II saw many other changes in the way that Guinness did business. The New York experiment and the acquisition of Irish breweries were two examples. Another of these was a reformulation of Foreign Extra Stout to increase its life and stability, and introducing measures such as pasteurization and carbonation. As Owen Williams described it, "Since 1949 [Foreign Extra Stout] has had a much more moderate hop rate, and has been made from a blend of two beers, the major constituent being used fresh, with a higher hop rate, but about 10 percent being specially matured by an accelerated process of maturation and with a very low hop rate. Foreign Extra Stout was formerly sold in a cask to a number of bottlers in Liverpool and London who sent it to be bottled to all parts of the world. Bottling is now largely concentrated in our own subsidiary, Guinness Exports Limited in Liverpool, and [its] condition is produced by carbonation, after which the stout is pasteurized so that no further fermentation can take place, and it will be unchanged however long it may remain in trade."

Despite the controversy over the issue of "tampering" with a beer whose formula was essentially unchanged for a century, the new Foreign Extra Stout was apparently well received because, by 1951, exports had soared to 90,000 barrels. Under Guinness Exports Limited, exports of Guinness stout for 1955 reached 140,000 barrels. They more than doubled during the next nine years to 300,000.

At the same time, the "home trade," reached 2.1 million barrels, with 50.4 percent of that in the Republic of Ireland, 36.9 percent in Britain, and 12.7 percent in Northern Ireland. Of the total, 96.5 percent of the sales were of Guinness Extra Stout, with the balance being of Guinness Porter, which—as we've seen—was sold mainly in Northern Ireland and not at all in Britain.

Meanwhile, Williams and Corran wrote, "the product variant brewed for much of the European market was Guinness Export Stout." As Corran explains, "Since the war, we have brewed a sweeter type of stout of equal strength to Foreign Extra Stout and specially designed for the Belgian market. It is sold in most European countries, and a little also outside Europe. It has a moderate hop rate and is generally bottled in the country of sale, either naturally con-ditioned or carbonated, and pasteurized like Foreign Extra Stout."

As Guinness moved out of the darkness of the Great Depression and World War II and into the light of a slowly dawning era of global prosperity, there were many exciting things on or beneath the horizon. Some were the unanticipated consequences of Hugh Beaver's nurtur-ing of a new generation of bright young men, one the accidental outcome of one of Hugh Beaver's hunting trips, and several were the audacious brainstorms of a jolly tyrant who came to Guinness as a result of the formation of its new export subsidiary.

Born in Celbridge, County Kildare, in 1725. Arthur Guinness founded the Guinness Brewery at St. James's Gate in 1759 and passed away in 1803 as one of Dublin's most celebrated citizens. *Image copyright of Guinness Archive, Diageo Ireland.*

Arthur Guinness II (1768–1855), was the second son of the founder. From 1803 to 1820, he was the second person to hold the title of head brewer at St. James's Gate. *Image copyright of Guinness Archive, Diageo Ireland.*

Benjamin Lee Guinness (1798–1868), the son of Arthur Guinness II, became a partner in the family business in 1820 and took over the leadership at St. James's Gate in 1839. *Image copyright of Guinness Archive, Diageo Ireland.*

Sir Edward Cecil Guinness, 1st Earl of Iveagh (1847–1927), was the third son of Benjamin Lee Guinness. He built the brewery into the largest in the world and took the company public in 1886. He was chairman of the public company from 1886 to 1890 and from 1902 to 1927. *Image copyright of Guinness Archive, Diageo Ireland.*

The main gate to the Guinness brewery has been one of Dublin's most recognized landmarks since the end of the eighteenth century. The medieval St. James's Gate was nearby. *Photo by and copyright Bill Yenne.*

A Guinness drayman takes a break from his work to enjoy a pint at St. James's Gate, circa 1910. Brewery workers were each supplied a daily allowance of stout. *Image copyright of Guinness Archive, Diageo Ireland.*

Monitoring the brew at "Number 9 Copper," one of the brew kettles at St. James's Gate in 1949. *Image copyright of Guinness Archive, Diageo Ireland.*

Through the early twentieth century, when barrels were made of American white oak rather than metal, the cooperage at St. James's Gate was almost as big an operation as the brewery itself. *Image copyright of Guinness Archive, Diageo Ireland.*

The coopers place a rope around the stave ends in preparation for closing up the top of the barrel. *Image copyright of Guinness Archive, Diageo Ireland.*

The cooper "blazes," or chars the inside of the barrel to dry it, set its shape, and seal the wood. In 1949, Coopers were still making barrels the old-fashioned way. *Image copyright of Guinness Archive, Diageo Ireland.*

The cooper setting the metal hoops onto the finished barrel. *Image copyright of Guinness Archive, Diageo Ireland.*

Wooden barrels being filled with Guinness stout in the St. James's Gate racking room, circa 1900. *Image copyright of Guinness Archive, Diageo Ireland.*

Barrels of Guinness stout, ready to be shipped to bottlers in Liverpool in 1949. *Image copyright of Guinness Archive, Diageo Ireland.*

During the 1950s, the use of wooden barrels was gradually
phased out in favor of metal. By the 1960s, metal barrels,
such as those seen here, were being used exclusively. *Image
copyright of Guinness Archive, Diageo Ireland.*

Testing the latest batch at St. James's Gate, circa 1949. Guinness master brewers still do quality checks as the matured beer is ready to be kegged for distribution. *Image copyright of Guinness Archive, Diageo Ireland.*

During the 1930s, artist John Gilroy created the artwork for the classic Guinness advertising. The Toucan is the most remembered of the menagerie of animals that he used in his illustrations. *Image copyright of Guinness Archive, Diageo Ireland.*

Mountains of wooden barrels, 30 feet high, in the cooperage yard at St. James's Gate. The world's largest brewery was an immense operation. *Image copyright of Guinness Archive, Diageo Ireland.*

A malt train passes Brewhouse Number 2 on the Guinness railway. Several of the brewery's large fleet of locomotives are visible in this photograph. *Image copyright of Guinness Archive, Diageo Ireland.*

Though the Guinness railway no longer runs, the James's Street pedestrian tunnel (right) is still very much in use as a means of access between the upper and lower sections of St. James's Gate. *Image copyright of Guinness Archive, Diageo Ireland.*

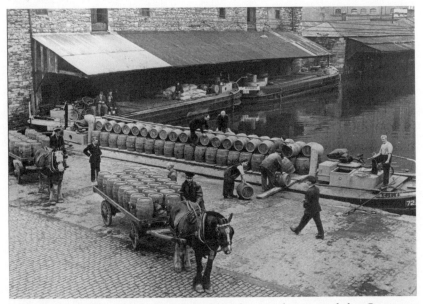

Loading barrels at the Grand Canal Harbor at the rear of the Guinness Brewery. Barley would have been brought up to the brewery from the country by barge. *Image copyright of Guinness Archive, Diageo Ireland.*

The crew aboard a Guinness barge as it makes its way down the River Liffey from St. James's Gate to the Port of Dublin. In 1877, Edward Cecil Guinness issued contracts for the first of a fleet of barges that would be named for Irish rivers. *Image copyright of Guinness Archive, Diageo Ireland.*

The busy yard at St. James's Gate with Guinness railway trains and horse-drawn lorries loading and transporting barrels of stout, circa 1910. *Image copyright of Guinness Archive, Diageo Ireland.*

In 1931, the company launched the steamship S.S. *Guinness*, the first ocean-going vessel of its kind to have been built expressly for bulk shipments of Guinness stout. The beer was carried to England for bottling. *Image copyright of Guinness Archive, Diageo Ireland.*

The passing of an era intersects the coming of an era. Horse-drawn lorries are seen here delivering the metal kegs that were finally replacing wooden barrels in the 1950s. *Image copyright of Guinness Archive, Diageo Ireland.*

Though Guinness did not bottle the beer at St. James's Gate, labels were printed there by the millions and sent to the export bottlers. *Image copyright of Guinness Archive, Diageo Ireland.*

The big Guinness brewery at Park Royal in north London operated from 1936 to 2005. *Image copyright of Guinness Archive, Diageo Ireland.*

The Market Street Store-house at St. James's Gate, seen here in the 1960s, housed fermentation vessels from its opening in 1904 through the 1980s. It now houses the Guinness visitor center. *Image copyright of Guinness Archive, Diageo Ireland.*

Arthur Francis Benjamin Guinness lays the foundation stone at the Guinness brewery at Ikeja, Nigeria in 1962. Benjamin served as chairman of the company from 1962 to 1987. *Image copyright of Guinness Archive, Diageo Ireland.*

The original 1862 Guinness label design featured the Brian Boru harp and the signature of Arthur Guinness. The design remains essentially the same today. *Image copyright of Guinness Archive, Diageo Ireland.*

Guinness Master Brewer Fergal Murray amid the stainless steel brew kettles at the St. James's Gate brewery. *Photo by and copyright Bill Yenne.*

Guinness Archivist Eibhlin Roche and Master Brewer Fergal Murray in the Storehouse at St. James's Gate. *Photo by and copyright Bill Yenne.*

Guinness Master Brewer Fergal Murray holds a pint poured at the tap in the St. James's Gate kegging facility where the final quality check occurs. He proudly describes this as "the freshest possible product. This is as good as it gets." *Photo by and copyright Bill Yenne.*

Great Men and
Great Ideas

History often records that great leaders arrive at auspicious moments. Such was the case for Guinness as the company looked ahead toward its Bicentenary in 1959.

When Guinness took control of the Alexander Macfee bottling company in 1932, it got the services of an energetic Macfee manager from Lancashire named Arthur William Fawcett. Having started with Macfee in 1912, Fawcett worked his way up to head the company, and he would later be chairman and managing director of Guinness Exports Limited. Dr. Arthur Hughes, the brew master who later served as managing director of Guinness (1966–1973), best described him when he said Fawcett had "an abrasive personality with imaginative promotional ideas."

Those who worked under him often found him a stern taskmaster. Those called on the carpet in Fawcett's office interpreted his initials, A. W. F., to stand for "Appointment With Fear." A study in contrasts, he was a compassionate dictator with a caustic temper who is remembered for introducing an employee roof garden and a pension plan that was very generous for its time.

If Fawcett was a tough guy, it was probably because of his many years at Macfee, where the centerpiece of the trade was selling Guinness to ocean-going ships. "The toughest skippers were the ones who would only pay 'on return,' " Fawcett recalled in a 1962 interview. "They pointed out that they still had to sell your goods, so they could not pay for them until they had got back to Liverpool. One could not talk commercial practice to them, let alone refer to the exorbitant profits they would make. One type of skipper would simply walk away implying 'If you don't like it, take your goods back.' The more impatient would pick you up by the seat of your pants and politely put you overside. Thank goodness, bulwarks were not too high and there was very little space between ship and dockside."

Fawcett himself ran a tight ship at Macfee and Guinness Exports Limited, but he often included cheerful handwritten notes with Christmas bonuses, which were frequently decorated with cartoons he had drawn. To promote employee health during the dark months of the year, he even handed out halibut oil capsules, which he cheerfully described as "your winter sunshine."

To the rest of the world, he was a promotional genius. Fawcett is perhaps best remembered for his publicity schemes, which made headlines and helped promote the product. His publicity stunts did as intended—they garnered a very great deal of attention. In 1958, he acquired 250 surplus gas street light posts from the Liverpool city council and gave them away to Liverpudlians living abroad who suggested ways to expand sales of Guinness. When gasoline rationing was introduced in England during the Suez Crisis of 1956, he bought a horse and cart, which soon became popular with the media. Under Fawcett, the familiar yellow Guinness delivery trucks were adorned with replicas of leprechauns, large bottles, or world globes.

Beginning in 1953, he distributed thousands of miniature bottles of real Guinness stout, which became a ubiquitous promotional novelty around the world—not to mention a hit with collectors. Designed specifically for the overseas market, the miniatures were still being produced into the 1980s, long after Fawcett had retired. Standing just 3.3 inches tall, the little bottles were made by Jules Lang & Son of London, and filled by the Crown Cork Company of Southall using a miniature filling system developed by Guinness.

Arthur Fawcett's most outstanding publicity achievement was unquestionably his ambitious "Bottledrops" of 1954 and 1959. The idea was based on the old notion of sealing a message in a bottle and casting it into the ocean, hoping that it would be found by someone, some day, on a distant shore across the world. Fawcett did exactly this, but on an immense scale, putting messages into 50,000 bottles in 1954. In turn, these were dropped into six locations in the Atlantic Ocean, four in the Pacific Ocean and one in the Indian Ocean. All of the drops were north of the equator except two each in the Atlantic and Pacific. The messages tightly rolled and inserted in the bottles were a booklet about Guinness and a signed and numbered document that explained the Bottledrop as facilitating research into the perfect way to seal a bottle.

"In my opinion," wrote Fawcett in his message in the bottles, "If all these operations are done correctly, the positive life of the efficient sealing will be at least 500 years . . . it is perhaps intriguing to stop and think that many of these bottles, floating in the oceans of the world, may survive even many of the people reading this particular memorandum."

A note addressed to those who found the massage asked that an attached, numbered form be filled out and mailed back to Guinness: "We will most certainly write you back telling you exactly when and where your particular bottle was dropped, sending also a suitable memento of the occasion. But, irrespective of anything else, please don't forget the important message that has come to you o'er thousands of miles: Guinness Is Good For You!"

Five years later, to commemorate the Guinness Bicentenary, Fawcett tripled the size of the Bottledrop, releasing 150,000 bottles—embossed with a design based on a Western Hemisphere map—into the Atlantic from 38 ships. These bottles contained a booklet and a full-color certificate professing to be "from the office of King Neptune, Monarch of the Sea," along with instructions for turning the bottles into table lamps. In his letter, "Neptune" stated that he had "permitted the House of Guinness to cast in, and/or upon my Domain the bottle carrying this document—but in precise particular, the Atlantic Ocean—and allow same free passage, without let or hindrance, to convey to you the story of Guinness Stout, and also to further the fascinating hobby of labology (label collecting) . . . so please try a bottle of Guinness stout, I am sure you will appreciate it, just as Guinness Exports Limited will appreciate hearing from you."

Guinness noted that the bottles were cast into the sea to "float maybe for a thousand years, perhaps to be picked up on some foreign shore by a new friend of Guinness or, as has already happened, by an ex-employee now living in America."

Guinness had expected to start hearing from people within six to nine months, but three months after the 1954 Atlantic Bottledrop, the first bottle was found in the Azores. From then on, the company was flooded with discoveries from as far afield as Ceylon, India, the Philippines, South America, and the West Indies. The numerous discoveries made headlines around the world, certainly underscoring the Guinness brand name. If every bottle dropped had a message in it, every bottle found had a human interest story attached as the letters began pouring in.

One letter came from an 11-year-old girl in the Bahamas, who wrote: "Dear Sir, How are you feeling? Fine I hope as I am fine. I received your letter and also the book. I was surprised when I opened that package and saw that it was a little book. I read that book every day."

Michael O'Sullivan, a lighthouse keeper from County Kerry in Ireland, wrote to say that he found a bottle while on the way to a fishing spot, and went on to say that "Myself and my partner do appreciate and enjoy a pint of your famous stout very often."

Lynn Smith of Sugar Land, Texas, picked up a bottle while hunting quail on Matagorda Island, and Renee Kopfer of Corte Madera, California, wrote that "Recently, while beach-combing in the Channel Island chain off the Santa Barbara coast I came across one of your Guinness beer bottles."

The British Consul in Papeete, Tahiti, observed that "The people who found the bottle remarked that it contained a sweet and pleasant perfume. I was therefore forced to demonstrate that it has a sweet and pleasant taste, too."

From Western Australia, Geoff Gibson wrote that "I was walking along the isolated beach south of the Mundrabilla Road House when I found your bottle. Myself and all the people of Mundrabilla (all five of them) love Guinness."

Chester Cooley, president of the Da-Lite Screen Company of Chicago told Guinness: "Recently I experienced one of the greatest thrills when I found a bottle on the shore of one of the very romantic islands in the Bahamas and, on opening it, discovered my trophy consisted of a scroll commemorating the occasion. . . . I read the interesting literature enclosed with your letter. I am reciprocating in turn by sending you literature descriptive of the products we manufacture."

Raymond MacNair of New Brunswick penned a note that read in part: "This was our first trip to the Arctic . . . while walking along the beach at Coates Island, I discovered two bottles which contained scrolls. My wife and I enjoy walking on beaches and over the years we have found a lot of different things but the two bottles found in the Arctic surely tops the lot."

For Arthur Fawcett, the Bottledrops surely topped the lot. They have been described as "the world's longest running advertising promotion," and this may well be true. Though the numbers of bottles being discovered dropped off after a few years, the bottles still continue to be found at the rate of about one or two a year.

Fawcett's Bottledrops were a deliberate—and very successful— effort to put the Guinness brand name into the headlines. Meanwhile, at the same moment that Fawcett was planning the first Bottledrop, Sir High Beaver, Guinness's postwar managing director was developing an idea of his own. In its planning stages, it was no big deal. On a whim, he conceived what he intended as a minor publicity item, but it inadvertently turned into a brand-building campaign of unprecedented proportions.

It all began with an incident that occurred in November 1951 on a hunting trip in Ireland's County Wexford. Beaver and a companion became embroiled in a friendly dispute over the fastest game bird in Europe. Was it a grouse or a plover? That night, when no reference book could be found to answer the question, Beaver got to thinking that there ought to be a book that answered this—as well as other such types of questions that crop up in friendly discussions at corner pubs.

When Beaver mentioned this idea around the Guinness office, a young colleague named Christopher Chataway—an Oxford-educated economist recruited into Guinness after World War II—recommended two men whom he knew who ran a fact-checking service in London. Norris and Ross McWhirter were twin bothers in their mid-twenties who had become sports writers in 1950. Working as a sports commentator for the BBC, Norris had first met Chataway when the latter was a runner in the 1954 race in which Roger Bannister first ran the four-minute mile. Oxford-educated and endowed with photographic memories, the McWhirters had founded an agency that provided sports statistics and other facts and figures for London newspapers. As such, they were ideal candidates to head Hugh Beaver's project.

The book was originally conceived of as an inexpensive giveaway item to be distributed at pubs in Ireland and the United Kingdom. Neither Beaver not the McWhirters had any idea how popular the book would be when the first edition of a thousand copies was published as a handout in 1954. The following year, no one was more surprised than Hugh Beaver when *The Guinness Book of Records* reached the top of the British best-seller lists by Christmas after having been published in August.

"It was a marketing giveaway," Beaver recalled. "It wasn't supposed to be a money maker," said Beaver.

First published in the United States in 1956, it sold 70,000 copies. Issued annually, the book eventually became a global best seller. With hundreds of millions sold in more than 100 counties, year after year, it became the biggest selling copyrighted book in history.

A Family Business at Two Hundred

During the 1950s, as Arthur Fawcett contemplated his Bottledrops and as Hugh Beaver and the McWhirter brothers nurtured *The Guinness Book of Records*, people throughout Arthur Guinness, Son & Company, were preparing for a milestone that the majority of businesses never have the opportunity to enjoy—the Bicentenary. Few companies survive a century, and still fewer survive two. Such a landmark would have been worthy of Guinness being on a short list within its own book of records.

In 1959, Guinness hit the dual century mark against the backdrop of a burst of substantial growth. In the early part of the decade, net profits hovered below the 1949 peak of just over £2 million as the

United Kingdom, the biggest market struggled to overcome the detrimental economic effects of the aftermath of the Great Depression and World War II. In 1954, the year of the first Bottledrop, however, net profits reached £2.39 million. In 1955, they reached £2.8 million, and in 1956, the number was £2.95 million. In the ensuing two years, net profits grew by a million, reaching £3.98 million on the eve of the Bicentenary in 1958. For the Bicentenary year itself, net profits would stand at £4.2 million. The Bicentenary marked the debut of Guinness advertising in Ireland. The company had advertised in the United Kingdom for three decades, but amazingly not on its home turf.

"Guinness didn't start to advertise in Ireland until 1959," Archivist Eibhlin Roche points out. "With the rise of lagers, Guinness wasn't getting their 90-odd-percent market share anymore and it was decided that they should start advertising. There had been discussions about this all throughout the 1950s, but they didn't want to introduce advertising into Ireland all of a sudden for a brand that was so prominent, so they waited until the Bicentenary and used that as the launch pad."

Of course, point-of-sale items such as pub signs had existed in Ireland previously, but as Eibhlin explains, "there wouldn't have been any drip mattes or the normal pub paraphernalia that you see now. You would not have had billboards or posters with the toucan or the other Gilroy circus animals as there were in the United Kingdom. Press advertising, bus signs, and poster advertising didn't start in Ireland until 1959."

Also on the occasion of the Bicentenary, Guinness management expanded to include two, then three joint managing directors. In 1956, Hugh Beaver would be joined by Dr. Charles King Mill, and in 1959 by Alan Tindal Lennox-Boyd, formerly the United Kingdom's Secretary of State for the Colonies, and the son-in-law of corporate chairman Rupert Guinness, the Earl of Iveagh. Lennox-Boyd had married Lady Patricia Guinness, known to the family as Patsy, in 1938. Typically, family members were no longer being tapped for management roles in the company, but, as we shall see in a later chapter, Lennox-Boyd's foreign policy expertise was an important, perhaps essential, element in the global expansion of Guinness in the 1960s.

As Guinness proudly looked forward to celebrating 1959 in style, so too did the Irish government. A postage stamp bearing the likeness of Arthur Guinness was issued to celebrate the importance of his company and its having thrived for two centuries. Guinness itself celebrated with a commemorative Bicentenary label design that was rolled out in Ireland and the United Kingdom on April 1, 1959.

The official Bicentenary Day was celebrated first at Park Royal on June 11, 1959, with a garden party for a thousand guests, but the biggest commemoration came a month later on July 11 in Dublin. Corporate Chairman Rupert Guinness presided over the affair, which included a concert with step-dancers, harpists, pipers, ballad singers, and traditional musicians of every kind. A special votive Mass was held at St. James's, the historic parish church near the brewery.

The official luncheon was a banquet befitting a company that has lasted since the era of Mozart and Voltaire. A piece in *The Guinness Harp* inhouse publication reported:

Bicentenary Day in the Refreshment Department was a day to be remembered; a day of hard work and long hours, undertaken with the determination that nothing should go wrong with the largest and most important party ever catered for. Difficulties were not allowed to exist and that spirit carried the day . . . the food arrived in [Rupert Guinness Hall] from James's Street kitchen. In this same room, 1,400 pieces of table cutlery, 1,250 plates, cups and saucers, 750 glasses had to be stacked and hand washed before preparation could be started for the evening reception of 300 VIPs. . . . On Friday evening the tables were laid, the bar set up, final checks and counts were made. The stage was set. The kitchen in James's Street was a hive of industry until 10 o'clock that night. In view were all kinds of food, cooked and uncooked; 80 ducks, with chickens, salmon, ham, lobsters, and sauces of various colors. . . . The pastry cook was packing up his pastry cases, hundreds of them, just large enough to pop into your mouth, all ready to be filled an hour or so before the reception. The vegetable cook was putting away his trays of cooked potatoes and beans; lettuce was trimmed ready to be washed, cases of oranges were ready for the final slicing in the morning.

Seán Lemass, Ireland's An Taoiseach (prime minister), spoke at the luncheon. In his talk, Lemass noted that the firm had been of tremendous benefit to Dublin and to Ireland. He went on to add that the importance of Guinness to Dublin was reflected not only in the scale of their commercial enterprise and the employment they gave, but that the company and the Guinness family had been exceptionally generous to Dublin through the years in terms of housing and parks bequeathed to the city.

Rupert Guinness, Lord Iveagh, responded by telling the city fathers gathered to hear Lemass's remarks that he was glad they had been able to help celebrate the Bicentenary because their predecessors were no doubt colleagues of *his* predecessors. His great great grandfather, Arthur Guinness, as well as being a brewer, had taken part in the life and work of the city of Dublin, and his successors had been progressively more involved in Dublin's civic affairs. After lunch, to underscore the family tradition of philanthropy, Lord Iveagh laid the cornerstone for a new recreation center at St. James's Gate. Known as the Bicentenary Center, this facility with its 25-meter swimming pool was considered state-of-the-art when it opened in April 1962.

Speaking at the cornerstone dedication, Hugh Beaver reflected on Rupert's earlier comments by again mentioning the fact that Lord Iveagh was the fourth descendant of Arthur Guinness to have headed the family business. He told the gathering of brewery workers and other guests that "Bicentenaries are not common occasions but they are not unique. In the 200 years since 1759, this great Guinness business has been directed from the top, controlled and inspired by just five people representing five generations of the

Guinness family. I believe that to be absolutely unique. I don't think it has happened in any other country or any other business. It is a very remarkable achievement, and it is in a very great measure due to this that the prosperity and prestige of the Guinness enterprise has grown and remained."

To this, Michael Farnan, chairman of the Guinness Foremen's Association, added: "We are fully conscious of the great part in the Brewery has played in our lives, and in the lives of countless people, also in the life of our country."

Meanwhile, Charles King Mill addressed members of the Belfast Licensed Vintners' Association at a Bicentenary luncheon in Dublin that was also attended by St. James's Gate head brewer Owen Williams. Mill joked with the northerners, who came for a private brewery tour, that he was sorry that it had taken "nearly 200 years to get you all down here. Viewing the brewery today, I hope, will give you an impression of the care we take to ensure that our product goes out to you in the best possible condition."

Frank Donnelly, chairman of the Association, was not joking when he replied that it was a nice gesture on the part of Guinness to invite them and wondered whether Arthur Guinness could possibly have foreseen the size of the business two centuries later. "People of every kind, the farmer, doctor, busman, lawyer, author, were all drinking Guinness today," he said. "It has something that appeals to the universal palate. . . . People coming to Ireland are surprised that Irish people are able to run such a large brewery. Guinness would hardly have survived the vicissitudes of 200 years, in which there had been two world wars, had its controllers not taken such an interest in their country."

As he ended his remarks, Donnelly said that he hoped that the next 200 years would be as fruitful for Guinness as the past 200 years had been. Certainly the next half century would see the importance of the brand and the beer increase around the globe. This was due in large measure to the steps first taken in the Bicentenary Year, which are discussed in the chapters that follow.

Two Hundred Years A-Brewing

Come all you thirsty tourists and travelers everywhere
Till I sing for you a verse or two in a grand old Irish air.
Now it's all about our famous Stout that is known the worldwide
    And made for you, this lovely Brew, down by the Liffey side.

They may boast about their frozen Stout and foreign Lager Beers
But If you want the best that has stood the test for o'er 200 years.
Take my advice, it tastes so nice and go home satisfied
With this lovely stout that we turn out, down by the Liffey side.
If you want to see our grand Brewery at the top of James's Street
    Don't make a fuss, just take the bus or travel on your feet.
That powerful sight is on the right, at the door there stands a guide
    Who will point you out where we make this Stout, down by the
    Liffey side.

Our barges neat at Watling Street rock gently to and fro
As winch and sling the barrels swing into the hatch below
With holds and decks full of Double X they sail down with the tide
All specially made for foreign trade, down by the Liffey side.

You may travel down to Cork's own town and kiss the Blarney
    Stone Or see Killarney's lakes and dells and come back through
    Athlone
But when the trip is done and your poor old tongue is feeling hot and
    dried
Just cool it out with our famous Stout down by the Liffey side.

We have Porter too, it's good for you and says so on our sign.
All working men, be it pick or pen, they love it at lunch time With
    cheese and bread its creamy head is Dublin's hope and pride As
    they loudly shout "A pint fill out" down by the Liffey side.

Go down the Quay and you will see the dockers sweat and toil
and watch them dash at "can a'hash"* their tongues and throats to oil
When the day is through and they get what's due to the nearest Pub
   they stride
For our famous stuff that builds them up, down by the Liffey side.

Now if you stray Glasnevin way when some old friend is dead
The mourners stand with hat in hand while the funeral prayers are
   said,
When the grave is filled, the tears all spilled, their eyes are quickly
   dried
With a pint or two in the Brian Boru, down by the Liffey side.

Our famous beer has brought good cheer to millions everywhere
It's Guinness Stout you will see poured out at the wedding, wake or
   fair
The guests all stand with glass in hand to toast the groom and bride
Sure its name is known in every home, down by the Liffey side.

Come fill your glasses to the brim and drink a toast with me
to the Noble House of Guinness and their world famed Brewery
We Irishmen are proud of them and their products true and tried
Long may they live and employment give, down by the Liffey side.

Notes: Written by Joseph O'Grady, published in the bicentenary issue of *The Guinness
   Harp* in 1959.

* "Can a'hash" was dockland slang for dinnertime.

Nitrogenation, the Really Great Idea

Today, we take that beautiful, creamy head on our pint of Guinness for granted. We enjoy our pints—so near to perfect nearly every time—without a thought of the little nitrogen bubbles that make it possible. Often, we forget that it wasn't always so.

When Frank Donnelly and others said in 1959 that they hoped Guinness's second 200 years would be as fruitful as the first, few could have imagined that the monumental technical achievement that would kickstart the next two centuries was right beneath their noses—and their palates.

As we've noted, few companies reach 200 years in business, but how many celebrate their Bicentenary by inventing a process by which a magnificent product will become as near to perfect as possible. In my first conversation with Guinness Master Brewer Fergal Murray, he told me that the nitrogenation process deserved to be a chapter in this book. As I followed him about in the magical world at St. James's Gate, and as I sought the words to explain the true essence of Guinness as it exists today as a brand, I came to agree with him. No story of Guinness can be told without this one word.

"The consumer wanted a more consistent, longer lasting head on top of the beer," Murray said, explaining the beginnings of the quest that ultimately led to nitrogenation. "It took Guinness a long time to figure out what would deliver that perfect head."

A journey of this kind has to have a beginning, and it began back in the 1950s—the decade of *The Guinness Book of Records*, the Bottledrops and the Bicentenary. The story is another one in which Sir Hugh Beaver serves as protagonist. As with *The Guinness Book of Records*, Beaver was the catalyst, the managing director who provided inspiration and the elbow room for craftsmen to do the work. We are tempted to say "to do their magic," but it is not necessarily magic. Of course, the results of skill, expertise, and hard work can seem like magic to those who enjoy those results.

With *The Guinness Book of Records*, Beaver's craftsmen were Norris and Ross McWhirter. With nitrogenation, the craftsmen were Michael Ash and his team. Like Chris Chataway, Ash was a member of the cadre of bright young men who joined Guinness on Beaver's watch after World War II, recruited from Trinity College in Dublin, or from Oxford and Cambridge. Chataway was an economist; Ash was a mathematician. Both were trained as brewers at Park Royal because only having learned brewing could they work with the numbers within a brewing company. One of Beaver's ways of nurturing such men was in informal conversations over breakfast at Park Royal. John Simmons and Mark Griffiths later called it "ordeal by breakfast," and perhaps it was. However, in at least the two cases cited, it was where Beaver first grasped the germs of monumental concepts.

The Guinness Book of Records was undertaken almost on a lark, a good idea that was unnecessary, but which couldn't hurt and could probably help. As we well know, it more than helped, it took on a life of its own and became legendary. Nitrogenation, on the other hand, was undertaken as a possible solution to a problem. The problem was typical of many companies: Sales are down, so how do we improve sales?

Despite the increasing net profits in the 1950s, sales of stout were becoming flat and starting to slump. The market share of lager—the ubiquitous beer in major beer markets from Germany to North America—was achieving major inroads in the United Kingdom and Ireland where ale and stout had traditionally enjoyed significant market share. Guinness then had a 75 percent market share in Ireland, but just 5 percent in the United Kingdom, where it was a guest beer at other brewers's tied houses, and where it had always competed against British ales. In Ireland, about half of the Guinness sold was on draught, but in the United Kingdom, it had always been, and continued to be mostly in bottles.

Sales are down, so how do we improve sales?

The rhetorical answer to this question was to increase draught sales. The problem behind the problem, however, was the complex way that Guinness was served on draught. Until the late 1950s, the typical way of pouring a pint of Guinness in a pub was by mixing beer from two casks, a high cask above the bar and a low cask beneath the bar. Of course, the more moving parts there are in a mechanism or system, the more opportunities there are for something to go amiss. Getting a good pint depended the right balance of parts and on the practiced skill of the bartender. Getting a perfect pint was not easy.

"It was very difficult to maintain a consistency," Fergal Murray explains. "Some pubs did it by mixing beer from one cask to another and others did it in other ways. Mixing from one keg to another led to problems. There was also an ongoing concern with temperature. If it was too warm, the carbonated stout would be too frothy, and if it was too cold, it was too flat."

In 1956, Hugh Beaver put Michael Ash in charge of finding a engineering solution to this elusive problem. Indeed, many within the company considered the quest to be a "mission impossible." It was considered by many to be less of a Manhattan Project than a matter of tilting at windmills. It was officially known within the company as the Draught Project, but many kidded Ash, calling it the "Daft Project." Though Ash had a team of 20 on his staff, he never felt as though he could assign more than two or three people to work on the Draught Project at any given time.

There were two fundamental steps to the eventual success of the program. The first was Ash's discovery that the key to creating a stable, creamy head on the beer was a mixture of nitrogen and carbon dioxide *within* the beer. The second step was to create a single, metal keg that could properly contain and dispense the nitrogenated beer. To accomplish the latter, Ash worked with Derek Lewis of Alumasc Limited, who produced countless prototype kegs and valves. They also worked together on a dispense system that would work with the keg to deliver a pint for which any publican could take great pride.

In 1958, Ash and his team were at last able to unveil for Hugh Beaver a system that was christened "Easy Serve." A better name might have been "Easier Serve" because the process was still complex. Technically, the Easy Serve keg was a single metal cask containing two sections, one with the stout and the other with a pressurized mixture of carbon dioxide and nitrogen. It was, in fact, easier to serve a pint with Easy Serve, and much easier to serve a perfect pint. However, the complexity of the system still needed refinement. Easy Serve was easier than the previous methods, but it needed to be easier still.

When presented with Easy Serve on the eve of the Bicentenary, Hugh Beaver was ecstatic. In January 1959, he and the Guinness board of directors decided that the system should be launched in the United Kingdom market during the summer to coincide with the Bicentenary festivities—and so it was. Meanwhile, Ash and some of the other brewers who were behind the development of Guinness Draught didn't want it launched in 1959 because they felt it wasn't ready.

As Eibhlin Roche explains, "the version of the mixed gas dispense system that was known internally as Mark IV, was test marketed in 1959, but the brewers weren't completely satisfied with it. Hugh Beaver wanted it to be launched because it was the Guinness Bicentenary and a great news story, so they went ahead in the United Kingdom. They deliberately didn't bring it into Ireland, which was a much more established Guinness market, until it was perfected."

Easy Serve was an important first step, but it was only a first step. Though the system was not fully refined—and formally launched in Ireland—until 1964, Michael Ash had achieved *the* key technical breakthrough—nitrogenation.

He had done so on a comparative shoestring. The company estimated that it had spent £20,000 to accomplish an engineering feat that would wind up netting billions.

Nitrogenation has so revolutionized our impressions of a pint of Guinness stout that it is hard to imagine that it has only been part of the story for half a century. Hard to imagine, too, is how long it would be before Guinness Draught as we know it today became the standard form of Guinness stout in Irish pubs.

"Many people don't realize that the beer has totally transformed itself," Fergal Murray says. "Today, everybody thinks that Arthur Guinness was drinking pints of Guinness Draught from nitrogenated kegs, but when Guinness Draught first came out, there were major moments of conversation. It took 20 years before Guinness Draught overtook sales of Guinness Extra Stout in volume terms in the Republic of Ireland."

The technical refinements that would be made in the keg and in the dispense system eventually led to the system that we know today. Today's keg of Guinness is a single-part keg—as is any standard beer keg. Inside, both carbon dioxide—which occurs naturally within beer—and nitrogen are present within the stout. The dispense system—unlike that of most beer kegs that are attached to a source of carbon dioxide—is a two-gas system that is connected to tanks of both carbon dioxide and nitrogen. The two gasses used in the dispense system maintain the same equilibrium within the beer that it had when it was put into the keg at the brewery. In the pub, a restrictor plate within the dispense system stimulates the nitrogen bubbles.

"Nitrogenation is all about bubbles," Murray says, explaining how and why nitrogenation makes Guinness Draught special. "What it does is to create a cosmetic look in a pint of Guinness. By doing this, it creates a different flavor profile and a different mouth feel. Nitrogen is in the beer, lying there dormant waiting for you to give it some energy."

As he has explained, the stimulated nitrogen produces the tiny bubbles that form the head when they are trapped by the surface tension of the beer. Aesthetically, nitrogenation provides the perfect head that is the hallmark of the perfect pint. For Hugh Beaver, though, nitrogenation was the solution to a problem of sagging sales as Guinness began its third century. For Guinness, nitrogenation was the revitalization that contributed to the achievement of legendary status for the world's greatest beer.

A Lager Called Harp

At the age of 201, the company that brewed the legendary stout also became a lager brewer. Even as Guinness was on the verge of revolutionizing the delivery of a perfect pint of the black liquidation with the froth on the top, plans were afoot to begin brewing a translucent straw-colored beer that was stylistically about as far as possible from stout on the spectrum of global beer styles.

Even the yeast used for lager differs from that used in ale and stout. The latter are fermented with top-fermenting *Saccharomyces cerevisiae* at cellar temperatures, while lager is fermented for a much longer period using bottom-fermenting *Saccharomyces carlsbergensis* at temperatures that dip near freezing. Lager, in turn, is traditionally served at cooler temperatures than ale or stout.

Lager originated in the early nineteenth century in Bavaria where brewers used very cold caves or cellars to *lager* (the German word for "store") their beer. Gabriel Sedlmayr of the Spaten Brewery in Munich is credited with having perfected and defined lager as a style in the 1830s, while Emil Christian Hansen, working at the Carlsberg Brewery in Copenhagen isolated the widely used *Saccharomyces carlsbergensis* yeast strain in 1883.

In the market today, there are a variety of subtypes of lager, ranging from darker colored bock, doppelbock, and dunkel to the pale helles. The most widely known lager type is the very light pilsner style (also known as pilsener or pils) that originated in the Bohemian (now part of the Czech Republic) city of Pilsen. The definitive brand is Pilsner Urquell, still brewed in Pilsen, but the style is used by nearly all mass-market lagers around the world from North America to Australia to Japan, and in such well-known European brands as Beck's, Heineken, and Stella Artois.

During the nineteenth century, lager became widely popular as a beer style throughout continental Europe, as well as in the United States, where the founders of the major brewing companies were German immigrants. By the twentieth century, lager was the dominant beer style throughout the world—except in Ireland and the United Kingdom, where the top-fermented beers continued to have a dominant market share. After World War II and into the 1950s, however, the popularity of lager grew rapidly, eroding the dominance of ale in the United Kingdom. Even in Ireland where stout, in general, and Guinness, in particular, had a commanding presence in the market, lager enjoyed substantial growth. Then, as now, lager was especially popular among the young, who favored the clear crispness of a cold lager to the complexity of fully flavored beers.

As Eibhlin Roche points out, "since 1799, Guinness had only produced porters and stouts, but with the rise of lagers, the company decided to get in on that themselves."

In 1959, during its Bicentenary, Guinness decided to stay ahead of the curve of the lager trend by creating its own lager. The company went straight to the source. Lager had originated as a style in Germany, and it was in Germany where the most highly regarded lagers were still brewed under the strict *Reinheitsgebot*, the purity law dating to 1516 that set exacting standards for ingredients and processes used in beer and brewing. With this in mind, Guinness hired a German master brewer, Dr. Herman Münder of Cologne, to come to Ireland to create a new golden lager.

As Dr. Münder was formulating his lager recipe, Guinness turned the old Great Northern Brewery at Dundalk into a state-of-the-art lager plant. The brewing water was drawn from the nearby Ravensdale Reservoir that is fed by soft springs from the Cooley Mountains in County Louth. As a brand name, Guinness picked its own logo, the Brian Boru Harp, and named its lager "Harp." As Eibhlin Roche explains, "It was a conscious decision to associate the lager brand with Guinness, so when Harp was chosen as the brand, it was launched as 'the lager brewed by Guinness,' as opposed to just a new lager in the Irish market. It was very much associated with Guinness when it was launched."

The brewing method, however, was strictly by the book—the German lager book. The first brew of Harp Lager took place on February 23, 1960, and the product soon entered the Irish market in bottles. It was in 1961, after having received a positive reception in Ireland, that Harp Lager was introduced in the United Kingdom. The draught variant of Harp followed in 1964, but the delivery system, like the brewing, was strictly in the lager style, and nitrogenation was not used. In the United Kingdom, Guinness initially marketed Harp in cooperation with British ale brewers, including Bass, Courage, Barclay & Simonds, and Scottish & Newcastle.

Through the coming years, Harp Lager became an integral part of the Guinness global portfolio. Harp Lager brewed in Ireland would be widely exported to continental Europe, North America, and elsewhere, and lagers based on Harp would form part of the product lines of the overseas Guinness breweries discussed in the next chapter.

Into Africa, Malaysia, and Beyond

As Fergal Murray has told us, consumers in Africa regard Guinness as their own, an African product. Many don't realize that Guinness originated in Ireland. Today, Nigeria is the third largest market for Guinness after Ireland and the United Kingdom, but Africa as a whole is a larger market than either Ireland or the United Kingdom—all because Guinness had the foresight to build a brewery in Africa—and then another, and so on.

Guinness was selling its beer in Africa in the nineteenth century, as well as in the Caribbean and the Far East. West Indies Porter appeared in the West Indies in 1801, and globetrotting Haines and Shand record their travels to many distant lands. However, overseas sales outside Australia and North America were minimal until after World War II.

It was during Arthur Fawcett's tenure at Guinness Exports Limited that the brand greatly expanded its market penetration into the Third World. By 1961, overseas trade was 12 times greater than in 1939. Singapore and Malaysia accounted for 20 percent of the export market, while Nigeria consumed half of the total volume of Guinness exported. With this in mind, it is little wonder that the second all-new Guinness brewery outside of Ireland, and the first since Park Royal went online in 1936, was opened in Nigeria in 1963.

If it was Fawcett's team that opened and expanded the Third World markets, the man who made it possible to actually open breweries there was Alan Tindal Lennox-Boyd. The husband of Patricia Guinness, the second daughter of Rupert Guinness, the corporate chairman, Lennox-Boyd was an Oxford-educated politician who had held several posts within the British cabinet. He was a member of Winston Churchill's government as Minister for Transport and Civil Aviation from 1952 to 1954, when he became Secretary of State for the Colonies. His tenure in the Colonial Office coincided with the pivotal—and often difficult—period of British decolonization, and the end of the British Empire as it was known for more than a century. He was instrumental in many aspects of this policy and, in the course of his work, he gained an intimate understanding of many of the soon-to-be independent colonies. When Harold Macmillan became Prime Minister in 1957, Lennox-Boyd remained as Colonial Secretary for two years, and was succeeded in 1959 by Iain Macleod. He then went to work for his father-in-law's brewery, joining Hugh Beaver and Charles King Mill in the triumvirate of joint managing directors. In 1960, when Beaver retired, Lennox-Boyd remained as one of two.

Philip Murphy, Lennox-Boyd's biographer, points out that his performance as managing director was "certainly dynamic and in many ways far-sighted." Murphy feels that like many other Western companies, Guinness's market share in some of Britain's former colonies was threatened by the advent of independence, as successor governments sought to promote domestic manufacturing through the use of subsidies and high import duties. He goes on to say that Lennox-Boyd recognized that "Guinness could no longer simply rely on exporting its produce, but had to invest in manufacturing within the developing world. His contacts among post-independence political leaders and Western businesspeople placed him in a good position to supervise this transition."

Investment in indigenous production also made sense if import duties were increased or if import restrictions were imposed by the newly independent governments. The first such investment in manufacturing made by Guinness was in Nigeria. In 1960, Guinness teamed up with the United Africa Company, a beer-distributing division of Netherlands-based Unilever, which was anxious to broaden its activities in operations in West Africa. The United Africa Company already controlled about a third of Guinness distribution in the region, as well as operating an entity known as Nigerian Breweries in partnership with Netherlands brewing giant, Heineken.

A subsidiary company called Guinness Nigeria was formed, in which Guinness owned a 51 percent share and the United Africa Company owned 49 percent. Ground was broken for a new brewery and bottling plant in Ikeja, a suburb of Lagos, then the capital of Nigeria.

The difficulties of building a state-of-the-art plant in the third world were daunting, but the technical problem of brewing Guinness Foreign Extra Stout in a tropical environment under conditions far different from those at St. James's Gate or Park Royal was immense. On par with nitrogenation in its economic importance, the breakthrough that solved this problem was one of the great technological achievements at Guinness during the twentieth century.

Fawcett and Lennox-Boyd were responsible for expanding the market and opening the doors, but it was Owen Williams, head brewer at St. James's Gate, along with Laurence Hudson, who made it possible for Guinness to have breweries in the Third World. Williams and

Hudson created Guinness Flavor Extract, a "concentrated essence" that could be brewed in Ireland and added into the brewing process at overseas breweries. Guinness Flavor Extract made it possible to ensure that the exact flavor of Dublin-brewed Foreign Extra Stout could be reproduced anywhere in the world. Fergal Murray, who worked for more than three years in Nigeria in the 1980s, explained it by saying "You have to make sure the beer meets the same standards as in Dublin."

In the 1960s, when this essence was first introduced for brewing Guinness in Africa, Guinness Flavor Extract comprised 8 percent of the content of each barrel of finished product, while the remainder of the content was beer brewed on site at the African brewery. By 1975, efficiencies were achieved and as Guinness developed experience and expertise using the essence, the proportion dropped to just 2 percent.

In January 1962, Rupert Guinness, Lord Iveagh, sent his grandson and heir apparent, Benjamin Guinness to Ikeja to lay the cornerstone for the Guinness Nigeria brewery, the company's second such facility outside the British Isles if you include the New York brewery that had closed eight years earlier.

Lord Iveagh was obviously hoping for greater longevity in Ikeja when he penned the message that he sent along with young Benjamin to be buried in the cornerstone's time capsule:

> If my beloved grandson, who is laying the foundation stone of this brewery on my behalf, were launching a ship, he would naturally wish "God speed, with health and happiness to all who may sail in her." Why then, should I not ask him to say something similar on this great occasion, and for what can be equally rightly called a great mutual adventure, with the same sincere hopes to all who may be employed in the brewery? May this eventually prove to be as beneficial to Nigeria as the original brewery, founded in Dublin by my ancestor in the year 1759, has been to Ireland.

On March 6, 1963, Alan Lennox-Boyd attended the grand opening of the £2 million Guinness Nigeria Brewery in Ikeja just three years, almost to the day, after the first site-survey team had come to here to take an option on what was then a piece of open country.

"I formed a great affection and regard for Nigeria and her people," Lennox-Boyd said, speaking of his time in the country wearing the hats of both Colonial Secretary and later as a managing director overseeing a construction project. "This was strengthened almost daily as we overcame problems of many kinds together. . . . It is a mark of our confidence in the future of this great people and of our trust in her people."

Overcoming problems indeed. The team headed by A. C. Parker—whom Guinness named to manage the Guinness Nigeria operation before and after construction—had more than their share of mud, rain, snakes, and materials shortages. As Guinness noted officially, "It is quite impossible to report all the difficulties that were overcome by the St. James's Gate and Park Royal brewers, engineers, builders, and managers in successfully setting up this first Guinness Brewery ever built overseas. The difficulties included a vastly different climate, a single high-gravity product (stronger than the average strength of the output from any other large brewery in the world), and no preexisting supply of local workers with the special brewing skills needed."

It had been difficult, but without Williams and Hudson and their invention of Guinness Flavor Extract, it would have been impossible.

When Lennox-Boyd invited Dr. Benjamin Nnamde Azikiwe, then Nigeria's Governor General, to speak at the formal dedication, the man known affectionately as "Dr. Zik," began by saying that Guinness stout was popular in that part of the world. Official reports of the speech mention neither applause nor chuckles, but we can assume there were both when he made this statement. He went on to observe that Guinness Nigeria employed approximately 400 Nigerians, many of them in technical roles and this certainly earned some applause.

"I congratulate the Board of Guinness (Nigeria) Limited on their foresight and wisdom in implementing this national policy," Nigeria's future president continued. "The establishment of this brewery is most welcome and should be regarded as another step forward on our road to economic reconstruction."

In the brewhouse, Dr. Zik "struck off a copper," turning a valve that enabled the Guinness Flavor Extract to move through the line into the next stage of the brewing process. Guinness's own report of the dedication noted that "the tour concluded with an obviously successful sampling of bottles of the new African-brewed Guinness, of which 150,000 barrels (36 gallons to the barrel) now can be produced each year at Ikeja."

The Ikeja brewery operated during the civil war that ravaged Nigeria between 1966 and 1970 and a further succession of coups and civil disturbances that went on for decades. The brewery continued to brew until 1998, when it was superseded by a larger Nigerian facility at Ogba.

Alan Lennox-Boyd's contacts also proved useful in Guinness's second overseas venture several years later. Site surveys looked at Malaya, which became independent from Britain in 1957. Renamed Malaysia in 1963, the country incorporated Singapore until 1965, when this prosperous city and commercial center became an independent country itself. In 1964, Guinness Malaysia Limited, later Guinness Malaysia Berhad, was formed as a company jointly owned by Guinness and local shareholders. The joint ownership was because, as Singapore's the *Straits Times* newspaper pointed out, the practice was "in keeping with the government's broad aims for the establishment and growth of industries that can contribute significantly to the country's economy and that will enable local people to participate in their ownership, direction, and management." The concept was familiar to that which Guinness had encountered with the brewery project in Nigeria.

On March 19, 1966, Lennox-Boyd and his wife, Lady Patricia, were on the stage when Prime Minister Tunku Abdul Rahman ceremonially opened the new Guinness brewery on 20 acres at Sungei Way New Village, near Kuala Lumpur, the Malaysian capital.

Earlier in the twentieth century, Guinness had been distributed in the area by Darby & Guthrie, supplied by Export Bottlers Limited and sold under the bulldog logo, and McAllister, supplied by Macfee and sold under the wolf logo. Beginning in 1966, the dogs and wolves departed and Foreign Extra Stout was sold under the Guinness logo, although initially it was under the curious brand name *Ginis Setaut*, which was the Malay phonetic transliteration of "Guinness Stout."

Brewed using malt imported from Australia and the United Kingdom—and concentrated essence from St. James's Gate—Ginis Setaut was sold in Malaysia, with an estimated 3,500 outlets in Kuala Lumpur alone, and exported to places from Borneo to Sumatra.

In 1968, Guinness Malaysia began brewing a lager called Gold Harp—known locally as "Goldie," to complement the stout. Over the coming years, additional lager products, including Eagle Lager and Guinness Pilsner, were also launched.

Meanwhile, Alan Lennox-Boyd engineered the enlargement of the small Overseas Planning Group into Guinness Overseas Limited, a new component within the company that would administer an aggressive expansion of international operations, including the new breweries, as well as a growing program of contract brewing arrangements. By the end of the decade, overseas sales under the umbrella of Guinness Overseas Limited were increasing faster than they were in Ireland and the United Kingdom. Australia and North America once accounted for two thirds of Guinness trade outside the British Isles. By the end of the 1960s, these traditional markets represented only 10 percent of the total export market for Guinness.

South Africa had been one of the original markets for Foreign Extra Stout on the continent. Indeed, it was one of the two countries to which Edward and John Burke first exported the brand in the middle of the nineteenth century. After the export bottlers were consolidated in 1950, Guinness Exports Limited continued to operate through wholesale houses as selling agents. In 1957, however, an agreement was signed giving bottling and marketing rights to South African Breweries Limited (SAB). From their bottling facility in East London, SAB distributed into a territory that included South

Africa, as well as the areas that now constitute Namibia, Lesotho, and Swaziland.

In 1962, discussions of contract brewing got underway, concluding with Guinness granting SAB a license to brew Foreign Extra Stout for distribution throughout the southern part of the continent. After several delays, the locally brewed Guinness was launched into the market on June 4, 1964, achieving immediate success. In the first year, sales were 30 percent over their target, but thereafter, production problems dogged the project, and brewing had to be discontinued in 1969. SAB continued to import Foreign Extra Stout from St. James's Gate until 1978, when Ireland severed trade links with South Africa over the issue of Apartheid. When Apartheid was terminated in the 1990s, Guinness resumed its contract brewing relationship with SAB.

Despite the disappointing experience of the New York brewery in the 1950s, Guinness still looked to North America, specifically north of the border, for a licensing arrangement. Lennox-Boyd took a personal interest in Canada, perhaps because the Guinness family—his in-laws—had property there. Discussions with Labatt Brewing, then one of Canada's two largest brewing companies, had actually begun as early as 1954, the year that Guinness's Long Island brewery had been closed. However, it was more than a decade before the two brewers formed Guinness Canada, a partnership with Guinness taking a 51 percent share. Beginning in 1965, Labatt brewed a specially formulated Extra Stout in Toronto and Vancouver.

In 1966, having staked out a position in West Africa with the successful Ikeja brewery, Guinness formed Guinness East Africa Limited, a 51 percent to 49 percent partnership with East African Breweries. The latter had an existing facility in Mombasa, a coastal city in southern Kenya, and the idea was to produce Foreign Extra Stout here for sale in Tanzania and Uganda, as well as Kenya. The operations were moved to Nairobi, Kenya's capital city, in 1971, where they would continue, except for a four-year period in the 1980s.

Noting the success of the Nigeria operation, Guinness decided to open its second African brewery in neighboring Cameroon. A site was selected in Douala, where the new 60,000-hectoliter facility was designed to brew, ferment, and package both stout and lager. Using Guinness Flavor Extract brought in from St. James's Gate, the first brew of Foreign Extra Stout at Duala took place in March 1970. The lager, as in Malaysia, was Gold Harp, the export variant of Harp. The following year, Guinness opened yet another brewery, based on the Cameroon model, in Kumasi, Ghana.

In Jamaica, Guinness Overseas Limited approached lager brewer Desnoes & Geddes, famous for its Red Stripe brand, about a possible contract brewing arrangement. This didn't work out, so Guinness decided to build a brewery on the island and formed Guinness Jamaica Limited. This facility opened in 1973 against the backdrop of civil unrest and an economic downturn that followed the election of a Marxist government. As Guinness Jamaica Limited struggled, Desnoes & Geddes cut a deal to contract brew for Heineken in Jamaica. In 1985, Guinness sold its Jamaica subsidiary to Desnoes & Geddes, who continued to brew Foreign Extra Stout under license. In 1993, Guinness PLC bought Desnoes & Geddes.

In Australia, Guinness grew its sales through a series of contract brewing relationships. From 1964 to 1974, Guinness had been associated with South Australian Brewing of Adelaide, who brewed Guinness Export Stout under license, mainly for the market in the Australian states of South Australia, Victoria, and New South Wales.

As H. S. Corran wrote in his 1964 update to Owen Williams's *Notes on the St. James's Gate Brewery*, the product variant brewed for the Australian market, as well as that brewed in Ireland and sold in Europe was Guinness Export Stout. As he explained, "Since the war, we have brewed a sweeter type of stout of equal strength to Foreign Extra Stout. . . . It has a moderate hop rate and is generally bottled in the country of sale, either naturally conditioned or carbonated, and pasteurized like Foreign Extra Stout. . . . Since 1964, Guinness Export Stout has been brewed and bottled under our supervision in

Adelaide, South Australia, by the South Australian Brewing Company Limited. Australian malt and hops are used."

In 1974, Guinness struck a contract-brewing deal with Toohey's, a major brewing company in suburban Sydney, that allowed for expanding Guinness Export Stout north into Queensland and south into Tasmania. From 1986, Guinness was brewed for the Australian market by Carlton United Breweries (CUB), later Carlton United Beverages, a subsidiary of Elders IXL. The latter, the brewers of Foster's Lager, became the Foster's Group in 1990.

By 1978, the total sales of Guinness Stout in the overseas markets exceeded two million hectoliters for the first time. Guinness continued modest growth in continental Europe and North America as well as in the Far East. Sales in the United States were made more problematic later in the decade by the strength of pounds sterling relative to the dollar.

In East Africa, Guinness activities were confined to Kenya, but by the 1970s, the brand was a household word in West Africa. In addition to the Guinness breweries in Ghana, Cameroon and Nigeria, the company had contract brewing operations in Liberia, Ivory Coast and the Gambia. In 1977, an enlargement of a big lager brewery in Benin City, Nigeria—complementing the original stout brewery in Ikeja, Nigeria—went online, brewing the Gold Harp brand. The following year, however, in accordance with the Nigerian Enterprises Decree, overseas shareholders reduced their share of Guinness Nigeria to 40 percent, with the Guinness share was now just 25.5 percent.

The global expansion efforts that began in the 1960s continue to bear fruit as Guinness continues to operate in the countries where it invested in building the key brewing facilities. Though licensing arrangements change from time to time, the technical and business model first developed in the 1960s remains sound, with Guinness still being brewed under license in more than three dozen countries around the world.

Diversification and Expansion

During the 1970s, Arthur Guinness, Son & Company Limited followed the example of many global corporations and diversified widely beyond its core products. Sir Arthur Francis Benjamin Guinness assumed the chairmanship from his grandfather in 1962 and became the 3rd Earl of Iveagh upon his death five years later. Benjamin, as he was known, oversaw the family business during the time it became a group of companies.

Though more than 85 percent of the Guinness Group's sales and profits remained tied to brewing through the mid-1970s, the company invested in subsidiaries such as the Callard & Bowser confectioners, as well as in activities from real estate to plastics and film production. The company's publishing division, where the flagship

165

product was *The Guinness Book of Records*, set records of its own, with more than 40 million copies sold through the end of decade. In addition to publishing the biggest selling copyrighted book in history to that time, the division also published related and spin-off works.

Through the middle 1970s, despite the global recession brought about by the energy crisis of 1974, Guinness continued to do well. The company grossed £414 million in 1976, up from £339 million in 1975 and £271 million in 1974, with profits up from £23 to £36 million in the same period. The increases were led by the brewing component. The other ventures didn't fare so well. Benjamin Guinness wrote in 1975 that "it is ironic that in our plastic molding business, where we have invested to anticipate future demand, we have been hardest hit by the recession. This emphasizes that investment by itself is not enough."

Also in 1975, Anthony "Tony" Pursell was appointed managing director of the Guinness Group. Having joined the company in 1948, he had held a number of posts within the firm before being named managing director at Park Royal in 1968. Five years later, he transferred to Ireland to become managing director in Dublin.

Though the plastics ventures did not fulfill the anticipated promise, Lord Iveagh and Tony Pursell took pleasure in the growth of the draught beer business, including Smithwick's Ale as well as Guinness Draught. By 1978, Benjamin Guinness was able to observe that, in Ireland, Smithwick's had "achieved the same dominance in the ale sector as Guinness in stout."

A formal five-year development plan that ran though 1976 involved many changes throughout the brewery. The largest single capital project was a new, £7 million brewhouse at St. James's Gate that was officially opened by J. M. "Jack" Lynch, Ireland's *An Taoiseach* (Prime Minister), on November 21, 1977. Meanwhile, Guinness's Irish Ale Breweries subsidiary exceeded previous sales records, as a new bottling line was brought online at the Dundalk brewery.

The company was investing in all of its facilities. As "Iveagh," which was how Benjamin signed his name, wrote to the company's shareholders, "The completion of the Development Plan by no means spells the end of modernization. We will still be spending very substantially each year to keep the brewery as a whole up to date and efficient."

With gross receipts or turnover up to £499 million in 1977 and £643 million the following year, Guinness continued its upward trend, buoyed by an upturn in the Irish economy—and despite continued recession in the United Kingdom.

In 1977, to help address the expanding export demand for its product, Guinness built the *Miranda Guinness*, named for Benjamin's wife, an ocean-going vessel especially designed as a bulk liquid carrier. Capable of carrying the equivalent of 1.85 million pints, she was merely the latest in the long roster of vessels that dated back to 1913 to 1915, when Guinness had acquired its first four vessels from John Kelly & Sons of Belfast. Another major round of fleet building had come in the mid-1960s, when Guinness acquired three ships that were the first to be designed to carry beer in transportable tanks rather that the traditional casks used in the trade. Built with air-conditioned holds to maintain an even temperature, these three ships were the *Lady Grania*, the *Lady Gwendolyn*, and the *Lady Patricia*, each named for a member of the Guinness family. Lady Gwendolyn Onslow was the wife of Rupert Guinness, the 2nd Earl of Iveagh. Grania Meve Rosaura, Lady Normanby, was Rupert's niece, the daughter of Walter Guinness and Lady Evelyn Erskine. Lady Patricia was Rupert's daughter and the wife of Alan Lennox-Boyd.

The *Lady Patricia* and the *Miranda Guinness* would be the last of the Guinness ships, continuing in service until 1993. When they were decommissioned, the volume of beer they once carried was shipped in 35,000-pint tanker trucks aboard conventional car ferries. In 1993, Joe Carroll reported in the *Economist* that "The *Miranda* will carry wine and olive oil in the Mediterranean, but *Lady Patricia* has been taken to the breaker's yard. There was much nostalgia and mourning as two familiar sights disappeared forever from the River Liffey."

The 1970s saw a continuation of the growing consumption of lager in the United Kingdom and Ireland that had been a major trend during the 1960s. Guinness responded with the development of a large lager brewing operation at the Park Royal brewery, which came online in April 1979. As part of creating a mechanism for the marketing of Harp Lager, Guinness formed Harp Limited (later Harp Lager Company Limited), taking on English brewing companies as minority partners in this new entity. Retaining a 70 percent interest, Guinness joined with Greene King & Sons Limited, with a 20 percent stake, and Wolverhampton & Dudley Breweries with a 10 percent share. Two additional franchisees, Courage Limited and Scottish & Newcastle Breweries Limited, who would also brew and market Harp in the United Kingdom.

As Guinness pointed out at the time, "The main responsibilities of Harp Limited are to brew lager, to provide marketing services and national advertising for the three brands in Great Britain and to exercise control over the quality, technical specifications and presentation of the brands wherever brewed or sold in Great Britain."

Guinness would have 100 percent ownership of the Harp brewing and marketing operation in Ireland (known officially as Harp Ireland Limited), which supplied the markets in the Republic of Ireland and Northern Ireland. The primary fixed asset of Harp Limited was to be the new lager brewing facility at Park Royal, which would brew not only Harp Lager, but the French lager Kronenbourg, under license from Strasbourg-based Brasseries Kronenbourg.

In the early 1980s, Guinness increased its share in the Harp Lager Company Limited subsidiary to 75 percent and, in 1990, became sole owner.

By the 1980s, the identity of Guinness was more and more that of a British, rather than Irish, company. According to the *International Brewers' Directory*, the annual output at Park Royal was more than double that of St. James's Gate. In fact, during this decade, this author observed in conversations in British pubs that may people assumed Guinness to be a British, rather than Irish, product. In a sense, they were correct. The company's corporate headquarters had been in London since incorporation in 1886, and the Guinness they drank in London had been brewed in that city for half a century.

During the coming decade, more changes would come as the identity of Guinness would gradually shift more and more away from being a brewing company.

21

The Watershed Decade

In his annual statement to shareholders on December 22, 1981, Guinness Chairman Benjamin Guinness, the Earl of Iveagh, wrote: "I believe that we will look back on the year under review and recognize it as a watershed for Guinness." In retrospect, he was correct. The year marked a significant internal reorganization that would set Guinness on a course toward major corporate changes that would play out during the coming decade. Benjamin Guinness's notion that the year had been a watershed, proved true for the whole decade.

The previous year, Guinness began the decade with an increase in gross receipts from £687 million in 1979 to £784 million in 1980. However, in the face of a global economic slump, profits declined from £52.9 to £43.3 million in 1981.

"It's been a tough year," wrote Guinness Group Managing Director Tony Purssell in his 1980 year-end letter to shareholders. He went on to cite the worldwide recession that had deepened as a result of the effects of the sharp rise in oil prices in 1979. "Many companies at this time are reporting a general downturn in profits, but within the Guinness Group we have had varying fortunes. The brewing companies overall have increased profits, but almost all the nonbrewing companies are operating below last year's levels and have reported lower profits."

In his own statement a year later, as he described that moment as a "watershed," Benjamin Guinness outlined a situation in which profits for the year to September 26, 1981 had fallen from £43.3 million to £41.8 million. He qualified this situation by noting "the strength of the brewing segment" of the Guinness Group. Though recession, taxation and unemployment continued to negatively impact beer sales in the United Kingdom in Ireland, Harp Lager gained market share in Britain, and sales of all Guinness products elsewhere in the world were on the rise.

"Brewing profits were ahead of our expectations," wrote the chairman. "This underlines the return which we now enjoy from years of investment in our world-wide trade names particularly Guinness Stout. We cannot expect in such difficult market conditions necessarily to see unbroken improvement in brewing results, but this year confirms that this is a market and product area in which we probably have unrivalled expertise. Brewing remains the cornerstone for the future of your company."

By now, one of the main problems in the Guinness bottom line was seen to be the group's diversification into businesses unrelated to brewing, which had made sense to company executives a decade earlier. Beginning in 1981, and continuing into 1982, Arthur Guinness, Son & Company Limited moved assertively to divest itself of unprofitable companies and those outside its core business in the beverage industry.

To get an idea of the scope of the Guinness Group's operations and business holdings, it is useful to examine a somewhat simplified snapshot of the company as it existed in September 1981 on the eve of the divestiture program. At that time, the brewing segment accounted for 68 percent of the total income for Arthur Guinness, Son & Company Limited, the parent company of the Guinness Group. This proportion had decreased during the 1970s from nearly 100 percent as the company had gradually diversified. Meanwhile, however, the brewing segment accounted for virtually all of the total profit.

General Trading, including United Kingdom retail subsidiaries, accounted for 21 percent of the income, while plastics and confectionery contributed 7 and 2 percent, respectively. The remaining slices of the pie were in leisure services and the film industry.

As had been the case for some time, the Guinness Group brewing business was under several regional umbrellas in the United Kingdom and Ireland. These were Arthur Guinness, Son & Company (Park Royal) Limited in the United Kingdom, Arthur Guinness, Son & Company (Belfast) Limited in Northern Ireland, and Guinness Ireland Limited in the Republic of Ireland. The latter incorporated Arthur Guinness, Son & Company (Dublin) Limited that handled operations at the flagship St. James's Gate brewery. The New York-based Guinness-Harp Corporation managed imports of the products into the United States.

Also under the Guinness Ireland Limited umbrella were Guinness's 100 percent share of Harp Ireland Limited, which brewed and distributed Harp and other lager brands in the Republic of Ireland. In the United Kingdom, the 70 percent share of Harp Limited that was owned by Guinness came under the umbrella of Arthur Guinness, Son & Company (Park Royal) Limited.

Other entities under Harp Ireland Limited were Guinness's 49.6 percent share in the Cantrell & Cochrane Group, a nonbeer beverage holding company, and Guinness's 66.67 percent share in Irish Ale Breweries Limited, of which the remaining third was owned by British brewing company Ind Coope. The components of Irish Ale Breweries included Smithwick's in Kilkenny and Cherry's in Waterford, which Guinness acquired in the 1950s, as well as Macardle Moore in Dundalk, into which Ind Coope had invested at about the same time.

Other entities under the umbrella of Arthur Guinness, Son & Company (Park Royal) Limited included Guinness Superlatives, the publisher of *The Guinness Book of Records*, as well as beer distribution organizations in Germany, Italy, and the United Kingdom, as well as malting and hop-growing operations, and a 28 percent share in Taunton Cider. During 1982, Guinness both increased its interest in Taunton Cider and launched its Carolans Irish Cream Liqueur in a number of export markets.

Based at Park Royal, but reporting directly to Arthur Guinness, Son & Company Limited, the parent company of the Guinness Group, was Guinness Overseas Holdings Limited. This component's major subsidiaries and associated companies included Guinness (Nigeria) Limited, with breweries in Ikeja and Benin City, of which the Guinness Group owned a 25.5 percent share; Guinness Malaysia Berhad, with its brewery near Kuala Lumpur, of which the Guinness Group owned a 50.01 percent share; Guinness Cameroon, with its brewery in Douala; Guinness Ghana Limited, with its brewery in Kumasi, of which the Guinness Group owned a 28.69 percent share; and Guinness Jamaica, with a brewery in Central Village, St. Catherine, of which the Guinness Group owned a 63.4 percent share. Shares of each of these companies were traded on the stock exchange of the country in which they were located.

Also under the Guinness Overseas Holdings Limited umbrella were smaller subsidiaries involving activities such as beer sales, marketing, general trading, and contract brewing. These were located in places such as Australia, Canada, Ceylon, Hong Kong, Japan, the Seychelles, and throughout Africa.

In 1981, the nonbrewing subsidiary operations of Arthur Guinness, Son & Company Limited included Callard & Bowser in

England, Clares Engineering Limited in England, Guinness Retail Holdings in England, Guinness Morrison International Limited with operations around the world, a share in Twyford Pharmaceutical Services Deutschland in Germany, and Twyford Laboratories Limited in England.

The plastics subsidiaries included Crystal Ware Products, Ferham Products, Micropol, Multiplastic BV, Penton Tools, Star Plastics, and the holdings of the Manchester-based White Child & Beney Northern Plastics Group. Other activities grouped under the Guinness Leisure Holdings subsidiary ranged from film production and distribution to holiday cottages in England and Wales. Guinness Leisure also had an interest in river, canal, and sea-going cruise operations in Corsica, France, Greece, Ireland, the United Kingdom, the United States, and the British Virgin Islands.

As Guinness moved toward divestiture in the early 1980s, the early spin-offs included Callard & Bowser and the Guinness plastics holdings. The company opted to remain in the business of retail stores, but decided to get out of the movie business. The chairman announced at the end of 1981 that Guinness would not be involved in the financing of any further films after what he described as "significant losses in this area."

The chairman also reshuffled upper management. In mid-1981, he moved Tony Purssell up to the post of chief executive, and a short time later to deputy chairman, where he served until his retirement in January 1983. As a co-deputy chairman, Benjamin Guinness named his first cousin, Simon Lennox-Boyd. Simon was the son of former managing director Alan Lennox-Boyd and Lady Patricia Guinness, Benjamin Guinness's aunt. As the new managing director for the Guinness Group, the board in October 1981, brought in a man from outside the company and family. Ernest Saunders, whose business reputation was that of a cost-cutter, had previously held management positions with Beacham, Great Universal Stores, and later at the Nestlé headquarters in Switzerland.

In addition to the divestiture strategy, Arthur Guinness, Son & Company Limited also took a number of steps during 1982 to halt the perceived decline in the company's overall performance. Among these were an efficiency program, savings in discretionary expenditures, and a reduction in borrowing, which was accomplished by a reduction in capital expenditures and in the level of working capital employed throughout the company.

To streamline operations in the brewing sector, all of the brewing operations in Ireland, the United Kingdom, and around the world were consolidated in 1982 under a single management entity that was called Guinness Brewing Worldwide.

During the 1980s, the lager sector of the business continued to increase, especially in the United Kingdom. In addition to Harp, Guinness began licensed production of Satzenbrau Diät Pils at Park Royal in March 1982. Later brewed at Dundalk, Satzenbrau would continue to appear in the product portfolio through the ensuing years. In 2006, it was launched by Guinness in Nigeria and Cameroon amid great fanfare under the name Satzenbrau Premium Lager. During 1983, Guinness responded to a trend within the brewing industry toward low-alcohol and nonalcohol products by launching its Kaliber, which was brewed in Ireland and at Park Royal, using a unique alcohol extraction process. In 1984, Kaliber was introduced into the U.S. market where such beers were garnering a great deal of consumer interest.

Also in 1984, Guinness launched two new regional lagers in Ireland: Hoffman in Limerick and Steiger in Dublin. Guinness also acquired the rights to Fürstenberg lager outside Germany. Based in Donaueschingen, the company was a true royal brewery, being owned by Princely House of Fürstenberg until 2004 when it was acquired by Brau Holding International AG, jointly owned by Heineken and Schörghuber.

As Guinness was spinning off nonbrewing subsidiaries, a new five-year plan was launched in July 1981 to improve and update operations at the St. James's Gate brewery in Dublin, and construction of an additional Guinness brewery in Nigeria was begun. On February 2, 1983, after a year of divestiture and cost cutting, Benjamin Guinness was able to report that the improvements were despite "the extraordinary costs which are the direct result of a number of important decisions which we have taken to rationalize our nonbrewing activities and to concentrate on our mainstream brewing activities."

During 1982, before-tax profits were up 18 percent to £49.4 million on a basis directly comparable with the £41.8 million for 1981. Gross income, meanwhile, was up 6 percent to £961 million for the 12 months of 1982. Profits within the brewing segment of the Guinness Group—Guinness Brewing Worldwide—were up 17 percent. In 1983, profits increased by 24 percent to £58.8 million, the best performance since 1979. Exports played a big part, Benjamin Guinness observed as he proudly announced that the Queen's Award for Export Achievement for 1983 had been bestowed on Guinness Overseas Limited.

To revitalize the Guinness brands, a Future Competitiveness Plan was introduced at St. James's Gate, consumer research was done and new advertising campaigns were launched in Ireland and the United Kingdom. For the United Kingdom beer market segment, Benjamin Guinness gave a great deal of credit to the "Guinnless" advertising campaign that was created by the London advertising agency Allen, Brady & Marsh. Launched in January 1983, the campaign punned off the old "Guinness Is Good for You" campaigned of half a century before by stating that "Guinnless *isn't* good for you." Guinnless, of course, is the condition of being without Guinness. The agency also created an imaginary "Friends of the Guinnless" organization to come to the aid of these unfortunates. Within three months, the Guinnless campaign had achieved 87 percent brand awareness among British adults and increased sales of Guinness Draught.

"After 10 years of decline, we anticipated only modest results for the first year," the chairman admitted in 1983. "However, I am pleased to report that the results of this superbly planned and executed campaign have exceeded our expectations. This confirms that, with the right positioning in the market, Guinness enjoys wide acceptance as a unique drink with consumers of all ages. Moreover, the standing of our brand with the consumer as a benchmark of quality and value is of benefit to the entire licensed trade with whom we enjoy an excellent relationship."

Guinness drastically trimmed its portfolio during the 1981 to 1983 period, spinning off nearly everything except brewing and its small stake in retailing. Having done this, Benjamin Guinness announced in 1984 what he described as "the second phase of our business plan—expansion."

At St. James's Gate, this included an £18 million capital improvement, primarily in the boiler house and fermentation facilities. On gross income of £923.7 million, before-tax profit for 1984 was £70.4 million. Profits in Ireland, Guinness's single largest market, increased 14 percent to £30.1 million. Sales of Guinness Draught increased significantly in both Ireland and the United Kingdom thanks to the continued effects of the Guinnless campaign.

During 1985 and 1986, Guinness followed up on the enormous success of the Guinnless advertising campaign with a jump from Allen, Brady & Marsh to the Ogilvy & Mather agency for a new idea. Ogilvy & Mather created the "Genius" campaign. These ads highlighted and conveyed the complex Genius qualities of the beer, such as its naturalness and wholesomeness, using commercials that focused on fire, the earth, the sun, and the moon. These television commercials were augmented by a theme that stressed the Genius qualities of the consumer. Another ad in the United Kingdom punned as it referred to the head on a pint of Guinness as the "Head of British Intelligence."

In turn, the Genius campaign evolved into the "Man with The Guinness" campaign that was launched in May 1987, and which incorporated some of the elements of the previous campaign. These often amusing commercials starred Dutch film actor Rutger Hauer, who had previously established an international reputation in such films as Ridley Scott's sci-fi thriller, *Blade Runner* and Sam Peckinpah's *The Osterman Weekend*. In the "Man with The Guinness" campaign, which continued for seven years, Hauer conveyed the dark and enticing mystery of Guinness.

As Genius segued into the Man with The Guinness in 1985 through 1986, the draught variant of the product continued to outperform the competition in the United Kingdom while increasing its share in the company's "target development markets," the United States and Europe. In the United States, where the Guinness had relocated its sales office from New York to Stamford, Connecticut, in 1984, Guinness products, especially Guinness Draught, found themselves in a unique and unexpected position. The volume of Guinness sold in the United States continued to grow at a rate of three times that of the imported beer market in general.

No wonder. By the mid-1980s, the craft beer revolution was spreading like wildfire, and microbreweries were suddenly proliferating, as American beer drinkers discovered the joy of complex and flavorful beer. At a time when most major imports were lightly flavored yellow lagers, Guinness could offer a complexity that stimulated the palate of this new generation of beer lovers.

In Ireland, where Guinness Draught sales were also increasing, company profits increased by 16 percent in 1985 alone, to £35.5 million. This was against the backdrop of the continued modernization program at St. James's Gate.

In 1984, Benjamin Guinness described the second phase of the Guinness business plan after divestiture as "expansion." This expansion included not only improvements in brewing infrastructure, but a new round of nonbrewing acquisitions, especially in the area of retailing. After a brief few years of selling off nonbrewing businesses, the company once again began acquiring nonbrewing businesses.

In August 1985, Guinness made a major acquisition that was the beginning of a major "expansion"—to use the word that Benjamin Guinness had emphasized a year earlier—within the beverage business, specifically whisky. The first of the Scottish distillers that would be acquired by Guinness between 1985 and 1987 was Arthur Bell & Sons, based in Perth. Founded in 1825, the company operated five distilleries in Scotland, four of which were located in the Highlands. Bell had established a reputation with four single-malt whiskeys: Bladnoch, Blair Athol, Dufftown Glenlivet, and Inchgower, as well as its Bell's Extra Special blended Scotch, one of the United Kingdom's most popular brands.

Also acquired as part of the Bell portfolio was the Gleneagles Hotels Group, which included the internationally celebrated Gleneagles Hotel in Perthshire, the North British and Caledonian Hotels in Edinburgh, and the New Piccadilly Hotel in London.

This acquisition was a major step back into the world of diversification that Guinness had appeared to have been ready to abandon at the beginning of the decade. While Bell was a diversified company with its hotels component, although it was primarily a beverage company. In its official statements, Guinness expressed confidence that its knowledge of the worldwide beverage market, as well as its proven capabilities could be utilized with a wider portfolio.

With this step, the business activities of the Guinness Group were now organized into four divisions. The largest of these was the International Beverages division, consisting of Guinness Brewing Worldwide and the Bell's group, which contained the distilling and whisky marketing activities as well as the Gleneagles Hotel Group.

Next was the Martin Retail Group, which managed a wide range of retail operations from the recently acquired Martin, Lavells, Lewis Meeson and R. S. McColl newsagent chains to Drummond's pharmacies to the long-held Clares retail services company and Hediard in France. Also acquired around this time were Champney's health spas at Tring and Stobo Castle in Scotland, which were under the Portman Health Group division.

The fourth division was Guinness Superlatives, which not only published the *Guinness Book of Records* and more than a dozen other related titles, also operated the Guinness World of Records tourist attraction that opened in 1985 at the Trocadero Center in London.

During the same year, Norris McWhirter retired after 30 years of having edited the *Guinness Book of Records*.

In the meantime, the brewing side of Guinness opened its own tourist attraction in Dublin. In 1984, the old hop storage warehouse at St. James's Gate was restored and opened for ROSC 1984, an international exhibition of modern art. (*Rosc* is an old Irish word meaning the poetry of vision.) Between 1984 and 1988, a number of art exhibitions were held at the Hop Store, which became the official Guinness visitor center in July 1988. For the first time since public brewery tours were discontinued several decades earlier, visitors to Dublin could catch a glimpse inside the magical world behind St. James's Gate. In 2000, the Hop Store would be superseded by a much larger visitor center, the nearby Guinness Storehouse.

Having added Arthur Bell & Sons to the Guinness Group in 1985, the company took an even larger step toward the world of distilled spirits in 1986. Spearheaded by the aspirations of Chief Executive Ernest Saunders for Guinness to be a widely diversified global beverage conglomerate, the company moved to take over Edinburgh-based Distillers Company Limited, a leading Scotch whisky producer. As Jonathan Guinness put it so eloquently in his book about the family business, Saunders had "a vision of a grand drinks company bestriding the world with its brands." The vision would come true, but the greedy Saunders would not be a part of it.

Formed in 1877, Distillers was a consortium of six whisky distilleries in Scotland, including Cragganmore in the Speyside, Dalwhinnie in the Highlands, Glenkinchie in the Lowlands, Lagavulin on the Isle of Islay, Oban in the West Highlands, and Talisker on the Isle of Skye. Distillers was a larger company than Arthur Guinness, Son & Company, so as the result of the 1986 merger, the Guinness family share in the merged company went below 10 percent. One hundred years after Edward Cecil Guinness first took the family business public, the company was again reorganized, this time as a proprietary limited company called Guinness PLC.

In the meantime, an ailing Benjamin Guinness stepped down as chairman in July 1986 and was given the largely ceremonial title of president. Saunders succeeded him as chairman while retaining the chief executive title. In January 1987, however, Saunders was asked to resign from the company following revelations that he had been involved in manipulation of the Guinness stock price. Having been investigated by the British Department of Trade & Industry, Saunders and three codefendants were charged and convicted in the United Kingdom in 1990 on various counts of conspiracy, false accounting, and theft and sentenced to prison. Saunders had his sentence cut in half on the grounds that he was suffering from a mental illness. A series of appeals was finally dismissed in 2002.

In January 1987, at a meeting attended by Benjamin Guinness, Scottish banker and industrialist Sir Norman Macfarlane (later Lord Macfarlane of Bearsden) was appointed chairman of Guinness PLC. Anthony Tennant joined the company two months later as chief executive. On April 23, 1987, Macfarlane introduced the corporate annual report with the words "1986 was undoubtedly the most important and the most traumatic year in the long and distinguished history of your fine company."

He went on to say that "The merging of two giant companies is difficult enough at the best of times, but continual external interest in the Company and high level media coverage makes the task even more demanding." He concluded his message by saying that "I believe that the tenacity and determination which have been displayed in overcoming the challenges and difficulties of the last few months leave us strengthened and better equipped than ever to achieve the goals that we have set ourselves."

Also during 1987, the Guinness PLC International Beverages division became two divisions as the distilling portion was split off from Guinness Brewing Worldwide and reorganized as United Distillers PLC. It combined Arthur Bell & Sons with the Distillers brands. In turn, the six Distillers single malts would be marketed as the Classic Malts Range.

On the brewing side, the Guinness Brewing Worldwide component Guinness PLC added to its range of lagers by inking a deal with Anheuser Busch, the largest brewing company in the United States, to brew its flagship brand, Budweiser, in Ireland. During the following year, 1988, Guinness PLC made a deal with Carlsberg, Denmark's largest brewer, to brew their lager for the Irish market. Also in 1988, the Harp Lager Company Limited subsidiary in the United Kingdom (75 percent owned by Guinness) acquired the Buckley Brewery in Wales.

Guinness PLC also entered into a number of joint ventures in the United States, Europe, and the Far East with the French holding company, Moët Hennessy Louis Vuitton, SA. This firm had been formed in 1987 when with Louis Vuitton fashion house merged with cognac producer Hennessy and champagne producer Moët et Chandon. By 1989, Sir Norman Macfarlane announced that Guinness PLC had a substantial investment in this French company, and that Moët Hennessy Louis Vuitton was "the largest shareholder in Guinness PLC."

In the meantime, Guinness PLC became involved in the ownership, management, and/or distribution of a number of major global spirits brands such as Dewar's blended Scotch whisky, Gordon's Gin and Vodka, Johnnie Walker blended Scotch whisky, and Tanqueray Gin, as well as a number of other well-known products.

By now, the spirits business represented the largest proportion of the annual income for Guinness PLC. In 1986, out of an operational turnover of £2.13 million, 50 percent was from the spirits trade and 44 percent from brewing. The following year, with an operational income of £2.38 million, 56 percent was from the spirits trade and 37 percent from brewing. The balance was from other commercial businesses, including retailing and a share in United Glass.

Though brewing constituted a progressively smaller slice of the corporate pie, Guinness PLC continued its energetic investment in brewing infrastructure. A new brewhouse in Dundalk opened in 1986, and as Macfarlane pointed out, "our ambitious upgrading program [at St. James's Gate] was completed in 1988 with the full commissioning of a new brewhouse and fermentation/maturation plant. The brewery . . . is decidedly 'state of the art'—amongst the most flexible in the world."

What the chairman had in mind was diversification within the brewing sector itself. In April 1989, in his last annual report before being succeeded as Guinness PLC Chairman by Anthony Tennant, Sir Norman Macfarlane pointed out that "While draught stout will remain the backbone of our business, we continue to develop and market other specialist, premium products which will help to keep us at the forefront of our industry. The importance of our program is underlined by the fact that just four years ago our entire production was dedicated to traditional brands. Products developed since then accounted for almost 10 percent of our total volume sold in the U.K. in 1988."

Macfarlane was speaking about a number of products, including the alcohol-free lager Kaliber, whose distribution was gradually expanding throughout the world where other Guinness products were familiar, and whose draught variant was first test-marketed in 1988. "The development of global brands is now a strong feature of the brewing industry and Guinness is uniquely well placed to compete," said Macfarlane. He was also speaking about a new lager called "Guinness Gold" that had been developed for the U.S. market, and that has since come and gone. He also was referring to Smithwick's AFB, briefly marketed as the only alcohol-free bitter in the world. Mainly, though, he was speaking about the innovative product that is the subject of the following chapter.

Anthony Tennant became the second nonfamily chairman of Guinness in 1989, a pivotal year for the world. The Berlin Wall came down and the world became a smaller place. It was the final year of the decade that began with Benjamin Guinness making his auspicious "watershed" statement that we quoted at the beginning of this chapter.

It had been a decade of immense change for Guinness, a decade that marked a true changing of the guard. In 1988, a year after

Benjamin Guinness had left the chairmanship for the ceremonial post of president, the men on the Guinness PLC executive board averaged fewer than five years with the company. In an August 4, 1989, personal letter quoted by Michelle Guinness in her thorough history of the Guinness family, Bryan Guinness, Lord Moyne, expressed a sadness in the loss of Guinness identity in the company—which had always been referred to by the family as "the Brewery." Wrote Lord Moyne: "the family must regret the end of their two hundred or more years of responsibility for the Brewery itself, especially at St. James's Gate."

Some mourned this watershed decade as a turning point. Certainly we all mourned the last years as Benjamin Guinness lost his long and difficult battle with cancer.

"When Benjamin Iveagh died in 1992, all family connection came to an end," wrote Michelle Guinness in her book. It was a time perhaps to wax nostalgic, but Irish wakes are not entirely soaked in sadness.

There are two sides to turning points. At the beginning of the decade, despite all the diversification, brewing still represented nearly 70 percent of the annual corporate turnover. In 1989, it was down to 35 percent—although that proportion did amount to gross receipts of £1.07 *billion*. Guinness PLC was now a diversified beverage company, but it was a powerful one, and one that contained a powerful brewing component.

The turning points that marked the end of the watershed decade may have been mourned by some, but there were other turning points in those years that were celebrated by many—and those many had smiles on their faces and freshly poured pints of Guinness Draught in their hands.

And therein lies the tale of the remarkable widget.

A Widget in the Pint

In the 1960s, nitrogenation had revolutionized the way that people enjoyed their pint of Guinness in pubs from Southampton to San Francisco. The creation of Guinness Draught revolutionized the brand and made the elusive Holy Grail of the perfect pint more attainable—at our local pubs.

Back in the late 1960s, a few years after the introduction of Guinness Draught, Tony Carey, the brewing director at Guinness in Dublin began looking into ways to put nitrogenated Guinness Draught into cans and bottles, and to place into those cans and bottles a mechanism to stimulate the formation of bubbles as the restrictor plate did in the dispense system used in pubs. It was a task far simpler said than done.

Working with Sammy Hildebrand, Tony Carey had spent a number of years studying the theoretical side of the issue. He finally determined that the answer would be some sort of internal chamber within a can that could discharge a stream of gas—nitrogen and carbon dioxide—that would trigger foam production to produce a head. This idea was patented in 1972 as the Guinness Acorn. The engineering of the practical can, however, would take many more years of work. It was an off-and-on process in which many prototypes were tried and rejected. During the 1970s, there was a lack of urgency to the project because the retail market for packaged beer in the United Kingdom and Ireland was still relatively small. By the end of the decade, though, this had begun to change.

In the meantime, Peter Hildebrand, Sammy Hildebrand's son, developed a syringe-type mechanism for injecting a stream of foam into a bottle. Known as the Creamer, this system worked, but it was a cumbersome and time-consuming process. The short-lived Creamer is now all but forgotten, although one of the devices is still on display at Guinness's Storehouse visitor center at St. James's Gate.

In the early 1980s, the project to create nitrogenation in a can was revived and given a high priority under the direction of Alan Forage. The Guinness Director of Product development, Forage had an undergraduate degree in botany, a PhD in radiation biology, and experience in the pharmaceutical industry with a specialty in antibiotics and enzyme production.

In Dublin, Forage was given a £5 million budget and tasked with developing a practical way to put Guinness Draught in a can and deliver a proper pint with a proper head. Standing on the shoulders—metaphorically, of course—of Tony Carey and the Hildebrands, Forage and his team explored a myriad of technologies. Among those working with Forage was William Byrne, with whom Forage would share the eventual patent. Like their predecessors, however, they would be frustrated by a number of dead ends.

Finally, in 1985, Forage and Byrne at last achieved success with what they called the In-Can System (ICS). Alan Forage explained the ICS as a plastic chamber insert with a minute hole that was placed in the bottom of a 500-milliliter can. "Beer containing dissolved gas is filled under pressure into the can and the can is sealed," Forage wrote. The gas was the nitrogen plus carbon dioxide mixture. "Once the lid has been put on, the pressures in the can and inside the chamber equilibrate and beer is forced into the chamber, which becomes partially filled. When a consumer opens the can of beer by pulling the ring-pull, the higher pressure in the can is released to atmosphere. The pressure drop forces beer and gas out of the chamber through the small hole. It is this which creates the characteristic surge in Guinness Draught."

During 1986, the ICS was evaluated through consumer testing, and Guinness authorized the initial test marketing by the end of 1987. In the meantime, the ICS came to be known simply as the "widget." Through the years, the term, like "gadget" or "gizmo," has come to be used when speaking informally about small mechanisms. The term was perhaps first used in a 1924 comedy play written by George S. Kaufman and Marc Connelly to refer to generic factory products. Within Guinness, this nickname caught on, and the ICS became the "Guinness widget."

The can with the widget inside was introduced in limited markets in 1988 and nationally in Britain in 1989. It was launched in Ireland and selected U.S. markets in 1991, and elsewhere soon after. To call the reception enthusiastic would be an understatement. At last, Guinness lovers at home could replicate the pub experience. Originally, the product was marketed as "Canned Draught Guinness" in the United Kingdom, and as "Guinness Pub Draught," in the United States, but it is now simply "Guinness Draught."

In April 1989, in his last annual report before being succeeded as Guinness PLC Chairman by Anthony Tennant, Sir Norman Macfarlane happily observed that "the star of our new product portfolio is Canned Draught Guinness. Identical to the draught product in taste, it also reproduces the distinctive creamy head."

Anthony Tennant continued the discussion of the can with the widget in the 1992 annual report, writing that:

> Since [1989], it has consistently been in the top ten of take-home beer products, and has also introduced consumers to [the in-pub variation of] Draught Guinness. . . . The unique design of the in-can system used in Canned Draught Guinness, for which Guinness Brewing Worldwide holds the patent, won The Queen's Award for Technological Achievement in 1991—the first time this has ever been awarded to a brewing company.

In the beginning, the actual widget was a plastic disk in the bottom of the can, but in 1997, Guinness moved to the floating widget, a small white plastic sphere 1.5 inches in diameter. Originally, Guinness Draught was available only in pint-sized cans, but in 1999, Guinness introduced bottled Guinness Draught with a bullet-shaped "rocket widget" inside.

From the moment that it was launched back in 1989, the media was abuzz. What was the widget? How did it work?

Fergal Murray gives us an excellent explanation:

> The nitrogen is inside the beer. What happens on the canning line is that the widget goes into the can. The beer goes into the can. The beer goes into the widget inside the can. The nitrogen is inside the beer that's inside the widget, which is inside the can. As the can is sealed, there is pressure inside the can from the gasses, nitrogen and carbon dioxide, inside the can. There is nitrogen under pressure inside the beer inside the widget inside the beer inside the can. When the can is opened, the pressure drops, so the nitrogen inside the beer escapes, and the nitrogen inside the widget inside the beer inside the can tries to get out. The nitrogen inside the beer inside the can dissipates in the initial whoosh, but in order to escape, the nitrogen inside the beer inside the widget has to go through a small hole and it meets resistance.

He went on to explain that this is exactly what happens when the Guinness Draught traveling from keg to tap in the pub hits the back of the restrictor plate:

> When the black beer from the keg hits the restrictor plate, the bubbles explode. When the pressure within the can is released, the nitrogen bubbles inside the widget act like a jet engine. The energy of the nitrogen going out though the hole creates the surge. When you pour Guinness Draught, it's not pure black. It's a sort of brownish color because there are nitrogen bubbles in it. This happens again whenthe beer hits the bottom of the glass. Then it surges more. The nitrogen bubbles cannot escape because the surface tension of the bubbles is so strong. The nitrogen molecules are held back by the beer molecules.

What's it all about?
The perfect pint at home.

A Growing Company and the Perfect Pint

During the 1990s, Guinness PLC—now marketing the cans with the amazing widget—continued to grow, with total gross income topping £4 billion in 1991 for the first time. The brewing sector represented about a fifth of the assets, around 40 percent of the income and 30 percent of the profits. Chairman Anthony Tennant reported that 1990 saw Guinness PLC emerge second only to Coca-Cola among the world's most profitable beverage companies.

In 1991, extending the influence of the brand globally, Guinness Brewing Worldwide established licensed brewing agreements in Barbados, Burkina Faso, Congo, Gabon, Guyana, and Tanzania. The following year, the company entered into license arrangements in the Dominican Republic, as well as renewing an earlier licensed brewing relationship with South African Breweries (SAB) that had been suspended because of the worldwide boycott of South Africa over its practice of Apartheid. With that oppressive policy moved into the dustbin of history, SAB now made freshly brewed Guinness available in South Africa, the largest market in Africa and one of the world's top dozen beer markets. In 2002, SAB became SABMiller with its acquisition of Miller Brewing of Milwaukee, Wisconsin, the second largest brewing company in the United States.

In the early 1990s, against the backdrop of major geopolitical shifts, Guinness Brewing Worldwide initiated new distribution agreements in Russia and Eastern Europe, and began contract brewing in Vietnam. Elsewhere in the Far East, Guinness Malaysia Berhad, which was 50.01 percent Guinness-owned, merged with Malayan Breweries Limited in which major shareholders included Heineken and Fraser & Neave. As a result of this 1989 transaction, Guinness PLC had a 25.5 percent share in the merged company, which was now known as Guinness Anchor Berhad (GAB). Fraser & Neave was a Singapore-based holding company (also partly owned by Heineken) whose assets included Asia Pacific Breweries, producers of the well-known Tiger and Anchor lager brands.

In 1995, GAB rolled out its Guinness Special Light Stout in Malaysia. It was described as being a "refreshing, easy-to-drink stout with less alcohol than Foreign Extra Stout," but offering "the added flavor and satisfaction that consumers cannot find in existing Malaysian beers."

During this same period, Guinness acquired and operated Spain's Cruzcampo brewing company. That country's largest and fastest growing brewer, Cruzcampo was known for lager brands such as Alcazar, El Lion, and Estrella del Sur, as well as Henninger, a lager brewed under license from the Henninger Brewery in Frankfurt, Germany. In 1991, the year of the Guinness acquisition, Guinness-owned Cruzcampo acquired a majority share in Union Cervecera, Spain's sixth largest brewer. Denmark's Carlsberg, a major shareholder in

Union Cervecera, became a 10 percent shareholder in the new Grupo Cruzcampo. Guinness later sold its interest in Cruzcampo to Heineken, and as part of this transaction, the Dutch brewing giant agreed to distribute Guinness in Spain.

At the corporate headquarters in London, meanwhile, Anthony Tennant was succeeded as Guinness PLC chairman in January 1993 by Tony Greener, who had been named as chief executive in 1992. Greener joined Guinness PLC from Dunhill in 1986, and succeeded Vic Steel as managing director of the United Distillers component in October 1987. He served as group managing director from May 1989 until becoming chief executive. Though he had reached the top via the spirits side of the group, Greener had a great deal of interest in the brewing side.

In a September 1999 article in *Forbes* magazine, business writer Dyan Machan recalls being seated near Greener at a luncheon in the London corporate headquarters. Having been served a tureen of foie gras and wild mushrooms, she noticed Greener, now Sir Anthony, frowning over a glass of French wine. When she asked "with typical American tact," whether a pint of Guinness could be had, she recalled: "His face lights up. 'Yes, I believe we can,' Greener says, pushing aside the cut-crystal wine glass. Normally not one to drink at noon, he sacrificed himself to please his guest."

After consuming his can of Guinness Draft, Greener, like so many consumers of the product, ripped the can in two, took out the widget, "which he rolls admiringly between a beer-drenched thumb and forefinger."

It was on Greener's watch, that Guinness PLC was involved with several historically important and memorable consumer relations programs. In 1994, Guinness launched the Perfect Pint Initiative in the United Kingdom and Ireland. The idea that the consumer should get a perfect pint every time may not be unique to Guinness, but it is interesting to note that in the history of the brand it is a consistently recurring theme. It was the case when Michael Ash and his team perfected nitrogenation in the 1960s, it was the case with the development of the widget, and it was the case once again when Guinness PLC cared so much that the corporation launched an program aimed at the concept of the perfect pint.

As Tony Greener wrote in his report to shareholders, "Its unique and distinctive flavor makes Guinness stout a taste that, once acquired, is hard to relinquish—and as loyal consumers know, appearance and presentation are key to the appeal and enjoyment of the brand. Our challenge is to ensure that in existing markets the consumer gets a perfect Guinness every time—and that in new markets we create the widest range of opportunities for potential consumers to acquire the taste."

Under this program, dispense system improvements were designed to deliver the beer in optimum condition, while a program of "trade and bar staff education" aimed to ensure that every pint or glass would be correctly served. The education included detailed training in the proper two-part pour and institutionalizing the "six steps to perfection" process.

The Six Steps to Perfection

Step 1: Select a clean, dry glass. Hold the glass at 45 degrees under the spout.

Step 2: Pull the handle slowly toward you and allow the beer to flow smoothly down the side of the glass (note: do not submerge the spout in the beer).

Step 3: As the glass fills, straighten the glass. Fill glass until full.

Step 4: Stand the glass on the counter and allow the gas to surge through the beer.

Step 5: To create the legendary head, push the handle backward slightly (this is known as "topping off"). The head should rise just proud of the rim.

Step 6: Close the tap and present confidently to the customer.

Meanwhile, similar promotional initiatives were underway elsewhere, including continental Europe, which had seen consistent volume growth of over 20 percent. The Guinness Guild direct mail service brought technical and promotional information—in five languages—to the owners of 1,500 establishments serving Guinness.

Also during 1994, Guinness PLC launched one of the most audacious consumer promotions in the history of advertising. The company decided to promote the pleasures of the brand by giving Americans a little more than just a perfect pint with its "Win Your Own Pub in Ireland" contest. "Win Your Own Pub" worked as a spin-off of the perfect pint concept. Guinness lovers were asked to describe the perfect pint in 50 words or less, beginning with the phrase "The Perfect Pint of Guinness is . . ."

The "Win Your Own Pub" contest was exactly that. As contestants read in the fine print, the winner really would become the owner of Connie Doolan's pub at Cobh in County Cork. After 30,000 entries were evaluated and a winner chosen, Tony Greener happily remarked that the competition "provided more than just the opportunity to sample the delights of a pint of Guinness in an Irish Pub for Jay Mulligan from Boston, Massachusetts—he actually won his own pub."

In a 2002 article naming the contest to a top 10 list of "Most Significant Promotions," *Promo Magazine*, wrote "Guinness agencies Creative Alliance and Weiss, Whitten & Stagliano knew they had a killer concept 'when we both had it on our lists,' says Creative partner Nick Lemma. The campaign that was pitched cost about $1 million more than had been budgeted, but after Guinness group marketing director Todd Stevenson heard it, 'He just told us, "Make it work." . . . Two weeks later, we were on a plane to Ireland.' "

And work it did. As Tony Greener happily wrote in his memo to shareholders, "The competition was so successful, it is being repeated in 1995."

And repeated it was. The winner in 1995 was Frank Gallagher, who relocated from Florida to take the keys to the Kilgoban Pub in

Bantry, County Cork. The following year, an Oregon woman named Shann Weston won the Seanachaoi Pub in Killaloe, County Clare. In 1997, it was Doug Knight, a Minneapolis musician who won Morrissey's in Cahir, County Tipperary. A New York paralegal named Trevor O'Driscoll won Finucane's pub in County Kerry in 1998, and Erika Lee of Portland, Oregon won O'Sullivan's Pub in Newcastle West, County Limerick, in the final contest of the essay series.

Even as "Win Your Own Pub" was garnering headlines concerning pubs within Ireland, Guinness Brewing Worldwide had embarked on another far-reaching program, the objective of which was "to facilitate the development of authentic, high-quality Irish Pubs outside of Ireland."

Recognizing that a large portion of its Guinness sales outside of Ireland occurred in Irish pubs, especially authentic ones, the company launched the Irish Pubs Initiative (later known as the Guinness Irish Pub Concept) to help people open Irish pubs around the world. As Tony Greener explained, "Professionalism and pride in the product are only part of the enjoyment of Guinness. Atmosphere and ambience are also important, and where better than the friendly surroundings of an Irish bar? It is no longer necessary to go across the sea to Ireland to find the perfect environment."

Initiated in 1992, the program soon spread to places such as Canada, Singapore, and Finland. It was extended into the United States with the opening of Fadó Irish Pub in Atlanta in January 1996, the first of more than 130 such pubs in America. Because of "tied-house" laws governing the alcohol industry in the United States, Guinness was unable to participate financially in the pubs, but its pub business development team could assist owners in creating authentic Irish pub ambience, and train the bartenders to pour a perfect pint.

In 1995, Guinness Brewing Worldwide took the Guinness Irish Pub Concept a step further with the launch of a twinning initiative, in which some of the best pubs in Ireland joined in "big brother" type relationships with pubs elsewhere across Europe. Initially, more that 60 Irish pubs "twinned" with bars in Belgium, Denmark, Finland, France, Germany, Holland, Hungary, Italy, Spain, Sweden, Switzerland, and the United Kingdom.

Hand in hand with its successful consumer awareness initiatives, Guinness Brewing Worldwide continued to develop innovative advertising campaigns to support the flagship brand. The "Man with The Guinness" campaign, which was introduced in 1987, came to a close at the end of 1994 with a television commercial featuring the music of Louis Armstrong. The campaign is credited with reducing the age of the core Guinness drinker from 35 to 45 years to 25 to 35 years, giving Guinness an 80 percent share of the U.K. stout market.

In November 1994, Guinness launched the "Anticipation" campaign in Ireland and the United Kingdom. The idea was to illustrate the careful and unhurried process of pouring a pint of Guinness. The television commercials that were released as part of this campaign featured actor Joe McKinney, who became known as "the guy dancing round the pint." The purpose of the amusing commercial was to show how you may spend your time while waiting for a pint to settle and to be ready to drink.

An old friend rejoined the Guinness advertising line-up again during the 1990s, though he was not featured on television. John Gilroy's famous toucan, who had made only a couple of cameo appearances since Gilroy's circus animals were phased out in the 1960s, was reintroduced in Ireland in 1994 as the Guinness mascot for the World Cup. Since then, he has continued to appear on various Guinness ephemera, from T-shirts to key chains and the like. As Eibhlin Roche told us, "the toucan and the harp are the most recognized Guinness symbols."

While the toucan was flying back into the hearts of Guinness fans, two of the songs featured in Guinness commercials would reach the British pop music charts during the 1995—Armstrong's "All the Time in the World" went platinum in the early weeks of the year, while Perez Prado's "Guaglione," the theme from the Anticipation campaign reached number two toward the end of 1995.

In 1996, the "Black and White" campaign was launched in the United Kingdom with the tag line "Not Everything in Black and White Makes Sense." The opening pair of commercials, entitled "Old Man" and "Bicycle," soon attained the highest rating for advertising awareness of any Guinness commercial ever, higher even that the Guinnless campaign of the early 1980s. The Black and White campaign was adapted for a variety of media, including posters, print ads, point of sale promotions, and memorable computer screensavers, as well as additional television commercials.

In May 1998, Guinness launched the "Good Things Come to Those Who Wait" Guinness Draught campaign, which was developed by Abbott Mead Vickers, the fifth advertising agency to possess the Guinness account since Benson's in the late 1920s. It was this campaign that formally defined the notion that it takes 119.5 seconds to properly pour and serve the iconic perfect pint.

"We have run some really successful ads in the past focusing on why Guinness drinkers are different, but this new work focuses on why the Guinness perfect pint is different," said Andy Fennell, the marketing controller for Guinness Great Britain. "Central to the development of the new campaign is the issue of time—the time that it takes to serve and anticipate a perfect pint of Guinness. This is, of course, not only unique to Guinness but is also a truth recognized by all beer drinkers."

Guinness also launched several new additions to its portfolio of product variants during the mid-1990s. One of these was Kilkenny Irish Beer, an ale similar to Smithwick's, but served using nitrogenation like that of Guinness Draught. The brand name is in fact a reference to the Irish city where Smithwick's was born. The draught form of Kilkenny Irish Beer was first marketed in the United Kingdom in 1994, and introduced in Ireland the following year. Packaged Kilkenny for the home trade would appear in the United Kingdom in 1996.

At the end of 1996, when Tony Greener wrote that the year "was a landmark year for Guinness," it was a lot like the end of 1981, when his predecessor, Benjamin Guinness, the Earl of Iveagh, wrote: "I believe that we will look back on the year under review and recognize it as a watershed."

Just as Iveagh's statement set the tone for the ensuing decade, Greener's set the tone for the coming year and for the future of Guinness. Greener observed that the corporation had achieved record profits and record earnings, and that the two main brands, Johnnie Walker Scotch Whisky and Guinness Stout had both achieved record sales. He went on to note that these results flowed directly from "the investments made in the past two years, particularly the £75 million increase in marketing expenditure to build the appeal of our brands with the consumer, and our substantial investment in building our companies in developing markets."

What truly gave the record earnings of 1996 landmark status was how they positioned Guinness PLC for the events of 1997, a year that would be one of the biggest landmarks in the company's history. In 1997, Guinness PLC merged with Grand Metropolitan PLC (known as "Grand Met") to form the world's largest multinational beer, wine, and spirits company.

As Erik Ipsen wrote in the May 13, 1997, edition of the *International Herald Tribune*, "A conversation over dinner on April 10 between the chairmen of two of Britain's leading companies [George Bull and Tony Greener] bore fruit Monday in the form of a plan to merge Grand Metropolitan PLC and Guinness PLC into a $33 billion conglomerate."

The new company, which was originally to be known as GMG Brands, united the Guinness PLC brands with Grand Met's spirits business and its Burger King and Pillsbury brands under a single corporate roof. The merged entity would rank as the world's seventh-largest food and drink company in terms of the total value of the shares outstanding. It would rank as Britain's eighth-largest company, based on market value. The new entity would control over half the global Scotch business, which was seen as the largest and most profitable category in the global spirits business.

Said GrandMet's Bull at a news conference: "We have got a tremendous range of complementary brands. We fit geographically and our management shares a common philosophy."

"Our strengths in developing markets will be one of the biggest attractions of these two companies coming together," Tony Greener added. Greener and Bull would serve as co-chairmen until Bull's planned retirement in 1998, when Greener would become sole chairman. In June 1999, he would be knighted for his role in making the merger possible.

As Ipsen pointed out, combining the respective beverage components of the two corporations would "form the world's largest distiller and vintner, a subsidiary that will contribute nearly 60 percent of the combined group's earnings. . . . The deal is a marriage of relative equals. As of Friday [May 10], Grand Met had a market value of £10.8 billion, compared with Guinness's £9.8 billion." Guinness PLC shareholders would receive 47.3 percent of the merged entity and GrandMet shareholders would get 52.7 percent.

The combined wine and spirits operations of the two companies would be rolled into a division to be called United Distillers & Vintners (essentially accomplished by adding the GrandMet brands to Guinness PLC's United Distillers component), but Guinness Brewing Worldwide would be excluded from this unit as a separate division. Both Pillsbury and Burger King would also be separate divisions.

The company would be listed on both the London and New York stock exchanges. In addition to the Guinness brand, the beverage portfolio would include leading brands in numerous product categories including Bulleit Bourbon, Captain Morgan Rum, Crown Royal Whisky, George Dickel Whiskey, Gordon's Gin, Hennessy Cognac, J&B Whisky, Johnnie Walker Whisky, Seagram Whisky, Smirnoff Vodka, and Tanqueray Gin. The single malt distilleries in Scotland included Blair Athol, Caol Ila, Cardhu, Clynelish, Cragganmore,

Dalwhinnie, Glen Ord, Glen Elgin, Glenkinchie, Knockando, Lagavulin, Oban, Royal Lochnagar, and Talisker. Among many other holdings, the company also owned the Beaulieu Vineyard and Sterling Vineyards in California.

On October 30, 1997, the companies announced that the corporation that was to be created by their proposed merger would be called Diageo PLC, rather than GMG Brands. The term Diageo, based on the Latin word for "day" and the Greek word for "world," was chosen to suggest that every day, everywhere, people celebrate with Diageo brands. The corporate slogan became "Celebrating life, every day, everywhere."

Guinness in the
Twenty-First Century

In an earlier chapter, we observed that in the 1970s and 1980s, as the company diversified, the Guinness identity shifted away from its roots as an Irish brewing company. Since the late 1990s, the pendulum has swung back. Now one of the crown jewels in the Diageo portfolio of global brands, Guinness seems revitalized with a fresh excitement about being, well, about being Guinness! Maybe it's the widget, or maybe it's the amazing new visitor center in Dublin, or maybe it's that something intangible and unquantifiable that has always been part of the mystique.

By the beginning of the twenty-first century, two billion pints of Guinness were being poured annually in more than 150 countries

around the world. According to the industry newsletter, *Impact:
Global News and Research for the Drinks Executive*, Guinness Stout
is the seventeenth largest selling beer brand in the world, and by far
the best-selling beer brand that is not a pale yellow lager.

Ireland and the United Kingdom remain the largest markets
in the world for Guinness, with Nigeria in third place. In fourth
place, the United States is the fastest growing Guinness market.
According to Jonathan Waldron, the Dublin-based Guinness Draught
marketing manager, "Our top four markets explain 95 percent of our
volume."

Though no longer the largest in the world, the Guinness Brewery
at St. James's Gate remains the largest in Ireland—and the largest
stout brewery in the world—with a capacity of 6.5 million barrels.
After 69 years, the huge Guinness brewery at Park Royal was closed
in 2005. It had once been Guinness's largest brewery, but as production at the site declined, the company decided to close it, and to
concentrate stout production for the United Kingdom and Ireland—
as well as for the United States—at the birthplace of Guinness in
St. James's Gate.

In Ireland, the company also has an additional 1.5 million barrel
capacity in Dundalk, as well as 1.2 million barrels at Kilkenny. At
Waterford, the former Cherry's Brewery has been upgraded to a
state-of-the-art special ingredient plant to produce Guinness Flavor
Extract for export to the 50 countries where Guinness is brewed,
either under license or at brewing companies in which Guinness is a
partner.

Overseas, the company still owns a share in Malaysia's Guinness
Anchor Berhad and it operates 10 breweries in six African countries,
including Nigeria, Ghana, Cameroon, Kenya, Uganda, and the
Seychelles. Africa is a key market for Guinness. Indeed, Africans
drink more than one third of all the Guinness in the world.

Today, as much as ever, St. James's Gate is the center of gravity,
not only for Guinness, but for its fans and devotees. Guinness aficio-
nados who have made the pilgrimage to St. James's Gate since the

turn of the century have been welcomed at the Guinness Store-house, the brewery's new visitor center. The Storehouse is the successor to the Guinness Hop Store that served as the visitor center from 1988 to 2000. When the Storehouse opened, the Hop Store was sold to the Digital Hub, an Irish Government initiative to "create an international center of excellence for knowledge, inno-vation and creativity focused on digital content and technology enterprises."

Just as the previous visitor center had served for hop storage, the massive Storehouse was once part of the process of producing stout. Built to house fermentation vessels and opened in 1904, the 125-foot-high, red brick building once contained the largest fer-mentation vessel in the world. Updated and expanded in the 1950s, the Storehouse was superseded in the 1980s by a newer facility across James's Street to the north. It reopened in its new incarna-tion in December 2000. As the Hop Store before it, the Storehouse contains a myriad of exhibits relating to the history and folklore of the beer, the brand and the brewery. It also houses the Guinness Archives.

The Guinness Storehouse now has the distinction of being Ireland's number one visitor attraction, with three million visitors in its first five years. It is topped with the Guinness Gravity Bar, which is the highest point in Dublin. Constituting the seventh floor of the Storehouse, the Gravity Bar is a nice place to enjoy a pint, while also enjoying a 360-degree view of Dublin itself.

When those people who are enjoying their pints at the Gravity Bar—or at the 150 or so Dublin pubs visible from the Gravity Bar—or in the 150 countries across the horizon—*what* pints are they enjoying? Jonathan Waldron explained, as we sat in the Brewery Bar one floor down from the Gravity Bar, that Guinness thinks in terms of a lead variant in each of its markets.

"Our approach to date has been that there is a lead variant in each market. In Ireland, the United Kingdom and North America, the lead variant would be Guinness Draught by a margin of about

75 to 80 percent," he said. "In Ireland, Guinness Extra Stout is drunk by an older population, including people who began drinking Guinness when Guinness was *only* Extra Stout. That is evolving a little bit as we see, for example, that younger consumers might like to enjoy Guinness Extra Stout with certain meals, such as with fish. They find the bite of the carbonation, plus the deeper tone, as a good balance with fish."

Waldron observed that in Ireland, Guinness has been so ingrained in the culture for so many years, that it presents an interesting marketing challenge. This challenge is to market a beer to younger people who may perceive it as being their "father's beer."

As he explains, "We will always strive to maintain a contemporary association with the brand in Ireland because everybody's father *did* drink it. On the other hand, in the United States, the average stout drinker tends to be younger and more highly educated than the average beer drinker because Guinness is perceived as a premium beer."

In the United States, the huge increase in attention to microbreweries has been a great boon for Guinness because they have revitalized interest in complexity and rich flavor in beer. As Waldron puts it: "The craft brew segment of the American market is great for Guinness in that those kinds of beers are drunk by people who are looking for a taste experience. We can *certainly* offer people a taste experience! There are some great beers out there, and the more popular they become, it's only going to help Guinness."

In most of the rest of the world, Waldron says that Foreign Extra Stout is by far the lead variant: "In Japan, we've only ever had Guinness Draught, but elsewhere in the Far East, where our big markets are Malaysia and Indonesia, the lead variant has always been Foreign Extra Stout, as it is across Africa. In North America, we see an interesting thing, which is that people in the Afro-Caribbean demographic favor Guinness Extra Stout. In the Caribbean, the lead variant is Foreign Extra Stout, which is unavailable in the United States, so they are getting close to that with Guinness Extra Stout."

Noting that Guinness sees the Foreign Extra Stout world as a potential growth area for Guinness Draught, he said that, "We're experimenting with launching draught in Asian markets. Guinness Draught has long been available in Hong Kong, and it is gradually becoming more available in upscale bars in some major Chinese cities. We have a draught presence in hotels and leading bars, but if we want to expand our business, we have to go for the man in the street. We've found that, whereas the older generation may be happy with the bite and the bitterness of Foreign Extra Stout, the younger generation has grown up with a sweeter palate, so Guinness Draught is a much more appealing product for them."

The fact that Nigeria is the third largest market for Guinness after the United Kingdom and Ireland underscores the importance of Foreign Extra Stout among the variants. On the other hand, the fact that the United States is the fastest growing market is important for the draught products.

"In time, I hope that the U.S. market will become the largest," Waldron said. "It's such a huge market. There is an established 'taste beer' segment, which has grown in recent years. Canada is a reasonably good market, but it is a much smaller market than the United States. In Europe, Germany is the largest but France, Italy and Spain are close behind. In Russia, Heineken brews Foreign Extra Stout under license from us."

While Guinness Draught, Extra Stout, and Foreign Extra Stout dominate the world market, Guinness also offers a number of other variants of the Guinness stout brands—as well as other products. There are several variations on Guinness Draught that are really the same beer, but listed separately in the product portfolio because of their packaging or dispense system. The canned and bottled variants are each listed separately from the kegged version because of their district packaging, while Guinness Extra Cold is actually Guinness Draught served about one-third cooler than Guinness Draught is usually served. Launched in 1998, it comes from the same barrel in the pub as Guinness Draught but it goes through a super cooler before being poured.

Among other stout variants are Guinness Special Export Stout, sold in Belgium with 8 percent alcohol by volume, and Guinness Mid-Strength, a low alcohol (2.8 percent) stout test-marketed in Limerick in 2006. As Fergal Murray described the latter, "you don't have to have the full alcohol content to have the same satisfaction and flavor."

Introduced in Ghana in 2003, Guinness Extra Smooth marked the first time that nitrogenated bottled beer was sold in Africa. Jonathan Waldron explained that "in most of West Africa, Foreign Extra Stout, the lead variant, was the *only* variant available, but consumer tastes change. Previously, beer drinking was a weekend or evening out kind of thing for African consumers. Now they might want to drink it after work, but they want something with less alcohol than Foreign Extra Stout. For this, we offered Guinness Extra Smooth with lower alcohol by volume. It differs from the packaged Guinness Draught available in Ireland or the United States because it doesn't have the widget technology. It doesn't surge like Draught Guinness, but it does have nitrogen in solution."

Just as there are several variations on Guinness Draught, there are variants of Foreign Extra Stout. In Nigeria, for example, the product is produced using locally grown sorghum, rather than barley malt. Another product brewed in Nigeria is nonalcoholic Malta Guinness, which is exported to other countries.

"The Guinness stouts are variations on a single brand, while Harp Lager, Smithwick's Ale, and Kilkenny Irish Cream Ale are separate brands that are under the same umbrella," Jonathan Waldron said, naming the principal nonstout products in the Irish, British, and North American markets. "We brew them. They come from Guinness breweries, but they're not the Guinness brand. We see them differently and draw a distinction between Guinness and those brands. Harp has done well in Irish pubs in the United States. It's seen as a way for people for whom Guinness is a bit strong to have an evening in an Irish bar and join in the Irish theme by having a glass of Harp. Smithwick's is going quite strongly in the States because it's a great tasting Irish ale."

Another separate product is Guinness Bitter, an English-style ale sold in a green can only in the United Kingdom in the ASDA supermarkets, a chain formed in the 1960s when the a grocery business owned by the Asquith family grocery chain joined with Associated Dairies & Farm Stores.

Meanwhile, Guinness is continuously experimenting and test marketing new products and variants. One example was a craft beer series that was test marketed briefly in Dublin and Cork in 1998. Branded with the name of the brewery rather than the Guinness name, they were St. James's Gate Wheat, St. James's Gate Pilsner Gold, St. James's Gate Wicked Red Ale, and St. James's Gate Harvest Dark.

"Since I've been here, Guinness has been constantly innovating or trying new things," Master Brewer Fergal Murray said. "That's what brewing is about. Relying on a consistent product in the global market, while at the same time keeping other veins open to see what the consumers say."

In so doing, Guinness works from its strengths, which include malt roasting, where Guinness is a leader in the industry worldwide. "Roasting is a specific expertise that we have," Jonathan Waldron says. "In roasting malted barleys, we believe that we can produce superior flavors to anybody else. Roasting is a linking theme in all of the Guinness beers. We aren't going to do something within the Guinness brand unless we can see something about roasting and something about texture in the product."

A recent example of Guinness using its expertise to develop new product variants was the Brewhouse Series, launched in October 2005. Being based on recipes that existed at the brewery gave the series a historical context. As described by Guinness Archivist Eibhlin Roche, the series consisted of limited edition Guinness stouts, "all based on the Guinness brand equity, all black and white, and all made from the same ingredients as the classic Guinness stouts. Each was launched independently as a special edition for six months each, and sold only in Ireland. Their authenticity was underscored by their being based on old Guinness recipes."

To this, Fergal Murray adds, "Guinness has such a rich heritage. We're still understanding what the brewers here did in the past."

Each beer in the series was a slight variation on Guinness Draught. Brew 39 had a slightly different taste, Toucan Brew was said to have a crisper note due to its triple-hopped brewing process, and North Star Brew was produced with a slight change in the blend of barley malts.

"The Brewhouse Series was not necessarily totally different," Fergal Murray explained. "Guinness has to be Guinness. There are some fundamental equities. It has to be black and white. It's our job to be the custodian of the product, and not our job to change the product. We want the consumer to endorse a small adjustment and enjoy it. These were slight variations on recipes that we had before, which we adapted to modern brewing technologies. It's experimental, an innovation to show the consumers other specialties that we'd like to show them. North Star, for example, is fundamentally the same as Guinness Draught, but sweeter, differently aromatic and more ale-like."

Another recent product that was definitely more ale-like was Guinness Red, which was test marketed in Britain in 2007. It was brewed using a lighter roasted barley to produce a rich red color and what Simon Garnett, the senior innovation manager for the product, described as "different flavors and a bittersweet taste."

Jonathan Waldron added that, "the idea with Guinness Red was that it was a more accessible taste who love the Guinness concept, but for whom Guinness stout may be too bitter."

Guinness continues to study new technology, as well as new product variants. As we have seen, some of the major technological breakthroughs through the years have involved dispense systems, specifically nitrogenation and the widget. The object of both was to use a form of energy to stimulate nitrogen molecules to form bubbles, which in turn form the perfect head. The energy in the Guinness Draught poured from a keg at the pub is the friction of the restrictor plate. The energy in the can or bottle containing the widget is the pressure drop. As Fergal Murray puts it, making a play on the old "Guinness for Strength" slogan, "Guinness is no longer about *strength*, it's about *energy*."

There are many forms of energy, and in 2007, Guinness called on a third in the launch of its patented Surger system for dispensing nitrogenated stout. The energy in this new technology is ultrasound. The sound waves stimulate the nitrogen, creating millions of bubbles. While the widget delivers the gases in regular canned Guinness Draught, the Surger sonically activates the gas within the beer.

Designed for use both at home and for bars with limited space, the centerpiece of the system is the disc-shaped Surger that, at the touch of a button, sends an ultrasonic pulse through a pint glass of Guinness, releasing the gases in the beer, which then settle into the pint with the creamy head. The beer is brewed to exactly the same Guinness Draught recipe, but it has a slightly different gas mix.

"Our innovation process is not just about the products, but internally as well," Fergal Murray said, looking at how technology and innovation have made Guinness what it is. "You don't see it or hear about it, but it's about the technology inside the brewhouse. It's about how our beer is made, and the condition of the raw materials. We've innovated in our way of milling, innovated in refrigeration, innovated in the way we keg. Our kegging facility is one of the most unique in the world. Very few kegging systems use nitrogenation. We have the engineering teams here to support unique systems, but Guinness has *always* done that. More than 100 years ago, our combined heat and power station at St. James's Gate was one of the first of its kind in the world. Today, we send our essence to more than 40 countries around the world to maintain consistent quality in our products. No brewer had even tried to do something like that. Then our people did research into those methods, and it was done. Adapting to the technology of the modern brewing world is critical. This is a twenty-first century brewery now."

But even in twenty-first century, it all comes back to passion. Looking around at the brewery buildings, humming with action as they were in the last century and in both of the centuries before that, he talks about his passion and of all the workers here at St. James's Gate. Gesturing toward the people lining up to go into the visitor center, he says "If you look at those 800,000 people who turn up at the Guinness Storehouse every year, you'll understand what the brand means in the world."

Inside the Gate with the Master Brewer

So the tale comes full circle. To conclude my story, I am here where I began and where so much of this narrative has taken place—at St. James's Gate. As far as consumers in Ireland, the United Kingdom, North America, Europe, and many other places are concerned, the Guinness they drink is still brewed within sight of the place where Arthur Guinness first brewed it, where his first Dublin brewhouse stood, here at St. James's Gate.

Fergal Murray, master brewer and inheritor of a tradition that spans a quarter of a millennium, imparts an infectious excitement for his product. I came to St. James's Gate with an enthusiast's zeal for the beer, and in the presence of such hallowed ground, one

215

cannot help feeling the same about all the centuries of heritage. You drink it in at every turn, savoring the richness of the heritage the way you savor the stout as it massages your palate.

In the beginning of this story, I wrote that a pint of Guinness is a magic thing, tossing off a statement easily used as a metaphor. However, I was soon to discover that this magic is not entirely metaphorical.

"Let's take a quick run around," Murray says. He has told me many things, but he promises that he will now show me what he cannot tell me. The tradition is not dusty and parked on a shelf. It is alive, and he feels that I must see this. The "quick run around" will unfold over several days. There is much to see. Guinness has more than 50 contiguous acres under its control overlooking the Liffey.

As we cross the brewery's yard, passing over the ground where Arthur's sons and grandsons and their sons brewed the black stuff—and where Arthur once defended his water rights with a pick in his hands—Fergal Murray conveys both his pride and sense of place about St. James's Gate.

"In its heyday, this brewery was a town, employing as many as 5,000 brewers, coopers, maltsers, carpenters, plumbers, engineers, printers, clock-makers, mice-catchers, and whatever," he says as he points out this vathouse and that storehouse. "They lived and worked as a family. Their lives were around the brewery. People worked here for 40 or 50 years, for generations. There are not many of those anymore, but that's the way the business operated."

Indeed, at its peak, St. James's Gate directly touched the lives of perhaps a tenth of Dublin's population, and indirectly most of the rest. Guinness was an integral part of life in Ireland's capital.

"When people left here after a day's work, they'd go into the pub and have a beer," Murray laughs. Where else would you likely have people heading home from the factory and stopping off to consume one of that factory's products?

Wow.

The first stop is where it all begins, at the place where Guinness starts to distinguish itself from other beers. There are a lot of dark beers in the world, but Guinness is unique. At a stout tasting I attended some months before visiting St. James's Gate—a tasting that was won by widgeted Guinness Draught because we weren't in a pub—we discussed those things that were characteristic of the style, and those things that we like. Characteristics of the style are the dark color and the nutty "roastyness." All stouts have this. At its worst, the "roastyness" in dark beers borders on—or crosses the border into—"burnt." Any cook understands the fine line between roasted and burnt, and the same rules apply to malt as to any other food. What everyone at our tasting agreed is especially marvelous about Guinness is the smoothness of the roast. As Jonathan Waldron has said, "Roasting is a specific expertise that we have. In roasting malted barleys, we believe that we can produce superior flavors to anybody else."

The tasting that I attended certainly suggests that he is right, and Fergal Murray is about to show me why.

The roasting house at St. James's Gate is located high on the hill above the Liffey, at roughly the highest point within the brewery grounds, at the uppermost point where Sam Geoghegan's railway once ran. On a blustery January day, it is invitingly warm inside the immense room that houses two huge roasters. Virtually all the malt for all of the Guinness worldwide is roasted here. All the malt for the brewing at St. James's Gate is roasted here, as well as much of the malt that goes into Guinness Flavor Extract for Guinness brewed abroad. The rest of the roasting for the latter takes place at the Guinness plant in Waterford.

"Essentially, anything with any color comes from here," Fergal Murray explains, proudly pointing up at the huge roasters. I'm reminded of the night that I stood beneath a Delta II space launch vehicle on a pad at Vandenberg AFB a few years ago.

Wow.

Inside these behemoths, hot air and 3.5 tons of grain rotate for about three hours, yielding 2.8 tons of roasted malt for brewing after the moisture is gone. About 18,000 tons are roasted annually at St. James's Gate. However, by weight, only 10 percent of the grain used in Guinness stout is roasted.

"There is no open flame to damage the grain," Murray tells me as we look inside a roaster that is between batches. "There are no inconsistencies, no hot spots, because the air is all the same temperature. The roaster ramps it up to about 233 degrees, then we flash cool it very fast with water. The whole idea is to get the grain to have a roast color on the outside with a nice light brown on the inside. That's our visual spec. We know that matches the brewing spec we want for our brewing process."

Naturally, each batch of roasted malt is taste tested, and naturally, he offers a pinch of beautiful, dark brown grains for a test of my own.

"It has a bit of chocolate notes as it first comes out and is cooling," he remarks as we nibble. "The chocolate disappears, but we like to see that at this stage that it has the 'Guinness mouth feel.' That's because of the roast."

The thought of "burnt" doesn't even come to mind. It is as though you're tasting something, such as nuts, that occur in nature with a roasty flavor. From here, the roasted malt joins unmalted grain, and the two are milled together into grist.

"Like any brewhouse in the world, we want to get at the lovely protein, carbohydrates, minerals, and vitamins in the grain," Murray explains as we enter the big St. James's Gate brewhouse. Built in 1994, it is still state-of-the-art. "The malted barley comes in, and we crush it in the mill. We want to get into mother nature's grain."

This grist is then mixed with hot water and sent through a Steele's masher. The porridge-like mixture, called mash, then drops down into the mash tuns, which have always been known at St. James's Gate as kieves. In old documents from half a century ago, brewery workers at St. James's Gate also had a term for the mash. It was "the goods." In those days, they also used to speak of each of the old kieves having its own personality.

The function of the kieves is to strain the spent grains from the mash, separating this from the liquid. Hops are then added to impart bitterness to the sweetness of the wort. Brewing beer is like cooking food. The object is to achieve delicate and pleasing balances of flavors. In beer, flavor is a balance of the sweetness of the wort and the seasoning of the hops. The latter may be bitter or flowery, depending on the hops being used. With Guinness, the object is bitterness.

"Guinness chooses its hops based on high alpha acid content," Fergal Murray explains. Some brewers select hops by their growing region of their type. Guinness is after exactly the right balance of bitterness. Brewers can and actually do measure bitterness in their beer using the International Bitterness Unit (IBU) scale. An IBU is one part per million of isohumulone. The higher number, the greater the bitterness. Bland, mass-market lagers might be as low as 5, while the most bitter of English ales may be as high as 80 or so. Guinness Draught is rated at 42, while Foreign Extra Stout has 65 IBUs.

As with the roasting of the malt, Guinness has achieved a complex balance of flavors in which bitterness does not equate to harshness. As Jonathan Waldron had told me, "Although Guinness Draught is actually high in bitterness units, the creaminess of the nitrogen masks that bitterness."

"All of the brewhouse steps are about maximizing the optimization of the raw materials," Fergal Murray says, discussing the ingredients as the hopped wort is sent to be boiled in the huge, enclosed brew kettles. "That's what brewing is about in the twenty-first century. We have to have the right color, the right hop levels, and the right balance of wort before it goes down to the fermenters."

The brewhouse process takes 10 hours. He tells me that Guinness does up to 100 brews a week, and generates about three million pints a day. There is always a brew going through the brewhouse, although depending on orders, every brew kettle may or may not be used every day. Brewers at St. James's Gate used to call the kettles "coppers," because they were made of copper. Today, stainless steel is used.

"At this stage of the brewing process, we're doing things very little different than any other brewery in the world," Murray smiles, using a tone of voice that makes you know that things are about to deviate from the usual very soon. "In the boil, this is where things start to be different from the rest of the world. This is now where we add the color. The roasted barley is added—in liquid form as concentrated extract. It used to be added in the mash tun."

Answering the obvious question, he explains that the concentrated extract that is added at this point in the brewing process at St. James's Gate is "totally different than the essence that is shipped abroad. This concentrated extract is for color. The essence that is sent abroad contains both color *and* flavor because it has been through the brewing process and has been fermented and matured."

We follow the wort as it is cooled to room temperature and sent to the fermentation tanks, where yeast turns fermentable sugars into alcohol and carbon dioxide. Here is where everything I've learned from other brewery tours begins to change.

"Down in fermentation, everything is different between Guinness and the rest of the world," Murray tells me. "With Guinness yeast, we step into a different zone. The Guinness yeast operates at 25 degrees centigrade, converting sugar to alcohol in 60 hours. No other beer in the world does it that way. We believe in conversion of raw materials as fast as possible. This is the opposite from what many other people think. They think that fermentation should take a long time, but Guinness never did that."

It's true. A typical ale brewery measures fermentation time in days, a lager brewery marks it in weeks. Lager often takes more than a month. Guinness measures fermentation in hours.

"Our yeast operates at a very high optimization," Murray grins, bragging about the Guinness microbes as a trainer brags about a thoroughbred. "It's like the Olympic marathon runner who can run the marathon in two hours, while average runners can take all day.

Our yeast has to be an Olympic marathon runner because it has an enormous job to do, an extraordinary job of conversion in 60 hours. It has to get in there, gobble up all that sugar and create the alcohol and the flavor at optimized speed."

Enormous too, is the job of managing the vitality of the yeast so that it can turn in this kind of performance. "Master yeast cultures are stored in liquid nitrogen and taken out every six months and fresh cultures are grown up," he says. "We put a new propagation into the plant roughly every six weeks. The same strain of the yeast species *Saccharomyces cerevisiae* is used in draught Guinness is used in Guinness Extra Stout and Foreign Extra Stout brewed at St. James's Gate. It's conditioned to perform the same each time. The African breweries use a slightly different strain of *Saccharomyces cerevisiae* because the plants and brewing processes are different. In the nineteenth century, even before the science of understanding yeast classifications had evolved, the Guinness brewery had isolated a strain that was 'doing the job of producing a perfect beer.' The guys in the laboratory took a sample of that, and applied the new technology in the early years of the twentieth century. Guinness established a new way of looking at yeast."

After 60 hours, Guinness Draught is sent to secondary fermentation for 24 hours, and then it is matured over the next four days. Murray promised that during fermentation things would become different, but it was astounding. Just 60 hours?

Wow.

Now, he is about to reveal that, as I have been watching the brewing process, there is something that my eye *hasn't seen.*

In the beginning of this story, I wrote that a pint of Guinness is a magic thing. In the beginning of this chapter, I added that this magic is *not* entirely metaphorical. Like a magician, who directs the eye to the obvious while the sleight of hand occurs unseen, Guinness creates magic. While the eye is on the familiar process, a second, parallel process has been occurring—just like magic.

"During the maturation process, Guinness adds in a unique brew that has been created in a separate, proprietary process," Fergal Murray reveals.

Wow.

He tells me only *that* it happens, and I know better than to ask *what* or *why*. "This brew comes through the same vessels, but at a separate time, and it is kept in a separate stream until it is blended in at the maturation stage. This is our secret, our *special moment*. What it does in lay terms is to season the beer. We're bringing out the flavor, like adding salt and pepper to food brings out flavor. This seasoning, this bringing out of flavor is what Guinness has always done. Guinness has always known how to get more flavor. The Second Arthur Guinness and his team were looking at ways to bring out flavor, and the way they solved it is the way we still do it today. This is where Extra Special Porter, now Guinness Extra Stout, started way back then."

This is the secret ingredient, the mystery, and the magic that has literally turned my brewery tour into a magical mystery tour.

Wow.

"This unique brew, the St. James's Gate brewing essence, has a slightly different profile than the rest of the beer," he smiles. "It doesn't get fermented in the same way, and it's stored differently. It's not that nobody else *could* do this, it's just that we don't tell anyone *how* we do it. We don't give out any specs. Somebody else could do something similar, but they wouldn't know *exactly* how to do it."

Is this extra ingredient the "Extra" that the Second Arthur had in mind when he named it *Extra* Special Porter?

As we leave the brewhouse and pass through the long pedestrian tunnel beneath James's Street toward the kegging facility, Murray summarizes what we have seen—and *not* seen—in the brewhouse: "The unique qualities are extra hops, that mean more value to our product; more color that means more value to our product; a fermentation process that creates alcohol as fast as possible and holds the flavor; *and* a unique essence."

After maturation, the next stage is to create the final product variants. Both Guinness Extra Stout and Guinness Draught come out of maturation as Extra Stout. For the draught variant, nitrogen is put into solution. At this point, the beer may be put into tanker trucks to be carried in bulk to be bottled or canned, or it may go to the keg plant at St. James's Gate. Passing a big black truck heading out to Runcorn or Belfast, where Guinness has packaging facilities, we walk into the kegging plant.

"Kegging used to involve several lines with men all over the place filling them by hand, and there was the train to take the filled kegs away to market," he says as we take ear plugs from a dispenser near the door. Indeed, Guinness used to have a *huge* barrel making operation. The Guinness cooperage once employed nearly as many coopers as there were brewers at St. James's Gate. Today there is automation, and the kegs are stainless steel, not oak.

"Now there are three carousels. The first takes the empty keg and gives it a first-stage washing. The second sterilizes the keg so that it is 100 percent clean, then we counterpressure it with the same mix of gas [carbon dioxide for extra stout, and carbon dioxide plus nitrogen for draught] as is in the beer. Everything is in equilibrium. What's in the beer is in the keg. Then we fill it."

It is here that the Guinness brewers perform their final quality check. In a room at the center of the labyrinth of keg lines, Fergal Murray pulls a tap handle, filling a glass with stout he proudly describes as "the freshest possible product. This is as good as it gets."

Wow.

As we savor this beer that is truly taken from *the* source of Guinness, he reflects thoughtfully that, "the brewhouse has done it's job getting the sugar from the cereal. Fermentation has done its job converting the sugar to alcohol, the maturation stage has done its job of giving the beer its flavor. It's nitrogenated and the brewing art and science is done. The final check is both a tasting and a visual check. We can guarantee our beer looking wonderful every single time because we know we have consistency of liquid to the right content of head. Behind that is the art and craft of presenting it to a consumer."

He says that the visual check is mainly about the size of the head. It looks exactly right to me. Of course it is.

"No variation is expected. No variation ever occurs," he tells me with a matter-of-fact smile. "The pint tasted today is identical to the pint tasted here a year ago. It can't be any other way."

Epilogue

As I was packing up my gear to leave the Guinness Archives after priceless hours and days of research behind the big black gate at St. James's Gate, Guinness Archivist Eibhlin Roche asked me, "Now, do you love Guinness as much as we do?"

It was a startling question. It was startling both in its easy simplicity, and in the depth of its complexity. Love at its simplest is a complex emotion. Love at its most complex is an enigma.

Certainly I had come to St. James's Gate with a love for Guinness, but Eibhlin was asking me to ponder whether I loved Guinness as much as those for whom it is their life's work. Certainly, her enthusiasm, and that of many others at St. James's Gate, had deepened my appreciation for this object of our affection.

Yet, *love* also implies a relationship, a passionate relationship. I had come to St. James's Gate having formed a relationship with the black liquidation with the froth on the top. Or so I thought. I realized now that, as with love, this was a deepening relationship that I had only just begun to form.

From the first moment that I sat down across the table from Fergal Murray, and from that wonderful morning as I dashed after him through the nineteenth-century pedestrian tunnel beneath James's Street, I was overwhelmed by his excitement for his product. Gradually, I became infused with his passion, just as nitrogen infuses his beer.

From the first moment that I sat down across the table from Eibhlin Roche at the Archives, I sensed her excitement for two and a half centuries of the history of this brand. On the day that she brought out the ancient Brewery Notebooks, with notations perhaps in Arthur's *own hand*, I felt her passion. As I poured through the documents in her archives, I began to feel the passion of all the generations who had passed through this majestic brewhouse and the one across the Irish Sea at Park Royal—the Guinnesses and the Pursers, Arthur Shand and Arthur Fawcett, Ben Newbold and Hugh Beaver, Michael Ash, Tony Carey, Alan Forage, and countless others. I felt the passion of all those who strived not just for extraordinary beer, but for a sweet, black liquidation of transcendent magic.

"The perfect pint is about the whole process," Fergal Murray told me one winter afternoon in Dublin as the sun hung low in the sky, and as we pondered the ethos of this elusive Holy Grail of the mythic perfect pint. "It could be a windy, cold day and you're dying of thirst. You walk into a pub, and that miraculous moment happens. The bartender looks you in the eye and asks, 'May I help you,' and you answer, 'I'd love a pint.' You watch him as he meticulously goes about the ritual of pouring and presenting you the perfect pint. You'll dream about that moment *for the rest of your life*."

When, in minute detail, Fergal Murray describes a publican scrupulously going about the job of pouring and presenting you the perfect pint, that's enthusiasm. When he tells you that you'll dream about that moment *for the rest of your life*, that's passion. Perhaps it's even true love.

As B. Traven has suggested, the mythic quest is more about the quest itself than it is about the object of the quest. The mythic quest is really a voyage of self-discovery, and it is therefore about the things we discover and the pints we drink along our journey. It is about the places where we go in our search for that perfect pint, and those with whom we share that experience on life's cold and windy days.

When you realize that you've spent your life on this mythic quest for your Holy Grail, your perfect pint . . . and that you'll be walking that road for the rest of your life . . . and that walking the road *is* the Holy Grail—that's the love of a great beer.

When you realize that millions have gone before you on this road, and that millions will follow you long after you are gone, then you know that the perfect pint that we all seek can truly be called the world's greatest beer.

Appendix A

Generations of the Guinness Family in the Leadership of the Family Business

First Generation

Arthur Guinness (1725–1803), the founder of the Guinness brewery at St. James's Gate, was head brewer from 1759 until his death.

Second Generation

Arthur Guinness II, the "Second Arthur" (1768–1855), was the second son of the founder and the second person to hold the title of head brewer at St. James's Gate, from 1803 to 1820.

Benjamin Guinness (1777–1826) and **William Lunell Guinness** (1779–1842), sons of the first Arthur, joined their brother, the Second Arthur, in the management at the family business around 1808. The Second Arthur, however, outlived them and control of the family business in the third generation passed to Arthur's sons.

The Second Arthur relinquished control of St. James's Gate to his son, Benjamin Lee Guinness, in 1839. However, the title of head brewer went to John Purser Jr. in 1820, who in turn was succeeded by his son, John Tertius Purser in 1840. John Purser Jr. was a partner in the company from 1820 to 1840, but John Tertius Purser was never made a partner.

Third Generation

Arthur Lee Guinness (1797–1863) and **Benjamin Lee Guinness** (1798–1868) were the sons of the Second Arthur who were brought in as partners in the family business in 1820. Arthur Lee lost interest in the routine management of the business, and Benjamin Lee assumed a lead role second only to the Second Arthur Guinness, who continued as titular head of the firm until 1839.

Fourth Generation

Owners

Sir Arthur Edward Guinness, Lord Ardilaun (1840–1915), the first son of Benjamin Lee Guinness, his brother, Edward Cecil Guinness, inherited the St. James's Gate brewery from their father, but Arthur Edward sold his share to Edward Cecil in 1876.

Sir Edward Cecil Guinness, 1st Earl of Iveagh (1847–1927), was the third son of Benjamin Lee Guinness. He built the brewery into the largest in the world and took the company public in 1886. He was chairman of the public company from 1886 to 1890 and from 1902 to 1927.

Cousins in Management

Sir Reginald Robert Guinness (1842–1909) and **Claude H. C. Guinness** (1852–1895) were fourth generation descendants of the first Arthur Guinness's brother Samuel, and brothers of Edward Cecil's wife Adelaide "Dodo" Guinness. Sir Reginald served as chairman of the board from 1890 to 1902, preceded and followed by Sir Edward Cecil. He also served simultaneously as managing director at St. James's Gate from 1894 to 1902. Claude served as managing director at St. James's Gate from 1886 to 1893.

Fifth Generation

Sir Rupert Edward Cecil Lee Guinness, 2nd Earl of Iveagh (1874–1967), the first son of Sir Edward Cecil Guinness, assumed the chairmanship on the death of his father in 1927 and served until 1962 when he was 85. Had it not been for the death of his son during World War II, he would probably have retired in 1949 at the age of 75.

Arthur Ernest Guinness (1876–1949), the younger brother of Sir Rupert, served as assistant managing director from 1902 to 1912, and as vice chairman from 1913 to 1947.

Sixth Generation

Arthur Onslow Edward Guinness, Viscount Elveden (1912–1945), was the second son of Sir Rupert Edward Cecil Lee Guinness. He was killed in action during World War II and never served as chairman as he probably would have. Arthur's father remained in the chairmanship until Arthur's son reached the age of 25.

Seventh Generation

Sir Arthur Francis Benjamin Guinness, known as Benjamin, 3rd Earl of Iveagh (1937–1992), was the only son of Arthur Onslow Edward Guinness. He assumed the chairmanship from his grandfather in 1962 and served in this role until 1987. After his retirement as chairman, he held the ceremonial post of president. He was the last member of the Guinness family to have a leadership position at the head of the family business.

Appendix B

Guinness Head Brewers

St. James's Gate

1759	Arthur Guinness
1803	Arthur Guinness (The "Second Arthur")
1820	John Purser Jr.
1840	John Tertius Purser
1867	George Arthur Waller
1880	William Purser Geoghegan
1897	F. E. Greene
1911	Edward Phillips
1923	Arthur Barker
1932	Alan McMullen
1937	(for one month) William Sealy Gosset
1937	Geoffrey Phillpotts
1947	R. S. Wix
1949	Cyril Buttanshaw
1956	Owen Williams
1960	Launce McMullen
1968	John Brown
1973	Richard Lloyd
1978	J. F. Carson

Park Royal

- 1936 William Sealy Gosset
- 1937 Morris Heycock
- 1949 Lance Shildrick
- 1953 Cyril Virden
- 1960 John Webb
- 1966 Tom Jennings
- 1972 Alan Coxon
- 1984 Frank Robson
- 1989 George Irons

Carson is recognized as the last person to hold the title of head brewer in Dublin. After 1984, there were brewhouse managers. The same transition occurred at Park Royal shortly thereafter. Today, there is no head brewer in the older sense of the title, but a number of master brewers, as well as an integrated multidisciplinary team that includes specialists other than brewers.

First brewed in Dublin in 1802, Guinness Foreign Extra Stout is the original export stout. It is the fastest growing of all variants. It is the key Guinness variant for Caribbean, Africa and Asia. Nigeria is the largest market for Foreign Extra Stout and is the third largest market for Guinness worldwide. (Diageo Ireland)

Guinness Extra Stout is the closest to the Guinness Porter originally brewed by Arthur Guinness now available. Guinness Extra Stout has been almost completely replaced by Guinness Draught and now only represents less than five percent of all Guinness sold worldwide. (Diageo Ireland)

The largest Guinness variant across the world, Guinness Draught was introduced in 1959. Thanks to the innovation of the widget, launched in 1986, Guinness Draught is now available in cans and bottles. The widget helps to form the characteristic smooth and creamy head and create an authentic Guinness every time. The widget works by sending a jet of nitrogen through the body of the beer. This knocks nitrogen and carbon dioxide out of suspension, creating the surge, which results in the creamy head. Guinness Draught in Cans is now available in over 70 countries around the world. (Diageo Ireland)

Bibliography

Bickerdyke, John. *The Curiosities of Ale & Beer* (Scribner & Welford, 1889).

Byrne, Al. *Guinness Times: My Days in the World's Most Famous Brewery* (Town House, 1999).

Davies, Jim. *The Book of Guinness Advertising* (Guinness Media, 1998).

Dennison, S. R., and Oliver MacDonagh. *Guinness 1886–1939: From Incorporation to the Second World War* (Cork University Press, 1998).

Gourvish, T. R., and R. G. Wilson, *The British Brewing Industry 1830–1980* (Cambridge University Press, 1994).

Griffiths, Mark. *Guinness Is Guinness: The Colourful Story of a Black and White Brand* (Cyan Communications, 2004).

Griffiths, Mark, and John, Simmons. *Believe* (Guinness PLC, n.d).

Guinness, Edward. *The Guinness Book of Guinness* (Guinness Books, 1988).

Guinness, Jonathan. *Requiem for a Family Business* (Macmillan Publishing, 1997).

Guinness, Michele. *The Guinness Legend: The Changing Fortunes of a Great Family* (Hodder and Stoughton, 1988).

Note: Any study of the history of the Guinness company and its breweries before 1939 is indebted to the thorough scholarly work done by S. R. Dennison, Patrick Lynch, Oliver MacDonagh, and John Vaizey with company documents, including brewer's calculation books, brewery memorandum books, correspondence with Lord Iveagh, head brewer's diaries, letter books, managing director's diaries, and papers relating to the agencies and trade and to various aspects of the running and administration of the brewery and its additional activities. All those of us who have come later stand on their shoulders.

Guinness, Michele. *The Guinness Spirit: Brewers, Bankers, Ministers and Missionaries* (Hodder and Stoughton, 1999).

Hughes, David. *A Bottle of Guinness Please* (Phimboy, 2006).

Ipsen, Erik. "$33 Billion Giant Guinness to Unite with Grand Met," *International Herald Tribune*, May 13, 1997.

Lutz, H. F. *Vitaculture and Brewing in the Ancient Orient* (G. E. Stechert, 1922).

Lynch, Patrick, and John Vaizey. *Guinness's Brewery in the Irish Economy: 1759–1876* (Cambridge University Press, 1960).

Machan, Dyan. "A Liquid Lunch," *Forbes*, September 20, 1999.

Marchant, W. T. *In Praise of Ale* (George Redway, 1888).

Mathias, P. *The Brewing Industry of England 1700–1830* (Cambridge University Press, 1958).

Mullally, Frederic. *The Silver Salver: The Story of the Guinness Family* (Granada, 1981).

O'Brien, Brendan. *The Stout Book* (Anna Livia, 1990).

Pugh, Peter. *Is Guinness Good for You: The Bid for Distillers; The Inside Story* (Financial Training Publications, 1987).

Ryder, David S., *Newsletter of the American Society of Brewing Chemists*, vol. 59, no. 4, 1999.

Sibley, Brian. *The Book of Guinness Advertising* (Guinness Books, 1985).

Vaizey, John. *The Brewing Industry, 1886–1952* (Cambridge University Press,1960).

Williams, Owen. *Notes on the St. James's Gate Brewery* (St. James's Gate Brewery (internal publication), 1957).

Wilson, Derek. *Dark and Light: The Story of the Guinness Family* (Weidenfeld and Nicholson, 1998).

About the Author

BILL YENNE is the San Francisco-based author of many books on historical topics, from Lewis and Clark to the Second World War, and of course, brewing history. The *Wall Street Journal* recently said of his work that it "has the rare quality of being both an excellent reference work and a pleasure to read." The reviewer also wrote that Mr. Yenne writes with "cinematic vividness."

Descended from Irish immigrants from County Clare and County Cork, he was recently featured in a History Channel program discussing the history of beer. He has also been a guest on Beer Radio on the Sirius Satellite Network, and he has visited and discussed brewing at important breweries from Portland, Maine, to Portland, Oregon, from Guadalajara to Prague, and, of course, in Ireland.

Once referred to by American craft beer pioneer Buffalo Bill Owens as "the American Michael Jackson" (the king of English beverage historians, not the king of pop), Mr. Yenne has written extensively on beer and brewing history for two decades. He is a member of the American Society of Journalists and Authors (ASJA) and the American Book Producers Association (ABPA).

Among his beer books are: *The American Brewery*, *Great American Beers: Twelve Brands That Became Icons*, *Beers of North America*, *Beers of the World*, and *Beer Labels of the World*, as well as *The Field Guide to Breweries and Microbreweries of North America*.

Mr. Yenne has also contributed articles to *All About Beer* magazine and has hosted numerous beer tastings throughout the United States. He was a member of an elite panel chosen to select the beers to complement each course of a formal dinner held at the Oldenberg Brewery. Afterward, Jay Maeder of the *New York Daily News* described his choice of a beer to accompany the entree of "Soused and Stuffed Chicken Breast Marinated in Mustard Sauce" as "perfect."

Index